Memory Maps

By the same author

Keepers of the House
The Slow Train to Milan
The Tiger
The Bay of Silence
Black Idol
Nocturne
Joanna

The Marble Mountain (*short stories*)
The High Place (*poetry*)
Off the Rails (*memoir*)
A Valley in Italy (*memoir*)
The Hacienda (*memoir*)
The Virago Book of Wanderlust and Dreams (*edited anthology*)
Southpaw (*short stories*)
Elements of Italy (*edited anthology*)

Memory Maps

Lisa St Aubin de Terán

Virago

A *Virago* Book
Published by Virago Press 2003

First published by Virago Press 2002

A CIP catalogue record for this book
is available from the British Library.

ISBN 1 86049 931 7

Typeset in Janson by M Rules
Printed and bound in Great Britain by
Clays Ltd, St Ives plc

Virago Press
An imprint of
Time Warner Books
Brettenham House
Lancaster Place
London WC2E 7EN

www.virago.co.uk

for Florence

Prologue

This book is a map of my memories, of all the places I remember most for having liked the best. Somewhere in a scroll I try to bury (but somehow cannot forget) there is another, parallel map of all my least favourite places: the sites of personal disasters. This, though, is a compilation of my favourite places. As I list them, they seem so disparate that I feel the need, for myself, to make some sense of why each of them is included. Some of them, like the valley in Torajaland, or the hidden beach on the Caribbean island of Nevis, would strike most people as magical by their sheer beauty, but others, like the railway embankment in south London, or the one-horse town in the middle of the Bolivian jungle, take a little more explaining.

Many people travel in search of something different, and to feel different, and in search of the exotic. I have travelled mostly out of an inherent restlessness, driven by the sense of being different myself. So I have been in search of those places where I might find people a little more like me, a sense of belonging, albeit vicariously, and traces of my own ancestry.

I am often asked where I am from. The short answer is that I am half South American and half Channel Island. The long answer (and a killer of casual conversation) is that on my father's side I am a mixture of Portuguese, Dutch, Carib Indian, African, Brazilian, Venezuelan, Scottish, West Indian and German, while on my mother's side, I am a mixture of Jersey, English, Irish and French. I can legitimately claim kinship in much of the world, not least because my family has travelled for generations weaving Africa, America, pockets of Asia and most of Europe into our family cloth. Perhaps that is why I feel almost at home in innumerable different places, and yet never quite at home anywhere in the world.

Although there is no one place that I can say I come from, I have lived for more years than anywhere else in Italy. From my earliest childhood, I have been a dedicated Italophile. My father, in a moment of poetic licence, named me Lisa Gioconda after the *Mona Lisa del Giocondo*, '*La Gioconda*' by Leonardo da Vinci. Having struggled through a suburban English primary school with such an outlandish name, I felt it was somehow my right to live in Italy. My name and my lasting affection for the place are the only rights I have to be here. I have felt more at home in Umbria than anywhere else, yet I stick out like a sore thumb and am most definitely a foreigner. Italians are very accepting of outsiders (so long as they do not hail from any of the rival Italian regions).

Somewhere in between the fairytale beginning and the Mafia movie ending, there were some idyllic years spent in a half-ruined palace in the woods. I have lived in Umbria for fourteen years, in the same place and in the same house. My daughter and my grandson were born there. I was so settled, I thought I had finally made roots. During those fourteen years, I spent a great deal of time creating a garden. What started as an act of faith evolved into reality. It seemed permanent, a legacy to whoever followed in our footsteps on this hillslope of S. Ilario di Quarata. I thought I would live and die here, and yet, *per forza*, as they say in Italian, I am moving on.

There has always been something random about my travels. I think I am more of a drifter than a traveller: a drifter with no sense of direction. Getting hopelessly lost has enabled me to discover not only the underbelly of so many places, but also to stumble upon the most wonderfully hidden sites. I can and do get lost anywhere, so lost that a dreamlike quality can overtake a simple stroll, and a trip to the end of whichever street I live on can become an adventure. Venice, where I lived for two years, is still the most challenging maze I have ever encountered. For the first five years of our Umbrian sojourn, Venice overlapped like an insistent tide as a second home. It lured us back at irregular intervals to explore its damp alleyways. When the family apartment in Venice had to be sold to feed the insatiable appetite of our ruined Umbrian palace, it was a decision (though made by me) that I never quite came to terms with. By having become Venetian citizens my family and I acquired the right, eventually, to be buried there. I had never thought about or cared where I might or might not be buried before moving to Venice, but it became something I greatly looked forward to: I would have a plot on the island cemetery of San Michele with the likes of Sergei Diaghilev and Ezra Pound. After a life of restlessness,

I would come to rest in the most romantic graveyard in the world.

Relinquishing that plot and its melancholy mists made me feel as though I had left a part of myself back there – a tessera in that great maritime mosaic. Since I left Venice, I have written about her over and over again. The island of San Michele became my place of pilgrimage, soon superseded by another watery shrine much nearer to my base, Isola Maggiore on Lake Trasimeno. At one end of the island, the immense and decaying Castel'Isabella encapsulates a sense of time suspended and distilled into beauty.

When I started this book, I knew that within a year I would, albeit temporarily, be a nomad again. The Umbrian palace was sold and my family and I would move out of its splendid front and derelict back by the end of the following summer. The manner of leaving Morra, our village, was a little extreme, but then so much of my life has taken place in extreme situations. The new owner razed its five acres of gardens to the ground. While we were packing, three hundred trees, the shrubberies, the maze of aromatic herbs, the hedges, rose gardens, lily beds, orchards, avenues and herbaceous borders were all destroyed. It took four days. Day after day during our last summer in 2001, neighbours came and wept in the garden, or climbed the marble staircase to wander through the rooms in tears. Ours was a noble house bought as a shell and then given glory. The garden was a wasteland transformed. It was the pride of Morra. For a decade, wedding after wedding and dance after dance was held on its manicured lawns and the air was laced with jasmines and wisteria, lemon flowers and roses. It will be a long while before such things can be repeated there. Gardens are about love and care. Yet all the fine moments shared at the Villa Quarata remain, as does the bond that has grown between my family and our neighbours: Maria and Imolo, Clara and the Signora Maria and all the good people of Morra.

This is a narrative, a mass of relative values learnt. Not least of these is that tears should not be shed on the losses of the wealthy: there are too many others worthier of pity. The reversals of luck of the lucky do not put them in the same bracket as the millions of people who struggle through their lives in genuine need. I am lucky to have what I have had, to have known whom I have known, and to have what I still have. I have extracted pleasure from even the basest of chores and enjoyed the fleeting moments of lightness in the interstices of the more onerous aspects of life.

I always look for both sides of the coin when I travel, and now I have seen the flip side at home. My love of Italy and Italians in general is undiminished, and of Umbria in particular.

I believe that the three essential things to take on any journey are a sense of humour, tolerance and curiosity. My bags are packed: two small suitcases and an old Olivetti typewriter. Most of the memories I have are good ones and this is not an end but a beginning.

1

I find it strangely comforting to think that the earliest form of human life was nomadic, and the earliest signs of civilisation were the building of houses in which to settle down. The first *Homo sapiens* were Australian Aborigines, some of whom survive today in their nomadic state, while those who have settled are still prey to walkabouts – that instinctive urge to take off and roam. Until the fifties there were Bedouin in the Arabian deserts whose lives had scarcely changed over the previous five hundred years. Like the Aborigines, they travelled unencumbered by things. Simple mud villages, on the other hand, became towns and then cities stuffed full of an ever-increasing surfeit of material objects and ornaments. What I see in myself is a mix of these two primitive trends. I am neither an Aborigine nor a Bedouin but I am a wanderer, one with a hoarder's love of houses and things. Some might say this is evidence of a schizoid personality. I choose to see it as a drawing together of the diverse threads of our species and a serendipitous reflection of the mix of race, class and culture that I am.

I think of myself as a drifter. I do not seek adventure so much as the comfort of moving on. Some travellers, like Thesiger, actively seek the challenge of hardship and danger. 'No,' he wrote, 'it is not the goal but the way there that matters, and the harder the way the more worthwhile the journey.' Some explorers are lured primarily by the thrill of stepping first into the hitherto unknown. Neither of these types is me. I go out of my way to avoid danger and will always prefer a hotel to a tent. Whatever hardships I have encountered en route have come courtesy of my own dysfunctional planning and research. It is this that has let me arrive in Guyana (my fatherland and formerly British Guiana) on the eve of a dictatorial referendum to abolish the constitution. I was just dropping in to say hello to my ninety-year-old granny. I'd been travelling in Patagonia for the last month and hadn't read any newspapers or heard any news of that country being in violent turmoil. The same lack of planning took my ten-year-old son and I to Barcelona on an impulse holiday on the day of the opening of the Olympic Games. Dipping dreamily in and out of life like that has landed me up in numerous places in the throes of strikes, mass demonstrations, epidemics and natural disasters.

These lapses have made me acquainted with what I call airport hotels (a euphemism for yet another night spent transiting in some airport), the underbelly of a couple of army barracks, and the view of a few cities as seen from their gutters. But, I repeat, I am not intrinsically drawn to thrills. I am someone in search of a quiet life. Mostly, I flee adventure, not least because I am aware of how I seem to attract both strangers and strange situations.

Since I am tracing here a memory map of all the places that have stayed with me and become a part of me, such was the impact they made, and since this is also a map of all my voyages of discovery and the getting to those places, I am exploring my own mind here, and unpacking a lot of luggage in the process. If I go back as far as I can remember, there was a time when, very briefly, I was a thrill-seeker. I was three years old and lived with my mother and three sisters in a large dilapidated house on a hill in Wimbledon called Ridgeway Place. Our front garden opened on to the ridge itself, with the pavement dropping almost precipitously to a fairly busy road.

In the days when we lived in Wimbledon it was a large, rather expensive village in the county of Surrey. Since then, it has become an expensive suburb of London, and London sprawls for many miles beyond it. I had a small tricycle, and for a couple of heady months I tried my hand at being an infant Evil Knevil: a death-defying stunt-rider. I used to crouch, standing on the seat, and free-wheel at great speed down the pavement and into the road at the bottom. By sheer good fortune, I never once fell off, nor did I hit any of the occasional traffic in the road. Such was the freedom of having a working mother and a negligent nanny!

After a few weeks of this sporadic stunt-riding, the joys of dare-devilry began to pall and I rather hoped for a parental veto to free me for more leisurely tasks. However, in a street of child-rivalry, it was the first time I had been anything other than a tedious tagger-on, and two of my elder sisters enjoyed displaying my talent to their friends. So, several times a week, I whizzed away. When the veto finally arrived and my little tricycle was confiscated, I seem to have had enough of driving for the rest of my life. At forty-seven, I still feel no desire to drive, be it a tricycle or a car.

Later, there was a transitional phase. Danger was never again to be intrinsically attractive, but adventure per se held sway for a couple of years. My family had moved further into darkest south London, and my sister Lali and I would sometimes set out on an adventure by intentionally getting lost. (This ability would come naturally to me later in life.) By this time, the tricycle was a thing of the past and Lali and I had graduated to bicycles. We used to pack our saddlebags with liver-pâté sandwiches, chocolate cake and small bottles of water, and take off into the unknown. Usually, despite our intrepid intentions, we'd spend long hours pedalling around the interminable streets of Clapham, Streatham, Brixton and Herne Hill and get very tired. We learnt that adventures were thin and few, while London was a sprawling metropolis full of thousands of streets almost all of which had a depressing sameness about them. At the end of each of our forays we pretended that the day had been really good fun and made plans for another one when the time should be right, convinced that somewhere out there was somewhere wonderful just waiting for us to discover it.

On one such trip, turning and cycling with no purpose other than to wind up in the middle of nowhere, we found ourselves on the edge of Wimbledon Common. The common is a large expanse of woods and dells dotted with ponds and great stretches of rough grassland. It was wild and big enough for us to have been expressly forbidden ever to enter it alone. A boy had got lost there once and died of exposure. On that day, however, we overrode whatever qualms we had, including the thought of being recognised by any of our former neighbours and denounced to our mother for being in Wimbledon at all. We had set out to seek adventure and the common had a pioneer-type allure.

As the bridle paths gave way to mere footpaths, and then just high undergrowth, Lali and I discussed how she, aged eleven, and I, aged nine, would defend each other in the event of attack. To this end, we found a hefty stick apiece. Carrying these and having to push our bikes over the rough terrain made the going laborious. When we came to a huge oak tree, we decided to abandon the bikes over its roots and continue without them. As best we could, we left a trail of broken sticks by which to return and reclaim them. Having come so far, we felt we had to find somewhere truly special to have our much-awaited picnic. I walked to the drum beat of my heart, speechless with fear of the murderous lurkers. From the time we had turned off the bridle path, we had not seen a soul. This, in itself, seemed proof of what a perilous course we were following. Grim-faced and tired from our ride and walk, we trudged on, each waiting for the grip of fear to ease enough for one or other to risk losing face and suggest heading home. Just as weakness and cowardice joined forces in me and I felt bound to be that wimp, we came to the emerald lake.

For years afterwards, Lali and I would reminisce about its enchantment. Had we not been together, we might have thought we had dreamed that green fairytale place. As an adolescent, I returned there, alone, several times. As an adult, I have tried to find it in vain. It was a circle some sixty metres in diameter which glistened from a distance like a small lake. As we drew nearer, we saw the rippling emerald surface was entirely made up of hummocks of bog moss, the delicatest of grasses, with pink filaments as fine as gossamer shimmering over them. The colour was startlingly bright and stood out the more as a glittering jewel for being surrounded by the other greens of trees and scrub.

When we walked barefoot on the moss it was deliciously cool and spongy. It felt like floating. It tickled and soothed. Butterflies and dragonflies shimmered over the emerald circle. In the middle, on an island no bigger than a kilim, a willow tree grew with cushions of bog cotton around it. We sat on its white fluffy mound and ate our rations in the dry while our feet stayed on the soft damp moss.

We stayed there for several hours, even falling asleep, such was the calm of it. I can pinpoint a change in my life to that day. It was my first full communion with a place. I loved it and in so doing I became aware of another dimension of love.

I was a child prone to intense introspection and depression. The jolly japes of childhood often passed me by. At four and five, when other children were out skipping and singing nursery rhymes, I was immersed in the English novel, with a preference for George Eliot, Jane Austen and Trollope. As had happened in my time as a kamikaze tricyclist, I sometimes tired a little of being the child prodigy. I was aware from very early on of being different. My family was different. My mother had married four times, nobody else's mother had. We had no man in the house, just women. We spoke with an accent alien to south London and got chased in the street for it. We wore, by parental insistence, fawn socks instead of the statutory white of every other child's. We were a family but we didn't look like each other, most noticeably because there was me: half South American and dark-skinned. I was often ill as a child and lived as a semi-invalid wrapped in my mother's big black fur rug as I read my way through the two thousand books she had managed to salvage from her previous lives and marriages. I devoured those books and was often happy reading, but from very early on I felt that there must be somewhere for me to be other than in the immediate choices around me. I knew it was out there somewhere and whatever book I was reading could come with me.

Playing with local children was an option I could slip in or out of because my sisters were popular and generous enough to allow me to join in their games. I was an outsider but with the chance of belonging to my sisters' gangs. Lali and I were close despite having very different characters. She played very naturally with the other children, while I often felt, when I joined them, that I was pretending to play. I have wondered whether I would have been so aware of these things if I hadn't worked my way through my mother's library. She worked with maladjusted children, graduating as a mature student when I was five. All her books on child psychology were on a low shelf between her battered paperback fiction and the hardback novels which reached up to the ceiling. I was about six when I took down Iona and Peter Opie's *The Lore and Language of Children*. I found it absolutely fascinating and then worked my way along the shelf with the help of the shorter Oxford Dictionary. I monitored my own behaviour as a child, and sometimes I went through the motions of joining in.

There was hopscotch on the pavement, drawn in chalk. There was skipping to rhymes, which I was good at. There was two-balls, which I was hopeless at. This was played against the red-brick wall of the bombsite that bordered our flats. Then there was exploring the bombsite for the umpteenth time. There was knocking on people's doors and running away, and there was the ultimate dare of running through the council flats across the road. It was the worst and the best. If you got caught, you got a kicking from the council-estate kids, or ear pulls and a shaking from their parents. If you got through, you got months of respect. It took about four minutes to run through the winding tarmac that lay between the drab grey blocks of the council estate. It was rife with delinquents and petty thieves, with gangs who merited the name and bullied all and sundry in our neighbourhood, from toddlers to grandmothers. At night, the cries of domestic violence drifted through the tall lime trees outside our flats and crept in our windows. My own mother cried at night sometimes, racked, I knew, among other things, by the shame of our being reduced to live in a flat in Clapham South. Such was the hierarchy of the suburbs that children from our side of the street were not allowed to play with the children from the council estate by order of a dozen separate parental bans. Although our family had no such ban, the council kids themselves found us all too stuck up to merit any form of social contact other than fighting, and I was twelve before I felt brave enough to defy the peer pressure of our side and befriend a wan, smelly, but very funny girl called Mary.

Our fear of the other side was real: some of us did get caught running through. I was caught once, though luckily only by a big drunk who shoved me up against a wall, breathed a foul cocktail over me and told me to 'bugger off'. In those days, the divide was as dangerous to our eyes as the Iron Curtain itself. It was thought heroic to run through. Even the bigger boys from our many blocks of flats were aware that they stood no chance of inviting the council-flat boys to a fight. Over there, they used broken bottles and bicycle chains. Only a few of us rose to the dare to run through. I did it to honour my sisters, Lali and Resi, who did so much to make me acceptable in the group and who had often done it themselves and because it seemed easier, ultimately, than getting proficient in two-balls. I ran through several times and still have nightmares about running that particular gauntlet.

2

I knew that there had to be more to the world than this, and I felt it my duty to find it. There were clues in books and clues in some of our visitors, my mother's friends who travelled and brought back their tales to her. As a family, we made forays, and as a child detective with a mission I surveyed everywhere with an eye to finding that better place. There were clues on those forays too. The furthest away we went was on our annual pilgrimage to Cornwall in the far west of England. It took sixteen mortifying hours by coach to get there and although I now know that some of the countryside traversed is truly beautiful, I was always too travel-sick to notice at the time. I used to get travel-sick on the ten-minute bus ride to school.

There were some wonderful times on those Cornish holidays: walking along little roads lined with wild rhododendrons, looking out from Land's End at the Atlantic Ocean lashing against the cliffs and then dragging out towards the horizon and America itself. There were thick yellow Cornish ice creams and hot lamb pasties that crumbled in your hands as you walked along the seafront. Yet, in between, like a drawstring threaded through each episode, there was the hovering presence of 'granny' Mabel waiting to explode. We went to Cornwall because 'granny' Mabel lived there and invited my mother and her four daughters to stay for free for two weeks every summer. But for this invitation, we could not have afforded to spend a holiday by the sea. That was the good news. The bad news was that we were all afraid of 'granny' Mabel, who was actually the mother of Lali and Resi's stepmother and thus not really any relation to me at all.

When I look back now, I see our two choices of accommodation as far from ideal, but then, as children do, we enjoyed the cramped, damp squalor of our sojourn. Usually we went to a small sweaty caravan in a wet field full of cowpats. My sisters argued a lot. A holiday wasn't enough of an excuse for a truce, so the arguments and fights spilled over into the tiny caravan. We liked the caravan most because 'granny' Mabel hardly ever came to see us there. When she did, she announced her arrival with strings of oaths and obscenities which were her normal way of saying 'hello, darlings', but which we took as a prelude to violence. Her wrath was astonishing to behold, even her affection was tyrannical, volatile and almost cruel. She was a one-legged wonder, a heroine of the First World War, a true eccentric, a one-time famous writer, an elderly nymphomaniac, a drinker and a blasphemer *par excellence.* She kept a wet, sticky cigarette glued to one corner of her heavily lipsticked mouth. She coughed what sounded like small reptiles up and down her throat. She grabbed us children and tried to smother us in her huge limp bosom. In her efforts to make us feel at home, she terrorised and tormented us to a degree that made it hard to relax on our annual jaunts to St Ives. One minute she would beam approval, the next minute she'd be swearing at me or Lali or Resi or our mother as though she hated and despised us. Then she'd laugh it off raucously and move on to some scurrilous anecdote while we'd be left trembling and distraught. Hers was a killer kindness. On the few occasions when we were invited to stay in her quaint fisherman's cottage at the top of Skidden Hill in St Ives itself, the daily proximity was a challenge. She kept her artificial leg and a spare in a cupboard in her bedroom, often asking to have it passed to her in bed. She also kept a chamberpot under her bed which seemed to be constantly full and which it was my duty to empty out in the tiny garden. Life was never dull with granny Mabel, not least because you never knew from one minute to the next what would trigger her displeasure.

Despite that, there were hours of dreamy contentment spent on Porthmere beach or, more often, on the small beach of St Ives itself. English people at the seaside tend to sit in their cars overlooking the sea with their windows closed tight while they chomp through their ritual seaside picnics. Anyone who has sat on an English beach on any but the rare days when the sun deigns to shine will know that the car-occupiers are driven by tenacity and experience. The tenacity is in persisting in wanting to go to the seaside, the experience is the remembered horror of being forced to swim in the ice-cold Atlantic and then to sit in near gale-force winds on the chill gritty sand while being brainwashed into believing that you were enjoying it.

Although the sea itself was wondrous, to approach it we had to change into bathing dresses knitted saggily by our mother. They were big itchy bags which could hold pints of cold sea water for hours at a stretch and invited the ridicule of everyone else on the beach, who wore sleek frilly nylon costumes. Our mother had a horror of what she called 'matière plastique'. Nylon fell into that forbidden category. Our swimsuits were invariably cold and damp even when we put them on. The two weeks a year we spent glugging salt water and seaweed did not turn me into a swimmer. That and the cold, but mostly the cold, made me hate going in with a vengeance. It was an ordeal that had to be got over. It was something I was told I would enjoy eventually. It was something I knew I had to do before I could get my kilt and vest and shirt and jumper and windcheater back on and enjoy the windy beach my own way, gathering shells and watching sea anemones in rock pools and scaling the low cliffs with my sisters.

Although Cornwall was the furthest we travelled, it didn't speak to me as other places did. I was looking for something, for an affinity, a feeling, a spiritual fulfilment funnelled through a place. My mother assured me that I would find school exciting. She was wrong. At the Dickensian infant school I enrolled in on Bonneville Road in Clapham, I developed a truanting routine for every day of the week. I spent my days on or around Clapham Common and I spent the one shilling a day dinner money exclusively on jam doughnuts – they were four to a shilling then. Sometimes I truanted to Clapham Common Old Town Library and sat with a row of depressives and alcoholics perusing the day's newspapers in the warmth of its reading room, suffused with the smell of ale and old age. I couldn't go to the public library too often, though, because the librarian was no fool and used to interrogate me. So I was free from school, but was that dour, chilly sojourn in suburbia what people meant by freedom?

Sundays were the best days at that time of limited horizons. Sundays were the days my mother, Joanna, and I spent on our own. Two of my sisters, Resi and Lali (known to this day in our family as 'the girls'), spent most of their Sundays with their father and stepmother on the other side of London. Our eldest sister, Gale, was eleven years my senior and had a social life of her own. By the time I was eight, she was away in Aberdeen at university. My own father was almost perennially absent, sometimes in faraway exotic places or else in his almost equally unapproachable house in Wimbledon where he lived with his new Cuban wife.

Thus Sundays tended to leave Joanna and I to our own devices, and our own devices tended to lure us to the Botanical Gardens at Kew. It was the cheapest and most charming way to spend a day out in London. Joanna's idea of a perfect Sunday was to lie in bed until well after nine, down about two pints of strong filter coffee and then catch the train to Kew. She'd pass through the old iron turnstile and march straight to the palm house. There under the tropical foliage in the damp heat she would unwrap her weekly luxury of a steak sandwich, open up her Thermos of yet more filtered Colombian coffee and dream of other climes. She was always happy to spend the entire day there, surrounded by hundreds of exuberant palm fronds while the steam heat rose up through the intricate cast-iron grids of the Victoria walkway. Her message, rarely spoken, was none the less loud and clear: we deserved to live among such plants and in just such a balmy climate.

Depending on the weather, our path to the palm house varied from a forced march through gale-force winds and even snow to a leisurely saunter learning the names in Latin of trees and shrubs from the entire world. Those days developed in me a lifelong love of botany and of gardening and an awareness of the vast variety of this globe. Since my mother's death in 1981, Kew Gardens has been of all the places in the world the one most redolent of her.

Whenever I return to London and have even a few hours to spare, I go to Kew. It was there that I got my love of trees and flowers. It was there that I first climbed into a hollow tree and felt a real sense of nature. It was Kew that developed my sense of colour, guiding me through the subtle, unimaginable variety of its iris garden. It was at Kew that I learnt how sweet a jasmine or a wisteria could smell, and how that scent could invade me with a sense of well-being. It was at Kew that Joanna talked of all the places she missed, of Italy and the Corentyne, of the Caribbean and the South of France, of New Zealand and India – all places she had never been to but yearned for with a visceral longing assuaged by their plants. She told me about all the explorers and botanists who had sent seeds and cuttings back to Kew and the cost in human terms of getting that living matter there. She told me about Humboldt and Marianne North and about the mutiny on the *Bounty*. She told me how the seedlings on board the *Bounty* had been watered even while the crew was dying of thirst and how the cruel and heartless Captain Bligh had loved and cared for his plants in a way he was incapable of doing for his men. On our bench in the palm house, she explained many aspects of the world to me. She called Kew Gardens an ambassador to the entire world. It was a kingdom at which we paid court: a mother and daughter with a bagful of sandwiches and acres of dreams.

3

When I was eventually caught truanting, aged seven, I was sent at great financial sacrifice to an exclusive private school. My new school was a revelation to me. I was very close to my mother, and although I didn't believe all she said about me I did believe most of it. She had told me that I was an infant prodigy – a genius the likes of which had never been seen before. It wasn't hard to hold my own on our road. And her friends, be they impressed or repulsed by my precociousness, at least acknowledged it. On the few occasions I had gone into my primary school (in the second year when lessons finally began), there was no competition: most of my classmates were either still learning to read or romping through bisyllabic *Janet and John.* At James Allen's Girls' School there were children who were better at me in lots of subjects. I had read a lot and done reading, writing and arithmetic, but things like science and French were utterly new and maths had leapt past the fields of addition and abstraction into realms which, to this day, I am incapable of grasping. For the first time in my life I had to try, and often, having tried my best, I failed.

I stopped playing truant. I started working hard and trying to please my teachers. And, although I was embarrassed to admit it to my sister Resi (a fellow truanter from a different school and in another part of London), I enjoyed school. I even enjoyed assembly and singing hymns, and I was so pleased with my new school uniform that I sometimes wore it in bed at home during the weekends when the girls were away and I had our shared nursery to myself. There was a spate of nearly two years in which I studied and behaved like the little angel my mother had always been convinced I was. I was nine when my lessons ceased to hold my attention and I began to read fiction and history secretly under my desk while keeping half an eye on the blackboard. This coincided with a time when my childhood illness peaked, giving me more and more time at home on genuine sick leave. My mother was working, which meant that I spent most of those days reading. Although my mother was unhappy at my being alone (not least because it was technically illegal for me to be so), those were the safest days of my childhood. And being away from the routine of school reminded me of quite how much I disliked that routine, while returning always drove home how much I disliked being told what to do. When I had been working to attain my own goals I had been happy there, but once I reached the top part of the class (in all but maths) and found I could stay there with very little effort, I was ready to move on.

I had a vague feeling of uneasiness and a faint awareness of wanting some way of getting out while still seeming to be in school. I often availed myself of the sickroom facility: I had a key and could come and go at will. Anyone caught shamming in the sickroom was in serious trouble. You could only stay there if you could show an injury or a temperature. At that time, I ran a fever every day, a low, steady fever which had covered me so many times that no one bothered to go and try to catch me out faking; that fever was mine. So I knew that if I could find a safe way off the vast school premises, it would be hard for anyone to prove I wasn't there because I could either be in the sickroom or whatever classroom I was meant to be in, or I could be going between the two by whatever rambling route I chose and thus be unfindable.

The solution came on a nature walk. The school was endowed with its own varied botanical gardens. There was a beach garden with sand which was watered only with salt water, there was a wood, and there were ponds and hedges with their appropriate growth, all in the middle of London. The hedgerow was thick and luxuriant and we were gathering things from along it to put in our nature folders. Under part of the thicket a cuckoo pint was growing and I half crawled under the hedge to take a closer look. Behind me, I heard our science mistress call out, 'Do be careful, Lisa, there is a hole in the hedge there and you could fall right on to the station platform.'

She laughed and we all laughed. I crawled out. But when the day ended, instead of going straight home I went back to check out this gap, taking an experimental tumble through the White Rabbit hole. Sure enough, after a rather uncomfortable roll, I landed up on the platform of East Dulwich station, whence, I noticed, passengers could make their way not only to Croydon but to Brighton.

Brighton was a mere fifty minutes away by train, and

Brighton was at the seaside. If I had to choose a beach to spend a lot of time on, it wouldn't consist entirely of grey pebbles and have wind so strong it blew me sideways. On the other hand, any beach was still a beach and the untamed crashing of the grey waves gave me a sense of freedom such as I had never had. When the biting cold eventually drove me off the shore I found that my dinner money was sufficient to buy me a pot of tea at the Grand Hotel which, as its name implies, was the grandest hotel in Brighton. I would sit for an hour or two beside a potted palm feeling incredibly smug for just being there where I shouldn't be, for having a foolproof alibi back at the school, for knowing that I could get home in time for no one to notice I'd been missing. Joanna was happy because I seemed to be so happy at school again. I had skipped a year and was due to enter the senior school in one year's time, something, I knew, which depended on my winning an academic scholarship to cover my fees. To this specific end I worked hard outside of school, harder than I would have done at school, and won one of the two available scholarships.

A lot more happened in the next year. Not least, my aunt Cicely died of cancer in London. She was my father's closest sister and married to a Guyanese novelist called Wilson Harris. During the spring of 1963, as Cicely fought for her life, Guyanese friends and relations gathered around her. And my father, Jan Carew, of whom I had seen very little in my life, came too. It was the first time I had a lot of contact with West Indians and Guyanese. It was the first time I became properly aware of the un-English side of me, recognising that much of what I found different in myself, in my way of thinking and behaving, was a shared commodity. When Cicely died, my mother (who loathed my father and never spent more than two minutes in his presence) found a way back to him through his grief. She had a heart so generous she would never let even strangers suffer uncomforted in her presence. Seeing Jan so broken, she comforted him. For the first and only time in my life, my parents were together.

Jan had had a number of novels published in translation behind the Iron Curtain and had accrued fairly hefty royalties, none of which, because of currency restrictions, could he take out of the Soviet bloc. He was invited by the Soviet Writers' Union to go over to Russia to spend his royalties there, and he suggested that Joanna and I accompany him on this trip. Although it would mean my missing a little school, I assured Joanna that it was a sacrifice I was prepared to make, and we set off for Leningrad by car.

Everything was new and exciting to me on that journey, from crossing the English Channel to Ostend to drinking thick creamy hot chocolate in a cobbled square in Brussels and cruising on motorways, stopping in Hameln of Pied Piper fame and sleeping under a feather duvet to jolting over the cobbled roads of Poland and then, last but not least, Russia itself. I had new clothes for the journey and this too was a source of happiness. Clothes travelled down our family from sister to sister until they got to me. Apart from the cardigans and bathing dresses which Joanna knitted me, I wasn't used to having my own new things. Jan's car was a lovely old silver Daimler which attracted a great deal of attention as we drove through Europe. Once we crossed into the eastern bloc, it attracted something like adoration. I had never felt so grand.

On the down side, by the time we reached Ostend, less than a day into our odyssey, my parents had fallen out. The front of the car was a hotbed of recrimination and argument. Having once been equipped with a chauffeur, the Daimler still had a glass partition, enabling the passenger in the back seat to ride in complete privacy. That passenger was me. I could lie on the beige leather seat with a cocktail cabinet and a little pull-out walnut table in front of me and a book or my own daydreams, and not hear a word of the bickering in front. Or I could keep the glass division open a chink and, hiding behind my book, give the impression of being oblivious to their ongoing row while actually learning interesting tidbits of family history and feeling at firsthand what it was like to have two parents close enough to fall out.

One night we camped in the Black Forest and I slept out on a carpet of pine needles and listened to the sound of nightbirds and the rustling of leaves intruding on the stillness of the dark dark night. Every day began on a note of reconciliation. I was only nine but not entirely unaware that my parents were doing more than talking in the little tent they had brought with them. However, at Ostend the Daimler developed a curious judder in its steering. This disappeared if my father took it over a certain speed. This speed struck Joanna as excessive. Every day the arguments would begin over the to-speed-or-not-to-speed question. By Kraków in Poland Jan had won that particular argument but, in so doing, lost the war. Joanna wasn't speaking to him, and at night, while I slept stretched out in utter comfort on the back seat of the car, Jan slept huddled on the front seat. He is six foot six.

In Warsaw we broke down and had to spend three days waiting for the Daimler to be repaired. For the last many hundreds of miles, instead of petrol as we know it a sort of muddy tar had been tipped into the tank. It was in Warsaw that Joanna finally began to relax. She and I wandered around the city, only meeting Jan for dinner. I could see her thinking this was much more what she wanted to do in Russia, although more must have happened on the road across the Steppes than met my eye because when we finally reached Moscow we stayed together for just three days and then split up for nearly three months, she and I returning by train while Jan shipped the car back on his own.

If I had been a little more of a capitalist at heart, I might, from that trip, have become a communist. It was to be some years before the irony of this was clear to me. Most of my childhood had been spent in the drab suburbs of London. Although we didn't lack food, for years, particularly when my mother was studying to be a teacher and living on a student grant for one, we lacked a lot of other things. We were broke, and gnawed by constant minor debt. After she qualified, my mother worked all day teaching, and then came home and worked for half the night addressing envelopes for a market research firm. Sometimes I would sit up with her and address envelopes too. Sometimes we did piecework on little wooden figurines for my sisters' stepmother's handmade toy factory. This was supposed to be a way of us girls making some pocket money but actually it eked out our meagre housekeeping.

Abbeville Road, our local shopping street, was studded with shops of indescribable squalor. The secondhand shops sold urine-soaked mattresses which they displayed on the pavement. There was a handful of better shops where we bought our groceries, but a pervading aura of want hovered over the high street. Further afield, in Balham, life was visibly treading people down to the point where dozens of them lumbered about the streets in a state of numb depression. By contrast, the Soviet Union struck me as a place of astonishing wealth. We stayed in hotels converted from palaces with enormous state rooms as dining rooms and bedrooms with marble floors, antique furniture, massive drapes, chandeliers and all the things I had only read about or seen in museums.

In Russia, we had people waiting on us hand and foot. Whatever food we wanted in Moscow and Leningrad was ours to command. Joanna grew merry night after night on champagne. I had never seen such plenty. We were fêted and spoilt and thoroughly pampered. It was summer and it was hot and I had never had such a good time.

We were guided round Moscow by a man called Victor Ramsez from the Writers' Union. In Leningrad, we were taken around by Veronica Spaskaya, who became a good friend to Joanna. Veronica drew me out of my luxuriant trance and taught me a bit about Russia. With hindsight, I realise she also taught me a lot about life. Before we left Russia, Veronica gave me a small black antique paliak box which, she said, was her one family heirloom, handed down from mother to daughter for generations. Both Joanna and I agreed that it would be wrong for me to accept it. When I told Veronica this, she sat me down and told me the following story.

It began with names: Leningrad, the city she had so lovingly showed us around, used to be St Petersburg, then, under Stalin, it became Stalingrad. The German army sent to Russia was the biggest army in the history of mankind. It swept across the Soviet Union, advancing at incredible speed. Literally millions of Russians died up to the point where the Germans reached the outskirts of Stalingrad. Those inside the city knew they had to defend it down to the last man. Unable to break through the defences, the Germans besieged the city, cutting off all supplies. Veronica was my age when that happened. She told me how after the food ran out, they ate all the cats in the city, and then the dogs and then the rats. In the end, they boiled up the soles of their boots to stay alive. Her entire family died in the siege, mostly of starvation. The Russians had sheer tenacity and winter on their side. The Germans began to die of cold and their own supply routes fell prey to the bitter weather. During the long retreat across Russia, chased out by the Russian army, hundreds of thousands of Germans died. Their army was both beaten and demoralised. It was their first major defeat and one that would, eventually, end the Second World War. Because of her own near starvation in the siege, Veronica was sterile, she could never have a child of her own. She told me she had been waiting to meet a girl whom she could talk to as she might have talked to a daughter. She insisted I take her little box, which I did, and which I treasured.

The effect of some of the things Veronica told me was immediate. For instance, I had no idea that the Russians had even played a part on 'our' side in the war. A sense of 'the Reds are our enemies' drifted through to the playground. They were the baddies. We were the goodies. We, the British, had won the war, everyone knew that, we sang it in our street songs:

> We won the war
> In nineteen forty-four

No one had ever mentioned the millions of Russian dead or their sacrifice.

Next there was the issue of freedom. Khrushchev was in power in Russia, bringing, it seemed, new hopes of freedom. Meanwhile, we in the West were so lucky to be free. I realised that I had something I not only didn't appreciate but had never been aware of. It was another kind of freedom to the one I dreamed of, one I had and Veronica didn't. It took many years for this to sink in, but it was she who planted the seed.

Next there was news. Veronica was hungry for it. For all the censorship and repression within the Soviet Union (though I was blissfully unaware of any such political restraint at the time), Veronica knew far more about what was happening worldwide than we did. She plied Joanna with questions and finding her little help she turned to me, grilling me for snippets of news. Joanna loved poetry, painting and fiction. She was a mine of information on the maladjusted child, but she shunned politics as 'boring'. This was something she had passed on to me. Politics was boring and poor Veronica gleaned nothing of any interest to her in that field from her sudden friendship with Joanna and I.

When Veronica discovered how much I read, she moved to the safer ground of fiction, wanting to know about all the latest English and American writers. She found it hard to believe that I had only read the eighteenth- and nineteenth-century English writers. 'But you could go to a public library and choose the books of any writer. Why don't you?' I didn't know, I had never thought to do so. And what, she asked me on another occasion, did I like best about Chekov and Turgenev?

Did I like Maupassant, she asked. I bowed my ignorant head in shame and left Leningrad determined to read differently.

Growing up on an island is a curious thing. You live and breathe an insularity. Such was the supremacy of English it hadn't dawned on me that people in other countries wrote books in other languages. On the shelves back in Clapham there was a section in French. They were Joanna's. I didn't speak French then and the notion of translations had eluded me. When I went back to England it would be to read foreign literature and to keep my ear open to foreign languages, to which end I made a little start in Leningrad, picking up as much Russian as I could. Veronica was encouraging me to make something of myself not because I was born needing only wings to fly but because I would work at perfection. I would like to say I went straight back and read John Stuart Mill, Rousseau and Russell and developed a social and political conscience, but it was not so.

4

From Leningrad, Joanna and I moved on to Sochi, a resort on the Black Sea. We were to spend five weeks there in a big hotel by the seafront with our days spent on the beach. Five weeks is a long time, especially when a family is divided. We both made friends on the beach and spent most of our days talking to them. Mine was an eleven-year-old Russian boy called Vovo. He spoke some English and he taught me some Russian. He also taught me to swim and gave me a social confidence that I had lacked. After my friendship with him I was able to make friends back in England more easily.

It was hot in Sochi, for Joanna and I staggeringly hot. After England, where a national prudery pervaded life, the abandon of Russian beaches was a revelation. Bikinis were in. They had not really come in yet in England. In Sochi, they had already graduated to micro bikinis sported by startlingly fat matrons. I had never seen so much naked flesh. Had I been there for a week only, I would have left with a sense of shock and repulsion at the sight of all those folds of flab. Staying five weeks,

I grew used to seeing women, in particular, celebrating the sun, at ease with their bodies, uninhibited by what others might think about their shape or beauty. No one changed on that beach as we did, contorting, English fashion, under a sewn-up towel. Men and women, boys and girls just changed right there in front of everyone.

I think it was there, on that beach, that I decided not just to leave London when I could, but to leave England. I didn't know where I would go, but it would have to be somewhere warm where people enjoyed themselves. I was a very physically inhibited child. I shouldn't have been, but I was. At home everything was very open, no one locked any doors. I sat and talked to Joanna while she was in the bath. I was encouraged to be open. But I never took a bath without locking and even barricading the door with the towel rack (since the lock was flimsy). I never changed in front of my sisters. I was incapable of getting out of my wet bathing dress without the covering of our tent towel. I came to see I didn't like being like that, but that was how I was.

When I thought of this somewhere else to live, Russia didn't cross my mind, probably, I suspect, because of its red caviar. I liked black caviar in small quantities with blinis and sour cream, but eating the big fishy globules of red caviar felt like swallowing coloured frogspawn. Every morning for five weeks breakfast consisted of a bumper bowl of red caviar, a couple of pints of very sour cream and a bowl of porridge. Lunch was identical except that in lieu of porridge there were boiled eggs, sauerkraut and bread. Supper, served very early, was red caviar, sour cream, a lot more boiled eggs and sauerkraut and huge fat snappy frankfurters that popped when you cut into them. Vovo was in seventh heaven when we arranged, with great difficulty, to invite him to our hotel for a meal – apparently we were 'lucky lucky'. Actually Joanna was severely constipated and I was ferrying quantities of red caviar around in a little velvet bag and then flushing it down our lavatory. The fishy smell hung around me. What with the famine at Stalingrad and Vovo's envy of our privileged diet, I felt like a criminal disposing of so much caviar, but leaving it on the table was not an option. We had tried it several times and had been stood over as by a prefect at school, defied to commit an affront against the national dish and legendary Russian hospitality. By the end of the second week Joanna and I were both secreting obese frankfurters in our pockets or up cardigan sleeves, attracting stares, of course, because who wears a cardigan when the temperature is 41°C?

On the beach old ladies came around selling tiny sweet grapes in bunches. They were seedless and gorgeous and Joanna, who was always obsessed by vitamins and eating mounds of green-leaf vegetables and a lot of fruit, finally felt brave enough to skip lunch completely. There were only two occasions in the entire time we were in Russia when we came up against the State. The first time was in Leningrad at a very grand hotel where we were staying. She and I went down to dinner all dressed up in our finery and took our seats in the formal restaurant, whereupon she was told that a woman and child were not allowed to sit in the restaurant without being accompanied by a man. Of all the people in the world to say that to, Joanna was about the worst. She didn't back down. There was no way she was going to back down, and I realise now that we were lucky it was Khrushchev in power and not

Stalin or we would probably have spent the rest of our lives in a gulag. Being of a shy and cowardly bent myself, I would have gladly slunk off to another restaurant, eaten in our room or, frankly, not at all. Not Joanna! She saw in that one rule a principle for all her life and all her sex. From a discreet preliminary request, it turned into a major incident with higher and higher officials being called and Joanna's voice increasing in decibels accordingly. Short of bodily dragging her out of the restaurant, (which prided itself on its fine dining and elegant ambience), there was no way they were going to win. In the end, we were moved to a table behind a pillar and ate our beef stroganoff in mortified silence.

Our second run-in with the authorities was over missing lunch in Sochi. On our second absence, Joanna was summoned to the manager's office and told not to do it again. When she explained that we had decided to stay down on the beach at lunchtime, she was told politely but firmly that this could not be so. After much discussion, a long, typed letter was produced in duplicate for Joanna to sign. In it she had to avow to be voluntarily absenting herself and her child from lunch 'despite being repeatedly pressed and invited not to'. That way, upon return to the Wicked West, she could not make the scurrilous claim that in the People's Republic of the Soviet Union people didn't eat lunch.

From that day on I lived in dread of being caught disposing of the red caviar. A long way down the sands, on the part of the beach away from our hotel, orphan children with shaved heads and dark smocks were taken out every day to play. I used to wander down there with Vovo. One day, after we had managed to invite him to eat with us, he invited me to venture a little further to where a man was selling hot corn on the cob. As we strolled back, barefoot and hand in hand, Vovo chewed contentedly on his sweetcorn. I took a bite of mine. It was rock hard. That one mouthful lasted me for the next half hour. Mercifully Vovo had to go back for lunch. I hid my inedible cob in our beach bag to get rid of back at the hotel. One thing about the beach at Sochi was that it was immaculately clean. Pensioners with spiked sticks and bags combed the beach daily, patrolling the sands for litter. Their vigilance would undoubtedly have uncovered an entire outsized cob of corn, and the waste would have been unpardonable, the slur inexcusable, and Vovo, whose parents had so little money, would know that I had spurned his gift.

That afternoon I flushed it down the lavatory bowl over and over again. It obstinately refused to disappear. Going very much against my squeamish grain, I fished it out, broke it up and tried again. Breaking it up was in itself no mean feat and wrecked our nail scissors. The bits were still quite big but I got a couple of them into the system before the water began to gather in the lavatory bowl and I realised that to block the entire sewage system in that rather large hotel would make us very unpopular, if not criminal. Over the next two days I took little spools of sweetcorn on the cob down to the beach, contrived to walk down towards the orphans on my own and dug deep pits in which to bury the offending vegetable. With only one spool to go, I gave up and chucked it into the sea while I was swimming. It bobbed around for days, accusingly, but, I was glad to see, not recognisably mine.

Towards the end of our stay Jan arrived to see us. The visit was not a success. He arrived looking bright yellow and half dead in the company of two boisterous Georgians. They were several days into a drinking spree and my father, for all his wild ways, has never been a drinker. He told me that if he didn't get down on to the beach and sleep for a couple of days his liver would kill him. Joanna was very unsympathetic, since she surmised, rightly, that much of his exhaustion was from having paid too much attention to too many girls. The Russian that Vovo had taught me was sufficient for me to follow the Georgians' rerun of the last few weeks as they sat swigging vodka on the beach beside their sleeping guest. Despite his dark skin, Jan took a dose of sunburn so extreme even Joanna relented and helped treat him. Then he was gone and I didn't see him again for months.

I missed him, as I have always missed him. When I was a child I knew instinctively not to tell that to anyone. Joanna struggled to be a mother and a father to me. She could not have loved me more, but the longing for a father was always there, to be sublimated, later, into a longing for his continent, for South America, the place I did and didn't come from.

Our return, when the time came, seemed like a hurried affair. Our flight back from Sochi was altered so that at the last minute we had to pack up and run. We flew back to Moscow in a small rickety jet which terrified Joanna but which I loved. It was only my second ever flight, the first having been in a slightly larger, less rickety Russian plane *to* Sochi. The trip was turbulent. Joanna had had a mastoid operation during the war and suffered from serious earache whenever she flew. On arrival she was determined not to fly home from Moscow to London. For once money wasn't the issue. We were still spending Jan's rubles as fast as we could. The funny thing was there was so little to spend them on. We bought furs and amber, gramophone records and books and there really wasn't much else to buy. Everything cost next to nothing so there was a fat kitty left. Out of this we took first-class railway tickets from Moscow to the Hook of Holland, and first-class tickets on a Dutch ferry to England. The two days that we had left in Moscow were almost entirely swallowed up arranging these tickets.

Even though Jan would ship back our books and records, we had a lot of luggage. Moscow station was a throbbing, shrill hub of turmoil. There were Tartars and Mongols and Chinese. There were people with children and people who had lost their children. There were soldiers, enough, it seemed, to go on manoeuvres. There were people smartly dressed and people dressed in what looked like brown sacking. Everyone seemed to be laden with luggage and a lot of that luggage seemed to be alive and clucking. Everyone getting on our train was carrying food, stuffing it through the windows in greasy packages interspersed with vast watermelons.

We were travelling first class. As far as I could see there were four classes on the train, but we were first and were ushered through like minor royalty. It was a slow train and a long journey. Even without an unscheduled delay at Brest Litovsk, the journey was one of several days. Unlike the passengers crammed into the lower-class wagons with squalid picnics eaten off their laps in crowded compartments on uncomfortable slatted seats, Joanna and I travelled in style. Our compartment was upholstered in blue satin and we slept on fine cotton sheets but we had no food, we had no drinking water, and it really felt as though we were going to starve. By day it was hot and the days passed slowly. Joanna and I played bezique, card upon card, in our little private sitting room, trying to fend off the sensation of thirst and the accumulating, overriding sense of hunger. At the end of the first-class corridor, our guard sat guarding a samovar of tea.

At Brest Litovsk all our money was taken from us and replaced with Russian traveller's cheques. These, as it turned out, were entirely worthless. This was to be a problem for Joanna in the long run, she couldn't afford to lose money. In the short run, it was a disaster. We had no rubles left so we couldn't keep buying the little glasses of Russian tea, the chai the guard was selling at a ruble a go. By the time we reached the Hook of Holland, our luggage was considerably lighter. Most of my clothes had been bartered for cups of tea to stave off dehydration.

Much of the journey was spent in 'if onlys'. On our first night on the train, we had eaten our dinner in the first-class dining car with the handful of other privileged passengers. The rigours of the last few days, the bustle of getting on the train and the excitement and heat had, quite uncharacteristically, robbed us both of our appetite. Instead of eating the four-course menu, we had both opted for a snack. We had left at least half a bottle of mineral water on the table and a debatable quantity of wine. As the hours and days wore on, this failure to have stocked up like camels about to cross the Sahara was the point of most regret. The entire dining car was taken off at Brest Litovsk.

Upon arrival in England, we were turning around almost on the same day to head down to Cornwall for a week with the girls. My appendix burst on the last night in our caravan there in St Ives, and my life was going to change. The one part of my childhood that I cannot remember day by day and hour by hour falls into the following period. More than memories of facts, I have only sensations, smells, memories of the texture of certain things, of expressions on people's faces. I know I travelled sixteen hours on a National Express bus with a burst appendix. I know I wouldn't like to do it again, but all I remember is the smell of banana sandwiches, sardine sandwiches and the smother of Horlicks every time the Thermos was passed backwards and forwards. I know a doctor came to our house in the middle of the night we arrived, and I know she left again without helping. I remember the feel of the black fur rug on my bed, the feel of a chocolate bourbon biscuit (my favourite) which I held in my hand for hours because I could not eat it but didn't want to put it down. I remember the sensation of waves, pages from Virginia Woolf's *To the Lighthouse* which I was reading when I fell ill. And I wondered how long it would be before Joanna realised that her darling was dying and whether she would be strong enough to bear that loss.

We had an excellent doctor, a Czech refugee who had walked across Europe fleeing the Nazis and worked with the dedication of St Francis to tend to his flock. He was Dr Tausig. But Dr Tausig was on holiday and in his place was a rumbustious Irish locum who smelt of whisky and peppermints. On her third visit to me, she called an ambulance since, as she gaily told me in her rich brogue, 'It's better to be safe than sorry.'

It took a year to recover, but after the first six weeks, by which point my life was no longer in danger and I was recovering from the two operations I had undergone, it was a year that was mostly much easier for me than for Joanna. I was missing school, but I loved missing school. I had to lie in bed all day and read, and I loved reading. The South London Hospital for Women was a great grey rambling Victorian building that looked like a prison with its barred windows. Sometimes, later, when I could get up for baths, I used to stare through the bars at the bare, skeletal common and feel like a prisoner. But I had just been to Russia and it had given me a lot to think about. I needed a lot of time to think. I mostly had my own room on the children's ward but sometimes, if someone more ill than me was rushed in, I got wheeled out onto a proper ward. The other children there didn't read. Visits were restricted to an hour a day in the evenings. I saw them pining in a way I wasn't. They found the food inedible. I liked it. I was used to being ill. I'd been ill since I was three. I had a high pain threshold. I had been making a big effort to keep going, particularly for the last couple of years, to not worry Joanna, to not make a meal of my constant fever and tummyache. While I was in hospital I didn't have to pretend. I was ill and allowed to be, and in some ways it was a relief. While the mess from my burst appendix was being scraped out, they discovered that I was riddled with tuberculosis. My main concern from day to day was not my health but what I was going to read.

5

One of the things I've done a lot of is travel by train. As a young child, I was a phantom commuter, riding up and down the south-eastern railway when I should have been at school. From the moment I boarded the Brighton train I felt safe. As its wheels began to turn, I had escaped, again. For someone who likes flowers, railway embankments are fascinating places. They lie undisturbed for years on end and attract a wealth of wild flowers that can make even suburbia pretty. South London's tracks were a jungle of rosebay willowherb and goldenrod, foxgloves and evening primrose. All through the autumn, banks of buddleia were alive with vanessid butterflies. And the first flowers of every season could be spotted crouching in the wild grass along the tracks. The first glistening celandines in January and the first bluebells in May, the first dog roses and the first morning-glories were all there, despite the grey smoky bricks and chimney stacks beyond them.

After my trip to Russia, I began to notice much more of what was happening around me. I began to observe how people lived, for instance. Before that I had had the very English way of not looking in through other people's windows. From the pavement on any street, there really wasn't very much to see. Houses had trim little gardens or abandoned dust patches or any number of subtle variations in between. Windows had curtains that got greyer and grimier as an area got depressed. What is different about travelling by train is you look into other people's back gardens: the ones that are normally hidden from view and that their owners think of as private and unseeable. And you look into back windows: the ones that don't have any curtains, the ones that people stare out of or lean out of or undress in front of. And the train went past allotments with their rows of flowers and vegetables, their ramshackle sheds and their solitary diggers.

It was only a fifty-minute ride to Brighton, or an hour and ten minutes at worst, but each of those trips was like a little piece of a jigsaw puzzle fitting into place, or not, but making itself known. So, paradoxically, I got to know London by escaping from it, and by listening to other people's conversations on the train I got to know about what life was like outside of my family circle.

Clapham really didn't have a lot to boast of. It had a hospital and a library, the common and a police station which sometimes won the prize for the best police-station garden. It had a murderer's house and a busy road and a big fig tree which, on a good summer, could just about ripen its figs (which in England is fairly miraculous). If the worst had come to pass during the Second World War, it also had a bunker running under the common in which Winston Churchill and the Cabinet and a few chosen ones could have sheltered from the total destruction of London. Every year, the common hosted a circus and a cattle show and a horse show and, by the serendipitous mixture of animal droppings, every year it had a plethora of cyllicybin mushrooms. The only really fine thing that Clapham had though, as far as I was concerned, was its Railway Museum.

Most museums announce themselves architecturally from afar. They are purpose-built stately affairs reflecting status and pride. The Railway Museum was a doorway in a drab suburb, but it opened onto an Aladdin's cave of locomotion. And there was something of a giant cave about the massive hangar-type structure in which all the wagons and engines were housed. There was a cast-iron monster brought back from Peking; there were the private royal compartments of Queen Victoria and Queen Alexandra. Right there in the heart of Clapham, which I hated, was a hangar full of trains, which I loved. I used to fantasise about hiding in the museum after it closed and spending the night in the cushioned luxury of one of those wagons. When I travelled back from Russia, the food problem was indeed a problem but it couldn't kill my pleasure in travelling in the sort of train I had only ever seen in a museum.

The next four years were less my favourite places than my favourite books. During this time I decided to become a writer and through reading I did a great deal of armchair travelling. In the letters of Lord Byron I discovered Italy and began to focus my dreams on one day getting there. It had been my idea to be a doctor, but my stint in the South London Hospital, seeing a lot more of my insides than I really wanted to and seeing a lot more noxious waste oozing out of my surgical drain than I ever wanted to see again, completely changed my mind. Doctors, I realised, had to see a lot of blood and pus; writers just wrote about it.

It wasn't until I was thirteen that I travelled abroad again. This time it was to Luxembourg. All my sisters were doing other things for the summer holiday, so Joanna decided that she and I would go abroad. Why we went to Luxembourg rather than anywhere else, I shall never know. We set off from Waterloo Station, catching the boat train to Ostend, then travelled on by train. To both of us, the location seemed as exotic as Xanadu. The idea of a Grand Duchy perching on the top of a hill surrounded by forests with little lakes but no tourists in bikinis and no silly dirty postcards, no caravans and no granny Mabels, seemed absolutely enchanting. We could speak French without having to deal with the legendary arrogance of the French and yet still eat French food that would slip down with good French wine.

And so it was, all that and more. Alas, the more included a veritable plague of midges. Since then I have travelled widely, but rarely have I come across a flying insect with a bite more vicious than those in Luxembourg. They were minute and black and looked thoroughly ineffectual, but their bite had such a kick to it we were forced to confine ourselves to quarters at the Relais Beaujolais with the windows hermetically shut and play endless games of bezique. The alternative was to sally forth wearing cotton gloves, hats and veils like a couple of Edwardian ladies. After a few days, it seemed sillier to travel abroad and stay locked in than to go out for walks in fancy dress, so we plucked up the courage and went into the forest. Most insect repellents are designed for mosquitoes and do very little for midges. Explaining this formed the gist of almost every casual conversation we had in the Ardennes. It is true of both midges and mosquitoes that some people are more attractive to them than others. Redheads tend to get bitten more than most and Joanna was a redhead. I also get bitten more than most, despite not being one. Those midges that didn't go for her took me as a poor second best. We took our veils off at our peril, and when we did other walkers could walk in peace. One of the few conversations we managed to strike up that went past the midge-veil-bite level was with a Dutch couple. When I say we, I mean Joanna, who always struck up conversations wherever we were with whoever else happened to be there. I was shy, almost ridiculously shy, and usually, if I had to choose between talking to a stranger or taking cyanide, I would have opted for the cyanide without a moment's hesitation.

However, the Dutch couple had a son called Fred as shy as me. Whereas Joanna accepted (although maybe never understood) that I was shy and so would never dream of urging me to speak to someone or make friends with them, Fred's parents encouraged him in stage whispers to go across and speak to me. Fred, meanwhile, was having none of it. Fred's father had worked with the RAF during the war and spoke rather wonderful English. Joanna and he were getting on like a house on fire, and within a couple of days she had extracted both his and his wife's entire life story, which she had swapped for a heavily edited version of her own. The Relais could, if requested in advance, provide a delicious picnic basket. Both families set off for a day in the hills, during which, to save

Fred the further embarrassment of being cajoled and then ordered to speak to me, I spoke to him. He was so grateful that we became friends, to the delight of all and sundry. When they eventually left Luxembourg, we exchanged addresses and wrote to each other. They lived in a place outside Amsterdam called Amstelveen. The smattering of Dutch I have grew out of that friendship.

I have a soft spot for Luxembourg, a fondness for its fine, glazed patisserie and its chocolates. I think of it as somebody else's dream: a toy town on a hill with its castle and all its slate-grey roofs. There is a softness built into its northerly, austere style. Its architecture is full of little, almost apologetic flourishes with its sandstone turrets and its quoins and balconies, carvings and crests. The villages are orderly, the trees are clipped, everything is clean and tidy, and yet I had the sensation that within all the beige and grey stone, so perfectly squared, there was something anarchic: a zest contained but not entirely smothered.

Luxembourg City itself was full of buildings that looked like town halls but were saved from dourness by these flourishes and also by the sheer height of their mansards and the variety and quantity of the little windows opening out of the slates. They gave the impression of another world up there, one of attics and students, garrets and impoverished dreamers living an entirely different life to the ones farther from the pale sky.

Liking a place often leads to fantasies, and the Grand Duchy was no exception. I imagined the student from Oscar Wilde's *The Nightingale and the Rose* living in one of the hundreds of attics. This was for no better reason than that they were there, and the roses in the garden of our Relais were particularly lovely, and the castle was a place that surely held the kind of balls the story spoke of.

Later, I used to wonder if I had overendowed Luxembourg with qualities it did not have because it was only my second foreign foray and inevitably tame by comparison with our Russian marathon. Beyond the glut of confectionery, was there really something sweet there? When I eventually returned, many years later, I was gratified to find there was.

Returning home I realised that it was not so much the place that had fired me as the fact that I had been happy there. Until that trip I had been shy, overly repressed and too prone to depression. (Shy, too, is the same word in Luxembourgeoise. We learnt it of necessity to cover my excessive blushes.) I had felt, before, moments of euphoria, but never a steady happiness. In Luxembourg, I became aware not only of feeling happy, but of wanting to feel so again. It was a new thread in my skein; a strand to twist and turn and keep refinding.

Wedged up in the Ardennes with its woods and midges, it is so tiny, most people miss that little tax haven. Though small on most maps, it is large on mine for having engineered another change: adding lightness to my own grey palette.

6

The Clapham that I knew when I was growing up has transformed now into a trendy and very expensive part of London. Abbeville Road, the slummy shopping street with its second-hand shops stocked almost entirely with stuff most people would burn, is now lined with delicatessens, cafés and restaurants. People dream of being able to move to Clapham with as much yearning, I'm sure, as I used to dream of getting away from it. However, when I lived there, no tourist in their right mind would rent something there. Only someone who had never been to London and had no idea where Clapham South was would pay money to stay there. Just such a tourist was my first husband, Jaime Terán, and his two friends, Otto and Elias. They turned up in London, went to an agency in the West End and asked for a house to rent or a flat no matter what the cost so long as it was in the centre. And, bingo! They were rented the top part of a maisonette in Abbeville Road for which they had not only paid a deposit, sight unseen, but also three months' rent in advance.

But for that, I could never have met Jaime or found myself farming sugar in the Venezuelan Andes. When I say that I bumped into a Venezuelan landowner in Clapham South, the full force of the absurdity of that statement, the sheer impossibility of such a claim can hardly be lost on anyone. Yet it was on Abbeville Road that he first saw me, aged sixteen, and fell in love with me. And then, with the tenacity of a limpet, he followed me, courting me, if such it can be called, with a dogged silence. This he interrupted from time to time not so much with a request as a demand to marry him.

I eventually did marry him, and just as everyone else asks why, I have to ask myself the same thing. I married him because I was bored, because he asked me to, because he invited me to Italy, because he said he'd die if I didn't and because he embarrassed me, following me around everywhere with his little pocket Collins dictionary and his loud voice saying, 'You marry me!' on buses and trains, at cafés and in front of my schoolfriends. Maybe, also, I married him because my friends and family saw something wonderful in him, something instantly charismatic which I couldn't see but didn't like to admit to missing. It was a little in the way of laughing at a joke you don't get, not wanting someone to think there is something wrong with your sense of humour. And I think, although I don't even like to admit it to myself too often, I married him to annoy his friend Otto, who, as hard as Jaime tried to get me to agree to stay with him, tried to get me to go away.

That's a lot of reasons for marrying someone. Usually, there's just one: love, or money. But love didn't come into it for me at that early stage. Also, for the record, although he turned out to be very rich, money didn't come into it either, because I had no way of knowing that when I finally agreed to marry him. The man lived in a horrible slummy flat in Clapham. There are few better ways for a millionaire to go incognito. All the reasons I married him put together would have been insufficient without his 'Let's go to Italy'. I had been dreaming of Italy for years, longing for it, plotting my future life there, following other people's lives there, particularly those of writers. I read the letters of Byron and Shelley, Goethe and Stendhal, George Eliot and Elizabeth Barrett Browning. I didn't love Jaime Terán but I did love Italy.

My first home there was in the attic flat of a sixteenth-century building on a little street near the centre of Bologna. It had three rooms, a kitchen and a bathroom. It had dipped, age-darkened terracotta floors, big stone fireplaces in three of the rooms (one of which was the kitchen), beamed ceilings and little Tuscan windows with wooden shutters that opened out over a palette of roof tiles ranging haphazardly from pale umber to rose madder with all the intervening hues.

Considering how much I had read about Italy, it shouldn't have come as a surprise, but it did, daily, hourly, and there was always more. The churches, the shops, the people, the pavements, the arcades, the markets, the squares, the cafés, the coffee, the chocolate, the smells, the wisteria, the colours, the frescoes, the towers, the alleyways; every bit of it, every brick of it was a source of wonder. I was sixteen, but I looked about twelve; and Italians are so nice to children. They treated me like a child, spoilt and petted me, gave me little presents and went out of their way to make me feel at home in the town.

Half the time I was in Bologna I was drunk with pleasure at the endless overload of lovely impressions.

Mine was a strange marriage, but I hadn't seen marriage from close up before. All my mother's had taken place before I was born and we had no near relations. So I didn't know what a marriage was supposed to be like outside of a Jane Austen novel, and I knew I had to make allowances for it being the twentieth century, and for Jaime being Venezuelan, and so old while I was so young. And I knew most people didn't get married with an interpreter to translate their vows as we had. Not having a common language didn't help. Living in a foursome with Jaime's two friends did or didn't help, depending how I looked at the situation. On the one hand, we had no privacy. On the other hand, Jaime spent most of his days staring into space or sleeping, so if I hadn't had Elias around (who was younger and a good friend to me), I would have had no one to talk to, to walk with, to explore the city with or to keep me from feeling lonely. In those early months, in fact, for almost two years, Otto, who had been a master of guerrilla strategy, conducted a guerrilla war with me. I have never argued with anyone else as much, or so much disliked, or been disliked by, anyone. But out of that war of attrition a friendship grew which has been the most important friendship of my life.

Otto was a scholar while I had a veneer of scholarship. He had spent nearly a third of his life as a political prisoner while I still lived blinkered by the notion that politics was boring. He was on the run from Interpol, a man in hiding, while I was a teenager with a penchant for fancy dress. He loathed what he called my 'prissy upper-class English ignorance' and I loathed him. Elias, on the other hand, the youngest of the group of three exiles, was handsome and funny, sweet and protective to me. Meanwhile, Jaime, the man I had married, remained an almost complete stranger. His lethargy, which had been remarkable in London, became almost total in Bologna. His one concession to not staying in bed all day was to go to the poste restante at the central post office and ask if there were any letters for him. It was a hollow gesture: there never were. He was waiting for money from the vast lands he owned back in the Venezuelan Andes, but the money didn't arrive and we sank into abject poverty.

For a couple of months Otto and, in particular, Elias tided us all over, shoplifting food and supplying our rustic Tuscan table. When it became clear that our situation was not going to improve, they set off for Sweden where they had been offered a job in a beer factory. The three exiles were the last hub of a group which had been politically active in Venezuela. They had an almost superstitious fear of splitting up. They invited, begged and bullied Jaime into going with them to Sweden to get some money together to get back on their feet. Their entreaties were in vain. It didn't matter how many times they pointed out to Jaime that he could lie in bed and sleep all day in Stockholm just as easily as he could in Bologna, he wouldn't budge, he wouldn't work and he wouldn't discuss it.

When they left, I began to see for the first time what an odd situation I was in. Sometimes we didn't eat for days. Sometimes our neighbours from across the landing would leave little presents outside our door: panna cotta, crème caramel, a little pasty or a fairy cake.

When life in Bologna got too difficult, or was seen to be so, we used to travel to Paris. Paradoxically, although we didn't have any money, we had a number of train tickets from Paris to Milan and back. Our earlier forays to Paris had resulted in square meals and baths. The one thing lacking in our own lovely flat was a proper bath. We made do with a big tub in the kitchen and an enamel jug to tip water over oneself. As time wore on, the situation in Paris deteriorated and our hostess there became almost as broke as us. With food measured out to hard rations, the invasion of four very hungry uninvited visitors was not always welcome. Despite this, we kept visiting because there was a luxury in just moving on, but our visits were more and more of the turnaround kind and sometimes didn't last longer than an afternoon before we'd be back on the train, chugging through France and up into Switzerland, crossing the Alps, dropping down to the Italian lakes and heading back into the monumental, architectural overkill of Milan's central station.

Friends of Otto's who had fought in the International Brigade in the Cuban Revolution made a small attic room in a slum tenement in Milan available to us. Sometimes, when we needed a change, we holed up in Milan, squatting in this anteroom to their own illicit stores. Every time we went back to Bologna after Milan, it was a great relief. Bologna was beautiful and we lived there in hungry comfort. Milan was grey and ugly and we lived there in squalor.

Bologna is one of those Italian cities that has got it all. It has fabulous medieval and Renaissance architecture and it has Roman remains. It has a great cathedral and yet is packed full with other exquisite churches. It has towers, great historic towers. It even has a leaning tower. It has a famous and historic university with an internationally acclaimed medical school. It has lovely piazzas, beautiful streets, fine shops, theatres, gardens, statues – everything, in fact, and yet it does not have the fame the Bolognese feel it deserves. Who talks about the leaning tower of Bologna? But it is there and it leans just as much as Pisa's. The Bolognese are very touchy about the way the world has failed to fully perceive the pre-eminence of their city. They are very sensitive about the way other cities stole all the glory. I have never known a city, town or village in Italy whose citizens didn't fervently believe was the centre of the world. Nor have I lived anywhere where this point was driven home harder than in Bologna. When I first lived in Italy, since Bologna was just about the only place I knew, and was certainly the only place I knew well, I was in complete agreement with its sons and daughters. And still, decades later, although it is no longer the fairest of them all, it stands well on its own merits.

After I left in 1972, I didn't go back for over twenty years. I had such fond memories of the city and I didn't know if they would stand up to the test of time. It was only when the film director Michael Austin, working on a film version of the novel I had set there (among other places), asked me to go with him to help him find locations for the film that I returned. The city has pillared arcades running through most of it. Rain or shine, pedestrians are forever seeing Bologna from a Renaissance loggia. Walking through the centre on that rainy afternoon in 1998, I felt invaded by memories which seemed to rise up from the marble pavements. It is a good place, a fine place. It had changed, but really not very much. When I saw the tearoom with its shelves of luscious glazed cakes signalling through the windows, cakes I used to spend hours staring at, my face pressed against the glass, fantasizing about the order in which I would devour them, we stopped and went in. How often can one as tangibly and easily fulfil a dream?

There are places that change people, that stay with them for any number of reasons. They don't have to be beautiful and they don't have to be nice. Bologna changed me, hugely. There was before and there was after. It wasn't a baptism of fire. It was a gentle change. I began to grow up there, to love, to communicate: I learnt Italian and most of my Spanish there. I had been living in a cocoon until I moved into its *centro storico.* I didn't break out of that cocoon entirely, but I stretched it and began to emerge. I became aware of many things and many ideas in that red-bricked arcaded city. Without its cradling embrace and intrinsic generosity I would, I am sure, see the world differently.

7

In my life there have been instances of misfortune, more, perhaps, than one would normally expect. More than compensating for these sporadic disasters have been instances of good fortune. While I was living in Bologna with Jaime, a stroke of such luck came our way. It was a swelteringly hot summer, so hot that the air was itself a blast of heat which ruled out opening any windows during the day. We lived in darkness with our shutters closed and only a faint electric light in our apartment. It was so hot that even the heat from a strong bulb seemed to tip the scales from bearable to unbearable. For several months, we had been alone. I read and studied, Jaime slept. Every evening, at about six o'clock, the heat in our rooms drove us out onto the slightly cooler communal landing. Here our two elderly neighbours, *la signora* Nadalina and *la signora* Berta, spent almost their entire day, leafing through a trunk of old court circulars and society magazines, gossiping about the royal heads of Europe and their families as though they were old friends and lived across the way.

Jaime and I had an open invitation to join them on the landing. It didn't take long to sort out which king had married which princess, duchess or actress and what their children were called, which was really all that was required to join in our neighbours' incessant talk. Royalty and high society were their favourite topics, but they had another one which ran like an undercurrent through their days. Everything in their darkly shuttered apartment was priced and labelled. Some things had price tags like old luggage labels tied to them, others were just catalogued in the old ladies' minds. They had a compulsive need to know both where things came from and how much they cost. Neither of the two went out for more than an hour a week for basic essentials, but they kept in touch with the world outside, vicariously, through its prices. No matter what, after an initial and effusive greeting, *la signora* Nadalina would launch into her enquiries about clothes, shoes, a book, a bag, a loaf of bread: 'Where did you buy it? What did it cost?' It was their chant, their mantra. It drove Jaime to distraction. I spent increasing amounts of time with the old ladies and found their obsessions eccentrically charming. Jaime had no time for other people's neuroses and found Nadalina's and Berta's contagious. He spent an hour with them every evening because they gave us tea and biscuits. Since this was often our only sustenance for the day, he sacrificed his neurasthenia for that afternoon tea.

By seven thirty the infernal heat that gathered in the basin in which Bologna is built began to fade and we would emerge from our airless twilight zone into the streets. There, Jaime would download the old ladies' chatter, muttering, 'Where did you buy it, what did it cost?' in Italian over and over again like a madman. On one such evening, when he chanced to be out on his own, he found someone following him. Otto, Elias and Jaime were all intensely paranoid, often with good reason, since they were in hiding. Normally Jaime was hyper-alert to anyone on his trail but that day, since he was in full flow, he didn't notice until the lady behind him had obviously been there for some time. He became aware of her because she was at his side and laughing. Her name was Franca, she lived nearby, she said she had never seen such a funny sight and invited him up for a drink. This was followed by an invitation to both of us to go to dinner.

Franca is blessed among women. Even if her hospitality had ended with the dinner (soup, steak, strawberries with blancmange, cheese, grapes and almond biscuits with coffee), it came at a point in our malnutrition and general malaise when I really didn't know how we would survive that summer. Jaime had stopped going to the post office every day. He couldn't be bothered and the effort of walking when you are hungry was too much. I didn't know what to do. I was seventeen and still stuck pretty much in my dreams. The only person I could turn to was Joanna and I knew she thought I was having a fabulous extended honeymoon in Italy. I knew she thought that because it was what I told her in my letters. She would have been appalled to hear that we had no money and no food. She would have been truly unhappy on my behalf and afraid also for my future. Her life had been a litany of disappointments. She was so proud of my success, of my escape and of my happiness, I hadn't the heart to tell her the truth. Into this scenario, Franca appeared like a fairy godmother. Within a week she had whisked us away to a little village just inland of the Adriatic coast. There, by the village of Bertinoro, Jaime and I were guests on her husband's ancestral estate.

Under any circumstances, at any time, Bertinoro would seem like a little slice of paradise. Coming as it did at that point in my life, it was nothing short of magic. The suddenness of our friendship and her insistence on our going down to the estate were such that Jaime was convinced we were being kidnapped. When the electronic gates closed behind us and the black limousine screeched to a halt in front of a huge ochre villa that gave every sign of being closed up, Jaime got out of the car with a 'we who are about to die' resignation on his face. All the way down, he had tried to convince me that we had fallen into a trap. Given his background, his wealth in Venezuela, his political problems and his proximity to Otto and Elias, I thought it quite likely that we would be having our toenails extracted for dinner and yet I couldn't bring myself to care. Every shutter on the villa was shut, but then, of course, all Italians keep their shutters closed against the heat of the day.

It wasn't a trap, though, and it wasn't a trick, nor did we stay in the sepulchral villa. The big house was the dower house. Franca and her family, her husband being the son and heir to the estate, holidayed in an enormous converted stable block. They had a fantastic library, beautiful sitting rooms, breakfast room, dining room and studies. They had about a dozen bedrooms, one of which was allotted to us. They had a massive covered loggia and a small round swimming pool surrounded by flowering shrubs and fruit trees. They had golden pheasants and peacocks roaming around the grounds.

They had an abundance of food from their home farm, wine from their vineyard and olive oil from their gnarled olive groves.

We spent a divine weekend. Jaime roused himself from his apathy and entertained everyone with anecdotes. I knew Franca had to get back to Bologna for Sunday evening. After a copious Sunday lunch, I packed up our things and waited for the signal to go back to the car. When it came, it was different. Franca was in the big Italian kitchen with her housekeeper, La Romana.

'We have to leave,' Franca said, 'but I want you and Jaime to stay on here for as long as you like. You must stay for at least a month. You need it. We don't use the house much and you're very welcome. La Romana will come every day and ask you for a food list. You are to tell her what ingredients you need and she will supply them.' I was just about to admit that we really didn't have any money to do a daily or even a weekly shop, when Franca interrupted me, she had read my mind.

'You are our guests. We would be offended if you paid for anything here. Really offended.'

I desperately wanted to accept her offer but felt it wrong to do so. Again, she was telepathic: 'You say you want to be a writer, well write, write here in our house. The best repayment you could ever give me is write well . . . Please.'

The idyll lasted for a month and three days. We could have stayed much longer but really felt it would not have been right. That month had the restorative power of years. Thirty years on, I can close my eyes and still conjure up the smells and tastes and sounds of Bertinoro. I savour the down of its peaches and their dribbling sweetness, the heavy scent of the wisteria cascading from a hundred-year-old twist of trunk. The cool, smooth feel of the fat black cherries. The tang of rosemary left in a daily sprig by La Romana on the kitchen table. Under the rosemary, wrapped in white greaseproof paper, would be the day's meat. On the centre of the table, there were always four bottles of wine and two of olive oil, virgin pressed, thick and green. I can hear the cockerels crowing at four in the morning, the church bells, the voices of workers on the estate making their way through the olive groves, the sound of La Romana singing in the kitchen. The buzz of bees in the wisteria, the splashes of peaches falling from their trees into the pool, the echoing of bells, the whisper of leaves in the breeze, the intrusive whirring of mosquitoes, the distant sounds of a tractor revving, the clicking of crickets in the scythed grass and the hush of the early evening broken only by the demented cries of the peacocks on the lawn.

Perhaps not surprisingly, it was at Bertinoro that Jaime opened his heart to me and finally told me who he was and where he came from, what he had done and what he wanted to do. He came from a place not unlike Bertinoro, but bigger, much bigger. He called it the Hacienda. He was born there, as his father and grandfather were before him and generations of Teráns stretching back for hundreds of years. Once upon a time they grew coffee on the *hacienda*, but for over a hundred years it had been sugar – sugar and avocado pears. I had known Jaime by then for well over a year, we lived together, we were married, and yet I scarcely knew him at all. He spoke very little. At first, I thought he didn't speak to me because I didn't speak Spanish. But I discovered later that he just didn't speak. No one could accuse him of having seduced me with his sweet talk.

While Elias was around I didn't notice much how I did or didn't feel about Jaime. After Elias left for Sweden, I was thrown back on Jaime's and my mutual silence. He may have been the mean moody silent type, but I must admit that I was not, intrinsically, a bundle of fun. I could be so with Elias, but when Jaime didn't want to speak, I'd just sit and read. When he took to his bed in Bologna and became so obviously leaden and depressed, I felt offended by his opting out. We were both in the same boat, both hungry, both tired of the heat, but he was more than twice my age and ought, I felt, to do something about it. I hadn't wanted to marry him, he had begged me to. I didn't much mind whether or not he entertained me, but I felt it was his duty to feed me. It must have been obvious from early on in London that I had the appetite of a horse. I ate about three times what most people did, and needed to. I grew pale and faint if I missed a meal. I had a quick metabolism, and he shouldn't have lured me to Italy to watch me starve.

Day by day, between the British Council library in Bologna, the two old ladies on our landing and my hours of reading in our flat, I watched him with increasing dislike. I even found myself missing Otto, and in his absence growing fond of him, going over his arguments without the heat and the personal insults and finding that much of what he had said made a lot of sense. I felt, sometimes, like the ancient mariner with a huge white albatross around my neck. If I didn't go to the market place and scavenge damaged fruit and vegetables, we would die. Why should I go? Why did I go? I didn't like my husband and I didn't like myself.

Bertinoro gave us a new lease of life. I wrote properly for the first time. When I say properly, I sat down and worked and actually finished a short story instead of leaving my work in progress as I had tended to do until then. I wrote a short story called 'The Landing' which was a fantasised narrative of the *signore* Nadalina and Berta. Ten years later, it became a chapter of my novel *The Slow Train to Milan.* Franca's words of encouragement made an enormous difference to me, as did the peace, the food and the countryside. When Jaime began to speak to me in Bertinoro, I began to fall in love with him and I fell in love with the *hacienda.* I promised myself that one day I would go and find it.

8

I went to Venezuela in 1972 and stayed there, farming in the foothills of the Andes, for seven years. By the time I arrived there I was 18 and my marriage was on the rocks. For most of the time I spent in the Andes I was, to all intents and purposes, married to the *hacienda*. It was a marriage full of passion and petty battles, love, hate and jealousy and all those unseen and unsung moments that cement such a relationship. As with any marriage it can be painted as heaven or hell depending on how the story is told, which bits included and which deleted. On the whole it was a good marriage, which I can look back on without bitterness. I have written a lot about the *hacienda* both as fiction and non-fiction. On whatever map I draw my memories the *hacienda* must always be the centrepiece. From within that centrepiece, I shall take the specific places there that I loved the best.

The first place I found on the Hacienda Santa Rita, as it was officially called, was a bank of white trumpet lilies which grew by the Momboy river. It must have been on my second day, taking my two beagle hounds for a walk, that I was drawn off the dusty track that led past the sugar factory towards San Pablo (a neighbouring estate which had once been a part of the Terán property) by a fragrance so strong it stole into my sinuses. I paused to investigate and followed my nose through waist-high reeds and grasses to the river. I picked an armful of the flowers and carried them back to the gecko-infested den I was trying hard to think of as home.

In a country without four seasons, one of the strange things to a foreigner is the way nature just keeps coming and coming, giving and giving. Those lilies didn't flower for a week and then fade; as some flowers faded, others took their place. During my first months on the *hacienda*, when I was particularly dazed and confused, I began to sleepwalk. Many times, I woke up in the small hours of the morning having sleep-walked to the river bank to find the lily bed in preference to my own.

During the early months on the *hacienda* I went through the hate part of my love–hate relationship with it. From the first day I had entered a strange world, with the added strangeness of Jaime locked in a schizophrenic episode in which he didn't seem to know who I was. Mostly I was alone on the *hacienda*. Not having the guts or the know-how to run away from it, I did the next most satisfying thing, which was to run away and hide. My first hiding place was behind the sugar mill. This mill was a great cast-iron cane-crusher powered by a hydraulic wheel. The millrace that fed the wheel ran along a high ledge behind the sugar factory, or *trapiche* as it was known. You can tell any teenage girl that crying doesn't solve anything, but it won't stop her tears. I used to cry a lot, and I used to really enjoy it. I'd look forward to it. I'd tell myself, I'm just going to wash these clothes and feed the dogs and kill those two trails of ants and then I'm going up to the *trapiche* for a cry. The millrace was noisy. I could weep, sob or even bawl in my little hiding place above the *trapiche* and even if someone happened to come by they couldn't hear me. To increase the pressure of the millstream, there was a series of boxed pools and dykes along its upper course. I found such a box, cut in stone with a cluster of maidenhair ferns growing round it. There was dense undergrowth on either side of it which concealed me completely.

Although at first I went there almost every day to cry, gradually I just went there to be alone and think. Years later, when my every move was monitored and I had no privacy at all, I used to track back by a circuitous route to that same spot and sit there for as many hours as I dared absent myself from my chores. From its safety, I could hear everyone calling me in vain.

In my second year on the *hacienda*, by which time Jaime had remembered I was his wife and we had had a baby, we moved from the little house by the river and the factory, *la casa del trapiche*, to the big house over the road, *la casa grande*. The *casa grande* was beautiful, built in the old Spanish colonial style with a courtyard and a pillared loggia, arched halls that led into each other, balconies and terracotta flagstones. It had a squat tower either end. One, which was older than the rest of the house, was reached by a winding wooden staircase. It became my study. The other, reached by a cantilevered green marble staircase, led to the master bedroom suite and a wide verandah. It had high ceilings and big shuttered windows. It is the custom to hang baskets of ferns along all balconies and verandahs. To have kept my end up with hanging ferns might seem a simple task for one whose hobbies were gardening and botany, but I found the ferns as delicate as an infant in intensive care and as stubborn as the donkeys we sometimes used to shift equipment into the hills. I can take a cutting from almost any plant, stick it in the ground and it will take root; I can take seedlings from any other garden and coax them to grow; I can graft avocado trees with a seven-out-of-ten success rate, but every time I took a fern into the big house it took one look at me and pined. Despite that, I always had some on the loggia, but it was by dint of cheating and constantly ferrying new ones down from the hills to replace the sick ones.

There is an ant in South America called a *bachaco.* It is a big red ant that lives and breathes to chew leaves. Moving in an army, battalions of voracious *bachacos* can strip an entire garden bare of any leaves overnight. They did this regularly to mine. Jaime's family used to say that he was a *bachaco al revés*, a red ant heading backwards. Red ants strip plants and then carry the leaves into their nest. They have big, cavernous nests which they stock as though against siege. Jaime used to carry everything out of his nest with the thoroughness and regularity of a *bachaco.* Thus, when I arrived at the little house, we had no furniture at all. Nosing around the outbuildings one day, I found a key which fitted the big door of the electric dynamo beyond the *trapiche.* Inside was a floor of mud two feet higher than its natural floor. Resting half buried in this mud was a carved wooden bench. It was nearly five metres long and very old and came, I discovered, from the cathedral at Trujillo. I never discovered how or why it came to be on the *hacienda*, but I did manage to have it dug out and brought down to my verandah.

On the little house, the verandah was shaded by a sprawling mass of bamboo three times the height of the house. Beyond it, the river Momboy hurried by. I sat for many hours on that bench. I sat there alone with only my dogs for company. I sat there with Iseult, my daughter, when she was born to that little house. I sat there with Napoleon, the turkey vulture who was my companion there. I sat there with Calichano, a peasant farmer with a festering leg who came to visit me sometimes and share his dreams of a tomato empire. I sat there with Comadre Elba, the thin old lady with a girlish whisper of a voice who had been both Jaime's and Jaime's father's nanny. I sat there with Coromoto, an eight-year-old child who was my first friend on the *hacienda*, and I sat there with José, Otto's younger brother and my close friend, who drove down from the high Andes about once a month to encourage me to keep going.

When we finally moved to the big house, the bench came too. The *casa grande* was beautiful and it was certainly big but whereas when he inherited it it was fully furnished with the Terán family heirlooms, by the time I arrived it too was completely bare. So once again, the bench took pride of place, and once again, I spent a significant part of my life sitting on it. In the entrance hall looking out over the courtyard, I learnt the history of the *hacienda*, which was the history of that part of the Andes. I learnt of the links between the fifty-two families of peasant workers, joined as they were by blood, by love, by fear or obsession, by debt, shared crops, shared mistresses, shared grief and incest. It was a lot to learn in a short time for a nineteen-year-old girl from another world. But it was a challenge I wanted to rise to, and although I often proved inadequate, I was as stubborn as the dying ferns. The harder it got, the harder I clung on. I felt that I could make the *hacienda* a better place and it could make me a better person. There was no evidence to support either of these beliefs, just a feeling and the fact that my name was Lisaveta, shortened in Venezuela to Veta, which comes out as 'Beta' – 'better'. Every time I heard my name called (which came to be every few minutes), it urged me on . . . better, better, better. Which was exactly what I was going to do.

Another favourite place on the *hacienda* was up a steep slope from the *casa grande*, through the terraces of avocado trees, up past the house of the old goatherd, Natividad, and on and up past the lemon tree to Antonio Moreno's house. Antonio Moreno was the foreman. He was tall and thin with hollowed cheeks where his back teeth were missing and his flesh had caved in. He was in his early seventies when I arrived but could have passed for a fit fifty-five. He was dark-skinned, Indian-featured and had the fierce enquiring eyes of a hawk. He held his mandate from Jaime's father, Don Cesar Terán, and then through Jaime himself, but he kept his power as foreman by his ability to inspire respect and fear in the other men. He always wore *cotizas*, a leather sole with a woven cloth strap, and he had toes like talons. He always wore a battered straw hat, which was a tremendous mark of status. He always carried a fine, sheathed machete on his hip. And on Saturday afternoons, like every other worker on the *hacienda*, he got paralytically drunk.

When he was about sixty, to the amusement of the workers,

he fell head over heels in love with a young washergirl in the big house laundry. They eloped and had five children, one of whom was my friend and companion, Coromoto. Antonio had weathered just about every imaginable calamity and had a wisdom and dignity I have rarely seen in any other man. From the beginning, he took me under his wing and I often climbed up to his house to drink muddy coffee with his wife, Zara.

I could never go past his house without stopping, which meant I didn't go to that particular favourite spot as often as I might because it had to include time for a social call. On the days when that was a possibility, I'd sit on Antonio's porch with its compressed dirt floor swept clean, with a garden at my feet comprised entirely of flowers in dried-milk tins. Zara had a lovely garden full of hibiscus and geraniums, jasmines and oleanders. She didn't have an easy life, but she had an extra room in her house, and the walls were papered with newspaper sheets and magazines, she had running water brought down in bamboo channels right to her kitchen, and she had pigs and hens and a cow. Also she worshipped Antonio and basked in the reflected glory of being the foreman's wife. So although she complained sometimes, her words were usually ones of doting praise for her man. Her tinned garden was planted in a brand of dried milk called Reina del Campo – queen of the countryside. The rows of many cans seemed to confer this title on Zara herself as they ran like a celebratory banner under her porch.

Beyond her house, in a spot originally shown to me by Coromoto and her little brother, there was a plateau with a tall bamboo where Antonio's cow grazed. Beyond that was a hillock with a huge frangipani tree. It had thick pink flowers whose fragrance was so sweet as to be hard to recall. I used to love sitting near that tree with a view of the *hacienda* across the Momboy valley. It was one of those places suffused with peace. Coromoto had pointed it out to me. She called it the calm spot, and so it was.

There were a lot of places on the *hacienda* to which I returned whenever I could, bits that I loved above others, but the ones I went to most were the ones in striking distance of the big house because I was always on call and could rarely take the luxury of riding to its farther domains many hours away.

I am a naturally calm person and for most of the time I lived in the Andes I refound and kept that calm. But there were times when, from a mixture of a seriously bad, sometimes violent, marriage to Jaime and the sheer volume of disasters that rolled across the *hacienda* with random force, I felt both desperate and demented. There were always between four and seven servants living in the house and usually two or three children whom I fostered. I was supposed to be the solid rock out of which order was carved from the reigning chaos. I couldn't be seen to weaken or despair. Every time I reached the end of my tether I found I could get back on track by running through the cane fields and up into a part of the *hacienda* where a rift was almost hidden by tall trees. If I had to choose one place above all others there, it would be this rift, *el zanjón*. The entrance from the hillslope was only a few metres wide and blocked by a thicket of trees. At first the *zanjón* was quite dark and didn't seem to lead anywhere so it was easy to miss it altogether or venture into a place where giant boulders blocked it. By climbing over these boulders, to a higher level, the fissure began to widen and the undergrowth thinned until there was what might have been a stone riverbed. On either side were orange trees and puma rosa, a pretty tree with hard red fruits like crab apples. Higher still was a canopy of tropical leaves through which a mosaic of daylight filtered. The silence in the *zanjón* was only ever broken by birdsong. The first time I ever saw the *zanjón*, there were bluebirds circling over it. I only saw these bluebirds a few times more and always over that enchanted dell. I used to visit it as a pilgrim would a shrine. In a distillation of memory, it is the concentrate, the essential oil, the essence of all I loved best of those foothills of the Andes. It had the lasting power to put my own ephemeral power in perspective, it showed me my own irrelevance. I used to run there and climb into the hidden rift and lie down on its ancient stones and feel as though I were receiving a primeval blessing, an assurance that life goes on.

9

The *hacienda* had been in the Terán family for nearly four hundred years. It wasn't mine by birth or right, but I felt that if ever anyone loved a piece of land enough to deserve it then the *hacienda* should have been mine. Or nearly, because it also seemed to me that it should have been Antonio Moreno's, the foreman's, who had worked on it for seventy years and not only loved it with a passion but knew every inch of it (which was more than I could claim). I have never left anywhere as reluctantly as I left the *hacienda.* Had things been different, had Jaime been different, I would never have gone.

Before I left I managed to pass a little bit of it into Antonio Moreno's name. I wished I could have staked a similar claim for myself and Iseult, my daughter, and lived on there. But they do things differently in the Andes. Sometimes it is a place with too much passion and too much rage, almost as though it reflects the elements. It wasn't safe to stay, so I did what I'd been doing all along, I ran away and hid. On that last time, though, I did it on a much bigger scale and fled to

Europe. Having abducted the five-year-old child Iseult, the last of the Teráns, Europe wasn't such a safe place for me either, so I spent the next eighteen months on the run.

Iseult and I lived out of a suitcase, travelling from town to town and country to country across France and Germany, Belgium and the Netherlands, flitting in and out of London to see my mother, slipping back to the continent to avoid whatever retribution was on our tail. As the year wore on and the fear of our last years on the *hacienda* wore off, and the spectre of Jaime's violence faded, we both longed for nothing more than to settle down. I was running out of money and out of steam when one of my sisters told me she thought I was mad to keep moving around, and that if I went to Norfolk no one would ever find me. She found us a cottage on Lord Walpole's estate near Aylsham and we moved in. It had two rooms up and two down, a chemical loo at the end of the garden and a big bath in an outhouse. It was cold, damp and up a dirt track. It was quaint, safe, and at the time perfect. Joanna moved in with us for much of the time.

Five days a week I cycled Iseult to the village school and then returned to write about the *hacienda*. On my way through London I had met a Scottish poet called George Macbeth. He used to drive all the way from the centre of London to the wilds of number 4 Dairy Cottages in north Norfolk to bring me presents of books or flowers or wine. I was very wary of getting involved with anyone. George didn't put any pressure on me. He just made himself useful, offered his services as a chauffeur and generally looked after me and Joanna while always trying to make friends with Iseult, who kept her distance and didn't like him. There had been a couple of interim boyfriends while we gadded around Europe whom she had befriended and been sorry to lose. One of the things about being on the move all the time is that I could love and leave.

The two most outstanding things about George Macbeth were that he was brilliant and he was kind. Kindness was something that had not existed during the nine years of my first marriage. I wanted to be a writer, and George was in the swim of the literary world. He took me to many readings and parties, receptions and prize-givings, introducing me to other writers. It was the world I had dreamed of. We always arrived like a couple, were seen as a couple, and without really making any decision to be one, became a couple. George bought a beautiful big house in Norfolk, the Old Rectory at Oby, so that Joanna, Iseult, he and I would have somewhere lovely to live. Such a house was what Joanna had always wanted. She'd talked about big houses all through my childhood. She hankered for Claremont, her family home in Jersey, lost by her grandfather to debt. She had missed being born there by only a few months and I think always felt cheated by it. She used to get the brochures from the National Trust of all the country houses in their care and fantasize about living in such places.

I wasn't ready to get into another marriage. I was still battle-scarred. Despite that, we all moved into the Old Rectory and were, mostly, happy there.

After the first months of running around after leaving Venezuela, I went back to South America. I had a romantic rendezvous in Argentina to keep. I also needed to spend a little time on my own. And I was sick of people saying to me,

'You are so lucky to have spent seven years in Latin America, you must know everywhere!' I spent seven years on the *hacienda*, out of which I got to see Mérida, three hours up the Andes, and Trujillo, two hours across the Andes, and the Colombian frontier at Cúcuta where we went twice, shopping; and Caracas, where I went to sell our avocados, and Valera, where we sold the sugar. Also, when Iseult was ill as a baby, I took her to convalesce at Playa Azul, and when she was a toddler, we stayed on the island of Margarita with her cousin, the poet Ana Enriqueta Terán. Sometimes, I shipped out with a couple of the maids and children to Gibraltar, a little lost port on lake Maracaibo that was only a couple of hours away. That was the sum total of my travel, not counting the trips up and down to our nearest village of Mendoza Fría. Machu Picchu, Patagonia, Bogotá, Lima and Rio just didn't come into the equation.

Since I was pledged to going to Argentina, I decided to get there through every country on South America's west coast, getting back via every country on the Atlantic side. I had to make an exception of Pinochet's Chile because I wasn't sure what Jaime's political past might do for me there. I also made an exception of Venezuela itself, being fairly sure what Jaime's wrathful vengeance would do for me *there*.

It wasn't a very sensible idea to travel on my own through all those countries, but I wasn't thinking straight, and I was getting tired of being sensible.

The heart finds ways to heal itself no matter what the odds. While I was putting all my time, energy and love into the *hacienda*, my own heart atrophied for all matters romantic, to the point, I thought, of no return. To compensate, I had my daughter, my writing, my family back in England and a few good friends. As a figurehead on the *hacienda*, as a mother, as a daughter, as a sister I could not have been more loved. But as a woman, from my nineteenth year, romance was dead, sex non-existent, and marital communication had dwindled to 'shall we or shall we not carry out his scheme to end all of our lives in a suicide pact and shall we do it now or later?' That was the main topic of discussion, but not one that cropped up very often because we hardly ever spoke to each other. There was another line of communication though, which was avocado pears. Even in the darkest moments, Jaime could and would talk about avocados. Ours was a plantation of sugar cane, but the cane was planted in the valleys. On the terraced hills, there were avocado groves which Jaime loved as I had hoped once that he loved me.

When the rational part of his mind stopped functioning and every day was played out in a theatre of uncertain violence and deluded schemes, he still found a way back to himself via the avocados. The groves of squat fruit trees had been his father's dream and it was one that Jaime honoured. He knew just about everything there was to know about planting, tending, grafting and producing avocado pears. He had nurtured dozens of varieties from the little wrinkled Fuerte from Mexico to the giant yellowish Hawaii, whose pendulous fruits could weigh up to three kilos a-piece. He also invented three new varieties of avocado, one of which he named after Antonio Moreno's mother, Florencia, and another which he named after mine, Joanna. I learnt as much as I could about avocado growing, partly because I was managing the plantation and needed to know all the ins and outs of our most lucrative crop, but partly because discussing it was the one way I could be close to the husband who lived in the tower at one end of the big house, while I lived in the other end with our bewildered daughter, waited on hand and foot by servants who lived in fear of their master.

There were good days and bad months. There was a year of silence which ended in a truce engineered by the avocados. When I went out to Venezuela, I knew very little about mental illness. It took me a long time to realise that there was nothing personal in my husband's behaviour. It didn't take me quite so long to learn to keep out of his way. Not being loved wasn't much of an issue at the time. I worked so hard and such long hours I had very little time to think about myself. When I did, staying a step ahead to stay alive in the big beautiful house was much more important. The nearest I came to love was a long and fairly innocent flirtation with Otto's brother José, and a long and very innocent affection for an Italian vet who visited me like manna from heaven every six months or so.

Three years before I left, José died in a car crash. His death drew me closer to Otto, a closeness that has lasted to this day. But the absence of José's love and romantic attention, his deep friendship, left a void, a no man's land I couldn't cross on my own. After his funeral, I shared my grief with a stranger who had been his close friend. Gradually, out of our shared loss, something like being in love emerged. We didn't see each other much, there was neither the time or the place. I lived under constant surveillance, imprisoned by a tom-tom of gossip which is the inevitable side-effect of living in a small, isolated and tightly knit community. We devised a way of writing to each other, with his letters arriving at the poste restante in Valera, the nearest big town. There was no delivery, there never had been. My letters from Joanna reached me slowly and uncertainly via the upland village of Mendoza Fría. It didn't arouse suspicion when I shifted my postal box to Valera, and it enabled me to write and receive long letters in relative safety.

Sometimes, when I took the avocados to Caracas to sell (a trip I made quite a few times since it involved bringing back substantial quantities of money in cash), I would give the lorry driver the slip for a few hours and contrive (through massive advance planning) to meet my lover. Sometimes, again with a lot of strategic planning, I would slip out of the big house after midnight, creep through the cane fields and across high scrub to the embankment over the road that divided the *hacienda*. At a certain point there was a bend invisible to all the prying eyes of all the huts and houses dotted across the hills. Dressed as a man, in black with a black woollen hat, I would slip under cover of the night into my lover's waiting jeep. Then he would drive up to the Páramo, the cold uplands of the Andes. I would stay crouched down until we left all the Terán territory, then spend a couple of hours under the stars.

10

I believe that true love can survive separation. I never trusted the love I felt in the Andes for José's friend. I knew it was like a fire that would have to be constantly fed and fanned. I had tried to convince my partner-to-be that my passion would wane unless we were together after I left Venezuela. My lover insisted he knew me better than I knew myself (which in some ways he did), but he could not know the depths of my repression or that the adolescent I had never been was determined to emerge somewhere along the line with all the fickle egocentricity of a teenager. At heart I am not fickle, but my heart then was a battered thing undergoing massive change. Apart from a bit of paper, my marriage to Jaime had been over for years, and yet my emotions were still entangled, if not in love, then in loss and rage. After leaving him, the longer I was alone, the more I felt myself changing.

When I finally met up with José's friend in Patagonia after many months of separation, we had already grown some way apart. Yet I felt this didn't warrant ending our affair; it could still work out if we started living together *soon*. It wouldn't, I was convinced, if we didn't. Our union depended on his getting another job. In a 'love conquers all' approach, I wanted him to chuck in the very good job he had and trust to luck. He spoke ten languages and had a Ph.D, so I reckoned there must be something out there for him. I knew I couldn't wait. He thought I could. I thought I had made it clear I wouldn't, but I hadn't.

I broke off our engagement and then, later, regretted it. Three years on, hoping that his love would still be true, I tried to get back together with him. It was not to be. My letter arrived, but his got delayed, went into store, unseen, and only emerged ten years later, by which time I had divorced Jaime and was happily remarried and living in Italy.

Our last (unhappy) meeting was in Norfolk when he came to stay at my little cottage. He was on a two-week pass from his job. Seeing him off at the airport in London was an amplified tug of war. While I begged him to miss his flight and stay on, the airline staff called his name over and over again. His absence on board became a security risk. His flight was fifteen minutes past its take-off time and waiting only for him. For about ten minutes more, the public address system was dedicated to him. He and all the rest of Heathrow Airport heard that unless he reported to Security immediately, the plane would be unboarded, all the luggage unloaded and every passenger would have to stand in the snow until each piece of luggage was identified. The full force of Security was tugging him onto the plane. I couldn't pull him back. We parted in silence and tears.

*

Timing is the great secret of humour and, it would seem, it is one of the great secrets of life. My timing was out when I left Venezuela. It wasn't often right when I went to Argentina. Perhaps that was why the good times stand out so clearly from my time in Argentina. Most of the journey was tarred with unease but there were precious moments, as welcome and miraculous as the finding of perfect rare shells on an empty beach. They were the days of what could have been, what might have been: the if onlys.

There was a night in Zapala, the Windy City, when we searched for an inn for the night that would take us without insisting on a marriage certificate. There, traipsing around the mostly empty streets with our two battered suitcases, we found a closeness that had been missing until then, and although our night itself started late, it was an aria whose high notes have stayed with me.

There was a walk through Palermo, the smart side of Buenos Aires, during which all my misgivings fell away. The next day we repeated the walk at my request only to find that *Paganini non ripeta.* Our intimate conversation strayed into a political discussion with each of us at the other's throat. I see now that my own inability to discuss politics (as clearly underlined by Otto) didn't really give him a chance to state his case. The days when I had boasted that I found politics boring were long since past. Living in the Third World showed me the practical lesson I had been unable to grasp through Otto's wrath: no living person can abstain from life. You have to choose. You have to be for or against the mass of people. Opting out is choosing to repress them. That much was clear, but so too was my certainty that love and art are ultimately more important than any political regime. This conviction never did slip into words too easily. It was expressed even more clumsily then than now. Having just spent seven years as a jumped-up social-worker-cum-district nurse, while trying to invent a new agricultural policy to boost the foothills of the Venezuelan Andes, I was determined to spend as much of my time as possible in the pursuit of love and art, at least for a year – a sort of gap year that students get after slogging through their exams and before going on to higher education. I was on sabbatical. The last thing I wanted to do was talk about politics, let alone fall out about them and pumice away the one love I had found to date.

There is a book called *Far Away and Long Ago* by W.H. Hudson which I read as a child and which instilled in me a love of Patagonia. I read and reread that book so many times, I knew whole chapters off by heart. It was about a boy and his brothers growing up in Argentina, and it had a timelessness and a sense of space that I fixated on. Some time around the end of my primary school the text of *Far Away and Long Ago* was set for an English exam. My answers quoted word for word entire passages of W.H. Hudson. It had been one of those exams I had come away from thinking, There is a God! Short of *The Mill on the Floss* or *Sense and Sensibility*, there wasn't a book I knew better or felt more passionately about. My exam paper was singled out as an example of bare-faced cheating. I was pulled up before my English mistress, the headmistress and my form mistress, like three black-capped judges waiting to pass sentence on my crime. I recall standing speechless with outrage before them and not uttering one word in my defence. I was shy, upset and even shocked. I left the room, having hardly heard what all my punishments were to be. Then I did something uncharacteristic. I went back in and stood up for myself. I challenged them, then and there, to question me on the book. They pooh-poohed me, but I insisted. They took two passages at random, started them, and I completed them verbatim. Nothing stands out in childhood like vindication.

Having stood my ground over Patagonia, I felt linked to that bleak landscape as to nowhere else. I was half South American, and Patagonia was in South America. My great uncle Frank had amassed a fortune in the railways there. I dreamed of Patagonia, of living there one day, cradled by its windswept emptiness. Now my lover and I were in Argentina, en route to Patagonia. Surely once we got there, far away down south, everything would heal and be all right.

My maternal grandfather was gassed at the Battle of Passchendaele and never quite recovered. After his release from hospital, the doctors told him he must always live in wide open spaces. I have never had such an excuse to cover my own longing for the great beyond but I have always felt both drawn and driven to those wide open spaces around the world as though somehow his condition had jumped a generation and passed into my blood as a genetic necessity. In Patagonia this theme song struck up its familiar tune. I had forayed into many wide open spaces, but south of San Carlos de Barriloche and beyond to the Horn was, is and will always be for me the ultimate expanse of bare beauty. Here time stops. The only things to move are straggling grass, fine as silk, and strange birds gliding like flaps of ribbon in the sky. It becomes a barren land able to sustain only a few sheep per acre. They say you have to be born Patagonian to live there without the wind and the emptiness driving you mad. They say the wind whispers people out of their minds. I didn't stay long enough or travel far south enough to put that to the test. I only know that all the days I spent there I heard the wind whispering and found it profoundly calming.

There were great rounded boulders and a palette of pastels such as I have never seen elsewhere in nature. There were pebbles pigmented like faded Renaissance frescoes, like the ragged façades of downtown Naples. Natural to the rocks were all those colours that shimmer on oily puddles and on the plumage of pigeons when they catch the sun. Some of the stones fitted in my pocket and were like dulled jewels, others had to be scrambled over, others were so big they had to be climbed. At lake Nahuel Huapí, the colours were stacked in endlessly varying shades of pink and red, mauve, maroon, sage and olive green, turquoise, beige, ochre, yellow, ranging from tone to tone, always doused with enough white to soften them. I've been told Nahuel Huapí is a sacred place. There was something overwhelmingly spiritual about it. My worries, wishes and doubts, even me myself became completely irrelevant there – no more than a speck of rock, though infinitely less durable.

I sat for many hours on a huge humped stone with my back against another and came away feeling changed. Over twenty years later I still cannot articulate exactly what it was, but I know that there was before and there was after Nahuel Huapí.

Cape Horn used to be the scourge of sailors. Proportionally more ships broke up and sank in its treacherous waters than anywhere else. Some of the ships that survived spoke in their logs of Patagonia in the days before it was uninhabited. The name itself is Spanish for land of the big-footed people: *pata*, meaning paw or foot, *patagón*, meaning a huge foot. The natives were supposedly giants, the gentlest giants imaginable. They welcomed the conquistadores with open arms and spectacular hospitality. The Patagóns astonished the Spanish not only with their size but with their complete lack of hostility. They lived in harmony, averse to any kind of violence. This made them absurdly vulnerable to their ruthless invaders. No matter what the provocation, the Patagóns offered no defence. So the invaders killed them effortlessly, stole their country and then discovered that only the Patagóns knew how to coax sufficient sustenance from their almost barren land.

Two of the big-footed giants had been taken prisoner and shipped back to Europe as specimens for the king of Spain. No sooner were they at sea than they began to pine. They died early on in the voyage. Their corpses were to be kept as proof of their sheer size, but as they decomposed in the tropical heat, the smell got the better of the crew. The dead captives were thrown overboard. By the time the next ship returned to Patagonia, the race of giants had been wiped out, whether by depredation alone or additionally by their exposure to European disease can never be known. The myth of the Patagón lives on. For some people, that is all it is, a myth. I believe in that one ship's log and the two faded giants chained to the deck who cried their eyes out and then died at sea.

11

After the Heathrow tug of war, I married George Macbeth. Two years later, in 1983, I left him to live alone with our baby son, Alexander, and eleven-year-old Iseult. Joanna had died of cancer and didn't need the big country house any more. After she died, I needed what I had probably needed all along – some time on my own. The only time I have ever lived alone was during my early days on the *hacienda* in the little house by the Momboy river with my beagle dogs and my turkey vulture. Nominally, I was living with Jaime, but as he was hardly ever there, I was alone. Since then, 'on my own' has come to mean without a lover or husband but always with my children. I was nineteen when Iseult was born and now, at forty-seven, my youngest daughter is ten. Even as one left to go to boarding school, there was always another one at home.

On my return from Venezuela, I had two friends in England. Both were friends of my father and both were people I had known as a child. One was the Polish painter Feliks Topolski, the other was my father's literary agent, John

Wolfers. The latter had also been my agent when I fled from the *hacienda*. He took my novel, *Keepers of the House*, and put it in a drawer of his office-house in Regent Square, London. On that day, Joanna and I had celebrated what I believed would be my imminent literary recognition. Whenever I asked John how it was going, he would shake his head sadly and explain what a tough world it was out there. Meanwhile he invited me to meet other clients of heady fame such as Jim Ballard. That period overlapped with my being more intent on hiding than publishing. I left my future career entirely in his experienced hands. Gradually John's large house became a second home to me, and his son Jojo became Iseult's good friend.

Eighteen months later, while repaying some of John Wolfers's hospitality by tackling some of the boggling mess in his study, I found my own manuscript, apparently untouched, in the same drawer he had put it in. When challenged John admitted without a glimmer of remorse that he had never sent it out to any publishers. 'It's not ready and neither are you,' he told me. We were close friends by then, although with many differing opinions. I begged to differ on the subject of my book: it was ready and so was I.

Eventually it was via George Macbeth that I found another agent, and it was George (after that agent had sent my manuscript round in vain) who helped find me a publisher. I didn't hold John Wolfers's bluntness against him. My mother, on the other hand, was mortally offended by it. She never forgave him, and since she died before any novel of mine found a publisher, she disapproved of our continued friendship.

John's defection had cut my readership down by fifty per cent, leaving Joanna as my sole fan. However, his challenging and occasionally outrageous opinions broadened my literary taste and he could be a fine, though cutting, critic. I took on board some of his comments for future prose, but refused to be swayed by his biting sarcasm on my first effort.

'Who did you want me to sell it to?' he asked me. 'The Mormons? Perhaps I could have sold it to them in Utah. It has to be the only contemporary novel that contains no sex at all! Maybe they'd have distributed it free in their Sunday schools ... And humour, have you heard of humour, Lisa? Dialogue? Little things we look for in fiction!' John Wolfers had a point. My next book would have all the above, but my first one was as it was, and I was determined to leave it that way.

John Wolfers had a house in Dielette, on the Normandy coast, where he spent his weekends and Jojo's school holidays. There came a point in John's own career when he decided that his intolerance did more harm than good to his illustrious clients, such was his increasingly cantankerous nature and his abhorrence of literary cant. One day when I was staying with him he announced, 'It's been a long time since I answered the telephone, and I really can't bring myself to listen to my answer machine any more. Given the choice of starting the day with hours of messages from whining authors or a little Brahms, I'm afraid my decision is predetermined.'

The upshot of this was a permanent move on his part to France. Jojo's mother had died of a brain haemorrhage, leaving John as Jojo's sole guardian. Man and boy would be moving to Dielette. All five floors of the house in Regent Square had to be dismantled and packed, its thirty years of accumulated junk and valuable antiques sifted and sorted. John didn't know where to start. As the time for vacant possession drew nearer, I noticed that, as with my manuscript of yore, John was not dealing with or touching anything except a gathering sea of fine wines and a cardboard castle of Gauloise cigarettes.

John had invited me to Normandy many times. He didn't approve of my leaving George. His dictum was 'shag whoever you want whenever you want, but marriage is sacred'. (Neither of us was sure where this left his own serial weddings!) Despite this, he offered me and the children a home. The inside of my head was almost as messy as the inside of his house, which was perhaps why I found it therapeutic to impose order on his chaos. I volunteered to pack his things up and to unpack them at the other end, spending five weeks in Dielette while he and Jojo settled in.

I was tasting my second year of literary success. I had published two novels and attracted a spotlight so strong I was uneasy under it. I talked about my past to so many interviewers that I began to despair of actually having a future. I was ready to flee the limelight and John's need dovetailed with my own.

Later, I wrote a short story based on our stay in Dielette. Later still, it became a novel. I called it *The Bay of Silence.* I could have called it *If Only.* If only we had travelled out with John and Jojo, instead of by train and taxi, we would have seen another side to Normandy than the sinister surface I perceived. We arrived wrapped in the miasma of our taxi driver's fear and paranoia. If only there hadn't been a nuclear reactor glinting over the otherwise fabulous beach. If only there hadn't been a sense of fear hovering over the village. And more than all of these, if only the house I had sheltered in to regain my calm and sense of safety had not been attacked by a gang of

Algerians who dragged the nine-year-old Iseult out of her bed and into the street to rape her. Although John and I managed to rescue her before this could happen, and our two families retreated into his home, that pretty little house didn't ever feel safe again. The village and even the police were hostile. So Dielette served to concretise my fears, to give direction to my malaise. The suspicion that some unspecified harm might befall my children hardened into the certainty that disaster was about to strike.

Iseult had been attacked but saved. I still thought, in those days, that lightning didn't strike twice in the same spot, so I believed that Iseult would now be safe. The child at risk I now believed was the other one, the infant Alexander, or Allie. I had to protect Allie from evil. I did my best but I knew, for once, that my best just wasn't good enough. Whatever was coming after us would find us harder to hit if we became moving targets. I had also seen enough horror movies to know that the bad bits happened to victims on their own. After Dielette, I surrounded us with witnesses, never leaving the company of strangers.

Now turn the coin. The other face of Dielette is of miles of deserted beaches backed by dunes, faced by an intricate lace of spume seeping up the sands. We set out every day for the white beach, filling our already laden basket with warm baguettes and thick ham, peaches and cherries, and bananas for Allie. We lay in the heat with a chorus of gulls squawking and circling overhead. We dug pits in the soft sand – pits big enough to bury us in while Allie played with the yellow piece of a wooden train, the toy he could not live without, content for hours under my large beribboned sun hat. Sometimes we made jaunts to the local market town and sat in cafés dawdling over huge melting ice creams. John and I made some excellent meals, and after the children were tucked up in bed in the rooms that seemed to wrap around the grand piano that was central to the tiny house, John and I would talk well into the morning.

The huge piano had been winched up from the street and hauled in only by dint of removing windows and knocking out stone. The tiny fisherman's cottage had once housed a concert pianist. Now the piano remained at the heart of the cottage which overflowed around it with beach debris, wellington boots and buckets, and drawings by Picasso and several paintings the National Gallery of London wanted John to bequeath them. There was a stack of priceless porcelain on one side of the kitchen, and a stack of empty wine bottles on the other.

Some of what John and I discussed in Dielette was sound advice from him to me which failed to penetrate the curtain of anxiety over my brain. Of all the friends I could have trusted, John was the most worthy. He had a loyalty to his own that was unshakeable. His, to me, absurd loyalty to communism in the face of its, to me, obvious demise was a case in point. Had I confided my breakdown to him, he would, I'm sure, have helped and sheltered me.

However, I was a master at hiding my feelings. I'd learnt how to as a child and perfected it on the *hacienda*. I've always had a calm exterior, and I usually have a calm centre. When that goes, I hide my feelings. For someone who prides herself on not caring what other people think, of being bigger than the '*Que dirán*?' ('What will people say?') that ruled Andean society, I take a strange amount of care in hiding things. For a long time, my definition of growing up was not crying at a shop counter. For years, a sharp tone of voice reduced me to tears. Becoming an adult meant being able to postpone those tears until I was alone. I am a born wimp who has forced herself to be strong.

As I began to crack up under my carapace, I didn't dare confess to the heinous fault of weakness. Out in the Andes, murder itself was less of a crime than a lack of courage. It was dishonourable to be weak. Dielette was a far cry from Valera. The circling gulls were not vultures, and I no longer had a community to carry on my shoulders. Yet the old habits were dying hard. It didn't help to know that many of my wounds were self-inflicted, or that my life was virtually beginning, not ending. I felt ancient although I was only thirty years old. I was relatively wealthy, physically healthy, moderately famous and pig stubborn. I had set my heart on Italy as a cure for all my ills. I would go to Italy and find the calm that was eluding me. That wrinkled boot between two seas became the be-all and end-all of my dreams. I had married a man because he offered to take me there. Now I'd go to Italy and fall in love. That was my plan. Like so many plans, it didn't work out as I had imagined. I did fall in love though. I fell in love with Italy itself – a place already so beloved it was almost a cliché.

Stendhal argued that unrequited love is love in its purest, strongest form. I do not agree. It is harder to sustain love through its daily mundanity than from afar on a pedestal. On arrival in Italy, however, I hadn't much experience of love, so

I managed to find the idea of rejection exquisitely sweet. When Sestri Levante gave me the cold shoulder, I turned the other cheek.

Had I arrived in Sestri during the summer season, it would have welcomed me with open arms. It had a tourist season as rigid and ruthless as a hunting season elsewhere. From mid-April to mid-September, twenty thousand tourists swelled the large Genovese fishing village, filling its hotels and *pensione.* When the tourists left, like migrating starlings, these establishments barred their doors, closed their shutters and the five thousand residents got on with the real business of living.

Outsiders out of season were resented. I was no longer the adored *bambina*, the child bride of Bologna. What did I want? Why had I come? Why didn't I have a life? And more to the point, why didn't I have a husband? What sort of fate awaited the poor angelic child I kept wheeling around in that pushchair? I was a threat, a vamp on the prowl for one of their men, be he son, husband or brother. I was up to no good! Some days I sat on the deserted Bay of Silence looking out to sea, wondering how they could be so wrong. On other days, I sat on the damp sand and wondered how they could be so right.

I had thought I could turn up in Italy and instantly find a live-in baby-sitter, given the national predilection for children. The English nanny I had taken to Dielette for Allie had rather fallen overboard there. I soon discovered that because Italians love their own families so much, they don't ever want to leave them. I found no one to live in; and for many months, I found no one at all. This meant, with Iseult away at boarding school, that Allie and I were alone.

After his bedroom caught fire one night while he was in it, trapped in the cot he was too young to climb out of but luckily old enough to call to me from, I decided we would be safer on the move. At night we slept on the Genova–Brindisi train. By day we were either in Brindisi on the Adriatic or in Genova on the Mediterranean. Alexander was just two and loved trains if anything more than I did. Believing I had no one to turn to, I turned to La Ferrovia dello Stato, the Italian railways, and let them be my nurse and keeper. I had to get better before Iseult came out for her Easter holidays and noticed that I was a couple of marbles short of a full set.

The motion therapy worked. The hours of panic receded, lulled by the gentle rhythm of the train and the quickening of a southern spring. Stopping and starting along the line, at Pescara and Ancona, Bologna and Rimini, all muffled by the night, I began to absorb the shock of Joanna's death. I had still been raw from it when Allie was born by a badly botched Caesarian. I thought then, and still believe, that my breakdown was triggered by an allergic reaction to whatever was put in the drip in my vein for ten hours before his birth. I felt it tampering with my mind at the time but was unable to persuade the locum doctor that it was the drip I was unable to bear and not the pain. The distortion, paranoia, panic and hallucinations began right there in the maternity ward. After the birth, they kept recurring, stirring up all my past in the process. And my entire past, when telescoped like that, is a bit more luggage than I like to travel with.

The almond trees blossomed in the south, daubing the bare fields and olive groves with candyfloss smudges. The pale winter sun began to warm the beaches at either end of the track.

One day, on a whim, I took the ferry across to Corfu. That was something I would do more during the spring and early summer, but for now I wasn't yet ready to be away from Italy. Whenever Italians return home by plane, a spontaneous outbreak of cheering and clapping applauds the touchdown of the aircraft. It struck me as strange at first, and then very sweet. On my return from Corfu, as the battered old ferry lumbered into the harbour and then rammed into dock, I felt happy enough to clap and cheer. The sheer force of pleasure at my reunion with the land I had chosen to live in made me realise that I had, finally, made a choice of my own. I was there because I felt like it, because I wanted to be, not because Byron or Stendhal had been there before me. It quite simply made me feel good. When one is going through a time of intense gloom, it is disturbing suddenly to feel happy, even fleetingly. That was the turning point, after which I began taking longer breaks from the train, spending one, two and even three nights in our rented flat in Sestri. It would only be a matter of time now before I was better. And I knew there wasn't time to waste or life would just go on without me.

They didn't exactly lay down a red carpet for me when I moved to Sestri Levante, but then why should they? The Sestresi and I were diametrically opposed. I wanted to stay. They wanted me to go.

The more that winter village excluded me, the more determined I became to be accepted. I felt I belonged in Italy, that we belonged. For once, I hadn't just thought it, I had packed up our trunks, upped sticks and moved there. I stopped commuting from Genova to Brindisi and set my sights on settling in Sestri.

It was a time of limited ambitions. The first was to get the woman in the grocery shop at the end of my street to say hello, to acknowledge me. Taking one step at a time, that was the Battle for the Buongiorno. Everyone talked to Allie (who was a baby and a late talker himself), but I wanted them to speak to *me.* We didn't have to have in-depth conversations: hello would do, and, who knew, maybe we would graduate to a 'how are you?'.

At Easter, Iseult came out for a month on school holiday. By the end of her first day she had made friends. By the end of her holiday, I could parade up and down the narrow, cobbled high street and swap a *buongiorno* with a dozen shopkeepers and several waiters. Iseult had explained who I was: a writer. Where before the women had shunned me and the men had been too afraid even to look my way lest the look be reported back home, Iseult had found us a sure footing on the first rung of their social ladder. As a direct result of her holiday, I was no longer a pariah and she no loner wanted to stay at boarding school. Both changes were welcome.

I could, of course, have been more easily accepted if I had compromised a little more, just as I would have stood out less in London and Bologna if I hadn't swanned around in outlandish ankle-length costumes which provoked hostility at worst and hilarity at best. In Caracas (which was ten years behind London, fashionwise), tight pastel slacks and mini-skirts were all the rage in the early seventies. By introducing the maxi hemline, I branded myself as patently mad. In Valera, I knew the high society called me *La Loca Lisaveta* behind my back. And out there, I knew that if I had only agreed to wear make-up (preferably lots of it), I would have fitted in much better than I did. But I wasn't prepared to give in on these minor points. I felt I had given in on so much, that I was too passive in other ways. I had to stand up for those petty vanities of my own, and they made me stand out the more.

It was my version of the German Jews' *Trotzjudentum*: Jewishness out of spite. I was different, I was ostracised, and I underlined my difference with visible banners. So in Sestri Levante, after the first few weeks when it became apparent how alarming my presence was there, I could have kept a lower profile, conformed a little, dressed down, killed the stilettos and cut the big hats. I was doing an 'if you've got it flaunt it' act. Yet I was only too aware of how little I'd got at that particular moment.

I felt I had let myself down, wasted so much time and betrayed my mother's faith in me. It might seem that I had done a lot, but *I* knew how much more I could have done. With my writing, particularly, I knew I still had a long way to go. I liked to make it look as though words and their mastery came easily to me. Up to a certain point they did, but the mastery was a laborious apprenticeship. The apparent effortlessness was an affectation. It was like doing very well in a school exam after months of truancy, implying I hadn't tried when really I'd spent my truant days swatting.

I was lost in the mystery of language. For years I had been working on rhythms, on ways of building up emotion and tension, of switching mood without altering the tone. I had been working out how to hone people, places, fleeting moments into a fluid prose which I envisaged but could not always grasp. I worked at layering so that successive readings of my work would keep uncovering more. I had learnt a lot about story-telling in the Andes. I knew that magic realism was the miracle of life drawn from the drudgery of every day. It wasn't a style or a recipe concocted out of certain wacky ingredients, it was a fantasy given birth to by a way of life. I had lived inside it, on the edge where those emotions that are universal (such as love and hatred, greed and grief, lust and fear) dictate life at a quicker pace than in the world I'd known before. It would have taken me decades to understand so much of human nature as I had thrust at me in Venezuela.

Whatever I pretended to be doing, I knew exactly what I wanted to do. In Patagonia, I had come across a Spanish translation of an Aymaran poet. He said,

> Poeta, no cantes de la lluvia,
> Haz llover!
>
> Poet, do not describe the rain,
> Make it rain!

I wanted to make things happen when I wrote. I wanted to make it rain.

Some of my novels and short stories are strands of what I want to say. They are trial runs for the big opus. Each time I felt I had enough skill to try out a new voice or angle (dialogue, humour, dramatic monologue, a more complex layering, or a metaphoric plot), I would experiment in print.

As the years pass, I have grown used to the idea of evolving my ideas in isolation. In the Andes, I had yearned for contact with other writers. Gnawing away at my writing on the *hacienda* (mostly at night, because the days were smothered in the life-cycle of sugar and the lives of its cutters) I used to dream of London as a city of letters. I imagined a café where writers gathered. London was to the written word what Paris was to painters. I fondly believed that once I escaped from the culturally arid Andes, I could just turn up, track down the café or bar where all the writers I most admired met with those I had never heard of but would be thrilled to meet, and it would be enough to walk in and be there. *Da daaa!* All the ideas that kept my brain racing would pour into the ears of people who could understand what I was saying, and who, in different ways, were doing the same things I was.

Alas London isn't like that. It hadn't been for a long time. There wasn't a league of literary alchemists meeting spontaneously in some café club.

The great minds were scattered. Sometimes, if I was lucky, I got to spend time with people I liked and admired and who inspired me. Sometimes friendships followed, as with Bruce Chatwin, Jessie Kesson and Ted Hughes (among others). The former lived all over the globe, Jessie Kesson in north London, Ted in North Devon. I kept on the move myself, bumping into other writers more by chance than design, savouring the moments and then chiselling out my own path.

There was a pub in Soho called the French Pub where artists gathered in the forties and fifties. Dylan Thomas, Louis MacNeice, Francis Bacon, Stephen Spender all drank there. I'd heard about it from my mother and read about it in endless memoirs. There was not, however, an equivalent essence of brilliance in any one spot in London in the eighties, no matter how much I had wished there was.

What one dreams of in exile is only a distant cousin to reality. I used to think I loved the English winters and conjured up nostalgia for slushy pavements, stewed tea and hot stodge. I was fantasising about being famous, and what could be easier than being acclaimed by one's peers? Had it truly been my intention to live in the midst of some kind of literary group, living in Norfolk and then bolting to Italy was not the best way to achieve it. My gripe with London was more about clinging to my native place from afar and then discovering, after that longed-for return, that I am a country mouse at heart. I was not shunned by London's literati. They did not gather at The Café, but they held parties, and I was invited into their inner sanctum. It didn't take me or anyone else long to realise that I am hopelessly inept at parties. I could dress gorgeously, but I was practically mute.

John Wolfers had warned me that it would be professional suicide to live further away from Bedford Square (the seat of publishing) than Hampstead Heath (some five miles distant). To live in Italy would be seen as positively subversive. It was one of the things we argued about in Dielette. I believed then, and now, that if my voice is strong enough, it will be heard wherever I live. If it isn't, time will tell, not me.

Meanwhile I have spent most of my life surrounded by people who read very little, write not at all, but who translate their world into stories. For the last twenty years, there has also been a coming and going of writers who came to stay. That for me is having my cake and eating it. I no longer feel the need to wear fancy dress to proclaim that I am an outsider.

I can accept the insignificance of my difference beside the importance of being the same.

My first year on the Italian Riviera was a bit like a playboy version of my first year on the *hacienda.* I was an outsider edging my way in to the centre so that I could back away again through choice.

12

We were to spend four years, in all, on the Riviera. My ultimate acceptance came when Allie began to talk. His first language was Italian, which we spoke at home so as not to exclude Rita, the housekeeper who joined us on a daily basis from that first Easter. She doted on Allie as though he were a late child of her own. Through Rita and her family my son also learnt the Genovese dialect. Like a court jester, Rita showed him off to the entire village: the English child in a sailor suit who had initiated himself into their jealously guarded sect. I basked in his glory: the mother who had allowed this to happen.

I moved to Sestri Levante entirely by chance. I'd been planning a move to Italy for a year. I found a house near Viareggio and waited for its occupants to finish their lease. At the last minute, those tenants decided to stay on, so my much longed-for rental fell through. The children and I were all packed up with nowhere to go. While giving a reading at Heffers bookshop in Cambridge, I made a friend. Both of us had just lost our mothers and were relieved to be able to speak of our bereavement. England doesn't do grief. Loss is something one is supposed to get over alone. To help this process along, friends shun you in their embarrassment and neighbours cross the street so as not to have to refer to the unmentionable. In the back of the bookshop in Cambridge, mutual loss jumped to how on earth life was supposed to go on. I mentioned that I had just lost my escape plan: the house, its tenants, and having nowhere to live in Italy.

The next day, from out of the woodwork, a flat in Sestri Levante emerged ready and waiting. I went because it was there. I didn't know beforehand that the village had two faces, a built-in schizophrenia that mirrored so well the split personality currently squatting inside my head. One face was a big, grand bay with a sweeping esplanade overlooking the Bay of Fairytales, the other was a tiny hidden bay whose peeling houses rose out of the sand behind battered fishing boats with stray cats scavenging in the guts and bones. That was the Bay of Silence: a silent, eerie place scored by church bells. Between them, like a grey fishbone, the main street either joined or separated them. There were two beaches, two bays: two worlds back to back with two faces.

After a while, I felt as though I were slipping in and out of my own mind, taking refuge in the past or the present at will. Sestri wasn't immediately friendly, but it was intense. I took my fear from Dielette, my fear for Alexander's well-being, my isolation in the two-faced town and the breakdown of my thoughts and worked them into first a short story and then a novel. It is the only macabre book I have ever written. Writing it was my therapy, my cure. I took my own incipient insanity and transferred it to another. Something was very rotten in the state of my heroine Rosalind's mind, but by the time I had finished with her I was almost well again.

It was a strange time for me to be there or anywhere. Sestri Levante is a strange place. Looking back, I see a serendipity in my having wound up there. I didn't straighten myself out alone, the book played a part, but it would never have happened without the help of the two people who watched over me like guardian angels until I got back on my own feet. It was another paradox. Short of choosing rural Calabria or Mafia-torn Agrigento in Sicily, it would have been difficult to pick anywhere else in Italy as initially hostile as Sestri. And it would have been difficult to find anywhere else in the world two people as kind and generous as my two saviours there.

Earning a slot for myself forced me to take root. It also gave me a chance to observe the darker side of my country of adoption before slipping into the beguiling ease so inherent in living in Italy. It was in the two-faced place that I wrote again, shook of the worst of my breakdown, and also it was in the wild hills behind it that I did, eventually, find love.

13

I travelled back from Sestri Levante to Norfolk expressly to have my portrait painted by Robbie Duff-Scott. Wanting this portrait was all part of my breakdown. I had become phobic about photographs. It wasn't that I felt they stole my soul (as some primitive tribes believe) it was just that I found them deeply depressing. I looked at my image and I couldn't see myself. But for the media rush, I could have dispensed with photographs altogether. As it was, I felt bombarded by this person who wasn't there, by an absence of myself. I was convinced a painting would be different. It could be my touchstone. Every time I felt myself disappearing, I could look at it and find myself again.

I tried to commission a portrait a few years earlier when I still believed I could nip my breakdown in the bud. The painting didn't happen then because of a misunderstanding: Robbie thought the letter he received from George Macbeth was a practical joke. The combination of my name, George's name (he was a Macbeth, Robbie a Macduff) and the improbable address of Wiggenhall St Mary the Virgin struck him as all too ludicrous to be true. It was only three years after receiving the request that he came across a magazine profile of me and realised the commission had been genuine. He wrote; I'd left; he waited and I returned to sit for him. We became friends, and a year after it was finished, Robbie came out to stay with us at the house I had rented in the hinterland of Sestri Levante in a semi-deserted hamlet called Velva.

The 'us' of the family on that holiday included George Macbeth to whom, technically, I was still married. Stories have a life of their own. Rumours do, gossip does, and lies do. Lies of omission are one thing, but active ones act. As a truanting child, I invented a kidney complaint to camouflage my comings and goings to Brighton. With details borrowed from a next-door neighbour, it became an immediately understandable alibi. My own diagnosed ailment – mesentericadonitis, was unknown and much too long to do the trick. It didn't help (after I was ten) when it was discovered that I had TB because tuberculosis – as anyone who has had it will know – is an illness that arouses suspicion and fear rather than sympathy. When Jaime found out I'd had TB, he told me I'd be shunned like a leper if I ever let on about it in Venezuela. By the time I was fifteen, however, in a self-fulfilling prophecy, kidney problems had become the bane of my life.

Despite John Wolfers's dislike of my first novel, *Keepers of the House*, it was published to a fanfare of media attention. The interviews and profiles continued under their own steam celebrating the Venezuelan past I was trying to recover from. My publisher assured me that it was necessary to keep giving interviews, that they were 'good for the book'. When I bolted to France and then to Italy, one of the things I was running away from was this publicity. After I left George Macbeth, despite my absence, the media interest continued apace. As a concession to George's distress at my leaving him, I agreed to pretend to be away in Italy working on a film version of my second novel, *The Slow Train to Milan.*

This lie was maintained both socially and publicly, together with the impression that George and I were still a couple. Of all my books, *The Slow Train to Milan*, has been the biggest film headache. It has been optioned, scripted, cast, discarded and picked up again nonstop for seventeen years. It has proved itself to be one of the slowest trains in history.

Another whiplash of that particular deceit was that Robbie Duff-Scott, who had fallen in love with me in a veritable *coup de foudre*, was under the impression that George and I were happily married. He had met us together, made the drawing for my portrait at our Hammer Horror house in Norfolk, dined at our table and read about our close union in several magazines and papers. For a year he wallowed in Stendhalian isolation, never venturing to mention how he felt. Meanwhile, I too was smitten with Robbie, but since he showed nothing but camaraderie for me, I kept my counsel, being primly opposed ever to making the first move in such matters.

It was not until Robbie came out to Italy and saw for himself that George and I were married in name only that he admitted his love. It was to be another year before we lived together, two before we married. However, from that holiday in the hills I foresaw fulfilment for myself, and a happiness that might almost match the fairytale romance I was fabled to be living. At last, it seemed, I would be able to give vent to all the passion I'd been bottling up.

Elements of my life are often compared to a fairytale. Every writer looks at fairytales; they are the first stories we are told. Having been labelled as 'of that ilk', I looked that much harder at the tales themselves. Hans Christian Andersen, the brothers Grimm, Perrault – all gathered versions of a recurring myth. Whichever version one opts for, they are cruel tales of trial and challenge, test and endurance, forfeits and sacrifice. Only the word itself, 'fairytale', implies something light and wonderful. The contents are invariably gruelling. One consistent link is that when they speak of love (once the mountains have been scaled and the thickets cut, the dragons slain and the prince and princess, or prince and peasant girl, finally get to embrace) the couple always 'live happily ever after'. What appears to be the end of the story is actually the beginning. The love story embarks where 'The End' leaves a void.

From the time Robbie and I became engaged, I lived my life in that void, that unknown territory, the most foreign of foreign countries.

Slowly, tentatively, I emerged from the chrysalis I'd spun for myself in Italy. It wasn't exactly a butterfly that emerged, but it was a version of myself ready to spread my wings. In this spirit I decided to accept a few, at least, of the invitations to read from my work that I had been so churlishly ignoring for the past two years. A lot of these were offers from literary festivals and universities. Through them, I began to travel in a way new to me. I made short, very organised trips to specific destinations where I was met, chaperoned and pampered.

Thrown in was the added bonus of meeting writers, critics and translators from all over the world in a less artificial setting than the literary gatherings of London (which I was too shy and socially inept to attend any longer).

I had been to many foreign venues as a groupie when I was first with George Macbeth, and then a couple more in my own right before cutting myself off in Italy. However, it was with Robbie that I really managed to combine business with pleasure because for the next several years every foreign tour or reading was made in his company.

There was one exception. Just weeks into our setting up house together, I went off to Brazil for three weeks on my own. Although I had invited Robbie to come too, he had declined.

14

The trip to Salvador do Bahia was my first return to Latin America since my rather reckless solo tour en route to the tryst in Argentina some four years previously. I had been missing the tropics, missing the heat and the rhythms, the sounds and tastes and smells, the spontaneity and the sheer disorder of it all. There had been times when I longed for a fix of cane fields and the smell of boiling sugar. The flat, muddy sugarbeet fields of Norfolk had done little to appease my craving. Italy had its own tapestry of tastes and smells and magnificent backdrops of scenery to hold me in its thrall and yet in my blood was a nostalgia for the tropics, like a small shrine which needed occasional offerings and actual pilgrimages to the source to keep it satisfied. Just being in Brazil was an emotional return.

I was not consciously aware of this need until I stepped off the plane into the blast of damp heat on the tarmac of Salvador. As a child, I believed I needed palm trees. It was not just that I liked them: I *needed* them. I needed to be near them – at Kew, in the Grand Hotel at Brighton, even in a suburban florist's, they sustained me. In Brazil, I rediscovered this need and logged it, permanently, for future reference.

On the *hacienda*, surrounded by mangoes and guavas, pawpaws and alligator pears, I had yearned for the soft summer fruits of Europe. With the Italian vet who sporadically visited me there I had conducted a curious love affair, with all our pent-up desire funnelled into a euphoric recitation of the names of these soft fruits. Perversely, when I returned to Europe, I hankered for tropical fruit warm from the tree. I longed for water coconuts in the way a recovering alcoholic longs for drink.

I had turned down invitations to many places since meeting Robbie because I didn't want to leave him and he had a distaste for travelling, for luggage, flying, trains and upheaval in general. But when Salvador do Bahia came up, despite being so much in love I knew the pull of South America would be too strong for me to resist.

Because it took me a while to persuade Robbie to live in Italy, I at first lived with him in Bristol. It was my first winter for two years spent in the cold. Being a painter of large canvases, it wasn't possible for him to take his work with him as I did. Nor was it in his nature to want to do so. He did not share my itchy feet nor feel the cold as I did. While battling with the elements in Bristol, the thought of my empty house on the Italian Riviera tormented me. I couldn't persuade him to visit it with me, nor could I bear to leave him for it.

'Work', however, was different, or rather it could be perceived to be so. Giving readings and lectures is a visitor's visa to escape. I recall saying my first half-truths to Robbie then:

'I really *ought* to go to Brazil' (that fabulous exotic place). 'It's work and I've been neglecting my work too much, you know.'

It *was* half true, but would certainly have been binned if instead of Brazil the venue had been Berlin or Brussels. Since I find the actual work part of being a novelist endlessly pleasing, the only element of sacrifice in my working life devolved to giving readings and lectures. Even there the sacrifice is minor. I also enjoy both and love travelling, so there is nothing arduous about what I do. I probably work much longer hours than people with a regular job, but that is my choice. No matter how much sheer slog writers put into their work, it is always a free choice. It strikes me that I am incredibly lucky to be able to spend my life perfecting something I love, in my own time and at my own pace.

Suffice it to say I was scarcely suffering for my art when I skived off to Brazil to spend three weeks poolside with a relay of piña coladas on the one hand and a pyramid of water coconuts on the other. I had imagined I'd be surrounded by jasmines and frangipani, samba and the rhythm of African drums. I would exert myself only to buy lovely presents for Iseult, Allie and Robbie. Then to ease my conscience for the gratuitously lovely time I had without them, I'd return one day with the children (as I tried to do everywhere I went without them).

There *was* a swimming pool and there *were* piña coladas and an abundance of water coconuts, but the blissful holiday I had envisaged was not to be. The conference of five hundred delegates degenerated into a riot by the second day. I had hardly had time to settle into my jet lag before our luxurious hotel was swarming with soldiers armed with riot shields and machine-guns trying to keep the two warring factions of delegates apart.

The problem lay in there being no simultaneous translation for the four hundred or so Brazilian delegates (who were Portuguese speakers and did not understand English). The sixty North Americans and West Indians were all English-speaking and were accused of having insulted their hosts. Which they had. A little tact on day one would not have solved the problem, but it would have avoided the scenes of violence and verbal abuse that ensued. Only four of the foreign visitors spoke or understood Portuguese. I was one of them. Everyone except for us, it seemed, had heated views on the issue. My holiday turned into a peacekeeping mission.

None of the delegates was quite as intransigent or potentially homicidal as the workers on the *hacienda* had been when one of their endless feuds had erupted. I had had years of training in diplomacy. Rather than let the crisis escalate into a blood bath, I helped the three other polyglots restore order before the Brazilian army did it for us. Every single event on that conference was sabotaged, and every act of sabotage had to be set right. It was one of the busiest times I have ever spent. Halfway through the conference I contracted (with what was becoming monotonous regularity) a severe kidney infection. It got so bad, I was advised not to risk the ten-hour flight back to England until I stopped bleeding.

Despite all the above, there were interludes when I got to see Bahia and I loved every minute of them. Salvador do Bahia was the first and foremost settlement in the Americas. It was founded by Thomé de Sousa in 1549 and Amerigo

Vespucci (after whom America is named) landed there. It is a city built on a grand scale, built not just as a trading station but as a statement of power and glory. It was built to reflect the majesty of the Catholic court at Lisbon. By the time the mostly seventeenth- and eighteenth-century centre was constructed, the merits of the rainforest behind it were known. It is a city of exotic palaces with floors of tropical hardwoods that gleam with a natural resinous sheen. There are ballrooms and staterooms, dining rooms wherein a hundred guests could sit and admire the wealth of Bahian society. It was a wealth so fabulous, people just didn't know what to do with it all. A Salvadoreño who was anyone sent his laundry to Paris on a weekly basis, despite the round trip taking from two to three months. Salvador was a place of ostentation and overkill.

It was also the centre of the Brazilian slave trade and had a slave population that outnumbered its white minority many times over. To this day, 70 per cent of Bahians are of African descent. So the music, the customs, the dancing and costumes are a weird mixture of Catholic piety and Condomblé, of monumental Portuguese architecture and riotous African colours. It is both sedate and sensuous.

Some cities, like Hamburg and the Hague, Zürich and Buenos Aires, are melancholic. No matter what takes place in them, they carry sadness in the air. Others, like Caracas and Milan, are chaotic. And some others, like Rome and New York and Salvador do Bahia, are intrinsically exciting. They exude excitement. In Salvador, this adrenaline rush is compounded by throbbing West African rhythms. Street urchins squat in the dusty streets thumping bongos and empty tins while radios from every tortuous alleyway up and down the hilly streets join the beat. Over the cries of vendors, the conversations shrieked across the streets, the tumbling rushes of laughter that erupted from some doorways and the drunken swearing that erupted from others was an orchestra of bells. Women sat in the streets gossiping. The streets were full, not as in Hong Kong and Ankara, of hordes of people going purposefully about their business; Salvador's was a shambolic crowd wringing passion out of each moment or wrapped up in the city itself, swaddling it in a langorous, sensual cocoon. The colours and shapes of all its wealth and the striking poverty of so many of its sons and daughters spilled over each other in the dust and heat and the shadow of black magic.

São Paulo is full of street children, Salvador's streets are full of children, noticeably so. Many of them wear the plain uniform of school. Many of them seem never to have set foot in one. They talk all at once and their voices are loud. Almost deafened by their competing vocals, no wonder the Brazilian delegates at the conference were so vociferous, I thought. It had to be no mean feat here to get heard at all. School was a privilege, university a rare prize. (Theoretically anyone who finished school was entitled to go to university. Catch-22 was how did you get to school?)

During my fact-finding missions around the hotel, I learnt that many of the Brazilian delegates had been waiting for years to attend our conference. They were on unpaid leave from their posts, were broke and out of pocket. They could not afford to attend the conference in previous years in its foreign venues. Now it was here. Now it was theirs. They had done slavery, someone informed me, they weren't going to do it again. They had things to say, important things. They asked only to hear and be heard at the conference. It mattered a lot to them.

By further merging with the crowd, I found out there were two rival factions within the local corps. One had helped organise the conference, the other was determined to close it down. Most of the rivals managed to sink their differences in the face of the new common enemy. There was a general loathing of the North American worthies who refused to understand what all the fuss was about, and made it worse by insisting on a bit more red carpet and more of the five-star treatment they were used to back in their star-spangled home towns. They, some of them, were arrogant and rude. From a starting point of doctoral theses, National Pride muscled in. Little flags were being waved and the local populace had been stirred up to help surround our hotel entrance, chanting anti-Yankie slogans.

One of the reasons I put myself out so much to help was the weasly spirit in which I had attended the conference. I'd come for a holiday – for a swim in the tropics. I became important because I spoke some Portuguese, I wasn't a Yankie, I didn't give a toss about the issues at the beginning and so I felt nothing either way. (I had skipped day one to lie by the pool.) I bumped into the incipient riot on the way back up to my nineteenth-floor room. Everyone else there from the foreign team was at least a respected university professor; most of them were deans and proctors. There was a solid wall of Ph.Ds on either side. The only truly disrespectful person, before it all went pear-shaped, was myself. I'd left school at fifteen and the only papers I had read were newspapers, while the only ones I'd written were grocery lists. The Brazilians insisted on calling me Doctor Terán and, since it was clear there would be no peace without cheating, I kept the honorary title for the days of the troubles.

There in Salvador, I also discovered the sheer power of an interpreter. It was a power I abused liberally. While one delegate shouted in one ear: 'Tell that jumped-up peasant to get back to his tin shack and stop interfering, goddammit! I have a doctorate from Yale here!', I would translate: 'My colleague is so sorry he has unwittingly offended you. What can he, on behalf of Yale, do to make amends?'

And while an equally irate Brazilian academic was shouting in my other ear: 'Tell that Yankie arsehole son of a whore I don't give a shit about Yale. He can't come here looking down on us. He can stuff Yale up his arse!', I would relay: 'This delegate had no idea you were from such an illustrious Yankie university as Yale. Now he knows you are from Yale, he hopes he can open a friendly dialogue.'

The crucial thing was to work all the recognizable names back into the text. The rest was utter fabrication for both sides. Had it not been, neither would have given an inch. Both were so touchy, if they had had an inkling of what the other was saying, some of the foreign delegates would have wound up in jail or prey to the trigger-happy National Guard.

The first-floor lobby, which was the main lobby, was under heavy surveillance by the National Guard, who had orders to shoot if things got any further out of hand than they had on the first day. The toughest part of the peacekeeping was calming the minor incidents in that lobby. Feisty and increasingly irritated US delegates (particularly some of the women) shoved the soldiers or pushed their primed machine-guns.

These stolid Americans saw the army presence there as a Third World joke and no threat whatsoever to their illustrious persons. These incidents tended to occur just before lunch when blood-sugar levels were low and tempers frayed from the morning session. You had to pass through the lobby to the main restaurant. I darted about that lobby like a demented budgerigar, twittering nonsense to the soldiers to distract them enough to loosen their grip on their triggers. I sunk to flattery and flirting, starting with a discussion on the fabulous structure of the gun to account for my colleague having dared touch the weapon. It sort of worked as a chat-up line. 'What a weapon! It's beautiful! Better than the Marines have in America! My colleague couldn't believe how you all have such costly guns. He was impressed, and so am I.'

When the likes of that wasn't enough, and it usually wasn't, I threw in how strong, gorgeous and virile the soldier himself looked. In the ensuing dialogue, I explained I didn't have a second of spare time until the conference was over but since I'd be staying on, of course I'd love a night on the tiles with whoever I happened to be placating. The one thing I had to do when the conference was over was get out of town. I had about thirty dates with thirty minor officials, one captain, and a couple of gorillas all set for the following week.

That conference of inflated egos and injured pride ended on the same note of farcical violence on which it had begun. The (Brazilian) flight due to ferry most of the delegates back to the safety of the Ivy League was late. So late that would-be passengers refused to believe the story of its delay or accept the airline's apologies. The visiting professors had had enough. They vented two weeks' worth of frustration against the glass wall that divided the departure lounge from the runway. Other planes were landing and taking off on routine domestic flights. Such a one had my name on its passenger list and was about to airlift me away from all my false promises. However, the delay of the plane for the pillars of academe seemed to the victims to be part of the dastardly local conspiracy against them. It was, they insisted, an act of revenge. It was a tactic they would not stand for. It was one they did not stand for. In a curious outbreak of mass hysteria, the professors began to hurl themselves bodily against the bulletproof glass wall.

There is something wild about Salvador do Bahia and its intermittent adrenaline surge. In its past it was the site of many slave revolts, and acts of gratuitous cruelty, acts of outrageous decadence, from its creole masters. It was the scene of sensuous escapes and frenzied dances. It heightens not only colours, tastes and smells, but also emotions. In the group of visiting academics, it had magnified outrage and then converted it into a simple primitive rage.

My plane arrived and I took my leave of a number of the professors who had shown grace under pressure. My last image there was of half a dozen apoplectic dignitaries hurling themselves at the glass like caged beasts. Behind them, in baffled surprise, were their colleagues. Some of these had been baffled for the duration. Some had arrived late, missed the riot and didn't realise that the army was occupying our hotel because of us. Some remained oblivious to the warring factions, only attending the conference when it was their turn to read their papers. Some had managed to stay poolside despite the peripheral commotion. Some whom I had run into around town also found and loved the charm and beauty of Bahia. Others saw in the same city only its ungathered garbage, its decay and squalor. In the great cathedral, there were those who saw the loveliness of the seventeenth-century Portuguese tiles and those who saw only their craquelure and the peeling paint of the stucco. If ever there was a conference of perception and denial, that was it.

15

The farthest afield Robbie and I travelled together was to the Melbourne Spoleto Festival of the Arts in the autumn of 1988. It was not a very flattering invitation because I was standing in for someone else. Nadine Gordimer was, at the last moment, unable to attend. I had the reputation of being willing to travel anywhere far away, which, at virtually no notice, was how my name came up. I was on holiday in Mexico at the time with the children when the organiser called up and asked me if I'd go.

'Hello,' he crackled down the Jaliscan line. He had heard I only travelled with my beloved and assured me that he would be welcome too. The engagement was for three weeks for three thirty-minute readings. They would arrange only the best hotels, all expenses, there would be lots of fellow writers he knew were my friends. The festival prided itself on its hospitality. Melbourne was a fine city: it had an art gallery with some important pre-Raphaelite paintings ... It was almost impossible to get a word in edgeways. My agent had already called briefly to ask if it was all right to give the festival my telephone number. I could hardly tell the breathless organiser (lest it diminish his sense of achievement) that he'd got me on 'hello'. I was going Down Under.

It had been the neo-magical qualities of the Australian tuppenny piece that had first endowed the place for me with its mystical air. From the grime of my primary-school playground in its south London backstreet, news spread that an Australian tuppence could not only get into a slot machine, but it could also roll out again after delivering the goods. This might have remained a mere unproven rumour had not a boy in the junior school got hold of three, which he was prepared to sell or barter. After a great deal of fighting, cheating and sago-pudding eating, I became the owner of one third of this treasure. Having rumbled many sweet machines with my minted boomerang, I finally lost it on Waterloo Station. That coin was enough to dispel Hilaire Belloc's image of Australia as a punishment worse than death, with New South Wales its ultimate torment.

When my mother fell in love with a New Zealand painter, whose trips into the Kangaroo Valley of London's Earls Court failed to ease his homesickness, Australia began to grow on the family map. The painter left to hitch-hike home across the world, while my sisters and I nursed our mother's broken heart. After several months of adventure and dysentery, the painter beached himself on the Sydney coast and then worked his way inland. He sent weekly bulletins back to our Clapham flat describing at length his bush experiences and the lure of that country that was holding him a voluntary hostage in its vast embrace. So Australia came to seem, to my seven-year-old eyes, something even more beautiful and fascinating than my mother. It was a rival, bewitching enough to steal her lover away and keep him dancing like an entranced marionette on its endless strings.

Had the painter returned sooner to his native island, we might all have emigrated to Hastings, New Zealand, and grown fat on natural butter. As it was, Australia stole him away and swallowed up our plans.

Together with some particularly heavy suitcases of Robbie's and mine, this was the luggage that I took to Australia.

After the tuppenny coin and the New Zealand painter, my early interest in botany had also fixed Australia as a place of extraordinary allure. From Captain Cook's logbooks from Botany Bay, it beckoned as my Mecca. No other country had such a rich heritage of plants. At least half the vegetable world, it seemed, was *australiensis.* The known species from that desert land fringed only by vegetation were mere tokens of what lay uncatalogued and still unknown. If there were nothing else, it was still the haj of botanists.

But of course there is so much else. It is a place of endless originality. As though it were not enough to have been the cradle of mankind, Australia seems able to change things for the better. Australians enhance the English language with a seemingly effortless flow of metaphors and wit. With spontaneous irreverence, they have distilled and expanded their mother tongue, become masters of lateral thinking, juxtaposed images as no English speakers have done before.

I wanted to see Australia's fabled flora and fauna. I knew it had more poisonous snakes and insects than anywhere else in the world. I wanted to see the duck-billed platypus, kangaroos and wallabies. I wanted to see the country that was overrun with rabbits and cane toads. To see the place where so many rivers and towns were called Murray (two of my sisters were Murrays). This was the place koala bears came from. The place where Aborigines felt their dreamlines and went on walkabouts. I wanted to see Hanging Rock. And I wanted to touch the ground that Patrick White wrote about. I also wanted to touch the sea on the other side of the world and to swim in the Pacific Ocean.

Like Hammond Hargreaves long before me, I set out to find gold there, and I did. After a few days I began to understand a little of the smile on the faces of its wandering sons. Here was a nation who had cheated fate and beaten the system. Where the French chose Devil's Island, with its mainland of steaming jungle, as a penal colony, England chose somewhere with a marked resemblance to terrestrial paradise. So the prisoners who survived the harassment of their officers eventually found themselves free men in a real land of opportunity. As Captain Cook remarked, 'The Earth and sea of their own accord furnish them with all things necessary for life.'

Cook also wrote, referring as above to the Aborigines: 'They may appear to some to be the most wretched people upon the earth: but in reality they are far more happy than we Europeans . . .' His views, alas, were not shared by many of the early settlers, who took the opportunity of eliminating and dispossessing as many native Aborigines as possible. When Queenscliffe, Victoria was settled as a town, many of the officers found that their wives and womenfolk refused to come and live there because of the rumour that they might have to see naked black men in the neighbourhood. The offending tribe was wiped out and the new town thrived.

Ours was a grand tour in which almost all my desires were gratified. The sheer pace of hospitality was such that I sometimes saw some of the above as an antipodean blur caught in an alcoholic haze. We flew for a little detour to Adelaide, where I gave a reading and we both got to hold a koala bear. I grew up with a toy koala bear sent as a present from Sydney. It was soft, grey and furry, and half the size of our cat. The real thing, outside Adelaide, was as big as a two-year-old child and just as heavy. Unlike my toy, his fur was as abrasive as a pot-scourer made out of wire wool. I staggered under its weight for a couple of seconds and then passed it, politely, to Robbie. No sooner had I done this than the grey bear rallied from its stupor and clung to Robbie's neck in an affectionate stranglehold. Having thus bonded, the koala refused to let go. The infatuation was not mutual.

While Robbie struggled to keep his balance, the park keeper explained that koalas live off the leaves of eucalyptus trees, which they eat in vast quantities. These then ferment in their stomachs, making them permanently tipsy. They slump around in trees like a huddle of grumpy old men at a gentlemen's club, snoring and wheezing. Their every movement is slowed by alcohol. The evening before our arrival in Adelaide, we had been on an all-night binge – a farewell party for the early flight. We were still drunk on arrival. The park keeper suggested that perhaps the reason why the koala wouldn't let go of Robbie was because he could smell the beer fumes and wanted to stay hugging a kindred spirit. Whatever the reason, it took nearly ten minutes to prise him off.

Most of our Australian visit was spent in Melbourne. The city is staked out like a specimen on a grid, with the Yarra river cutting through it. It has the Macedon hills on one side and the coast on the other. It began in 1835 as a city of rectangles within a square mile. It has grown a lot since then. Beyond the display of Victorian brickwork known as Flinders Station lies an arts centre, theatre and a great deal of undiscovered (by me) territory. Flinders himself was a great explorer: it was he who circumnavigated Australia and proved New Holland and New South Wales were not separated by a sea. The only exploring that I did, though, beyond the long shadows of Flinders's statue, was to track down and buy a genuine Driza Bone: a floor-length brown oilskin stockman's riding coat. I wore this for an entire winter after my trip, convinced that it had an off-the-wall elegance. Only after someone sent me a photograph of myself standing in St Mark's Square in Venice in what looked like a corseted tent did I lay it aside. To be fair to it, although it didn't suit me, I was dry as a bone inside its rigid canopy.

Our main task at the Arts Festival seemed to be to mix and mingle and have a good time. At this we did our best not to disappoint. Even the formal interviews had a different feel to them Down Under. An hour-long television interview about my writing went so smoothly it evolved into a pub crawl with the presenter. It was one of the occasions when I was definitely drunker than my spouse. I have no recollection of how he got me back to our hotel. And I have very little recollection of what I said for the show. One thing I do remember is that what was usually a glass of water on these occasions was actually a tumbler of neat scotch. It was replenished so generously and often by my Irish host that I was legless before we came off the air.

I know at one point we were in a pub and the conversation was very good, quick and funny the way Australians can be. I remember regretting not being able to join in much, such was the concentration needed to stay on my high barstool. And I remember inadvertently dropping the sweeping tail of the antique ivory-velvet tailcoat I was wearing down the lavatory of that bar, together with the museum-quality Flanders lace it was edged in. I remember washing and wringing out the drenched part in a squalid basin and then teetering back into the crowded bar, confident that nobody could notice my mishap. Meanwhile, the silk velvet had managed to retain several pints of water which it trickled behind me. For how long this ensued or what anyone made of it I have, mercifully, no recollection.

Another interview was for the *Melbourne Age*. It was conducted by Rod Usher, a fellow novelist whom I had met several times elsewhere. He lived outside Melbourne on the coast at Ocean Grove and invited us to spend a couple of days by the sea. I wanted to swim in the Pacific and we needed to get away from the frenzied social whirl of the city. With Rod and his wife, Angela, we went for country walks on which I saw wild freesias and wood anemones and innumerable exotic trees with staid English names like oak and ash. There too I saw the flashes of antipodean birds plumed in scarlets, blues and greens, also with plain names like thrush and robin despite their subtropical hues. It seems that when the first settlers arrived, they were so homesick for the English countryside that they named the new exuberant species with all the old names they missed from home. Only the gulls stepping gingerly over the sands like teenagers on stilettos were the same old seagulls that colonised everywhere from Brighton to Brisbane.

I had read how immense Australia is but had no real sense of its true size until I went there. It started on the plane when the pilot announced: 'We have now entered Australian airspace. Welcome to Down Under.' Six hours later, we landed. Later we drove through maroon-streaked eucalyptus forests, charred in places by past fires. We drove on and on and on. Even the scale of the fires was huge. Ash Wednesday, admittedly the worst fire for years, had consumed more acreage than the entirety of some small countries. Here were the wide open spaces with a vengeance. It was the same along the coast. There were beaches hundreds of miles long – thousands of miles, for all I knew. Land in Australia is as daunting as the sea elsewhere. Only the fringe is tamed, only the hemline. The bulk of it is a huge untameable landmass oblivious to man or beast.

There is a theory that the ozone layer is being pierced by the accumulated gas expelled by Australia's millions of sheep. Man evolved in Australia, survived in its outback against all the odds. The Aborigines have, again against all the odds, preserved their culture while ignoring every technological advance. Having provided the beginning, perhaps it is fitting that the single natural phenomenon most threatening to our survival should also originate there. Given the unique

Australian sense of humour and all the jokes about sheep and Sheilas (Australia, where men are men and sheep are scared etc.), perhaps it is fitting too that such a catastrophe should be caused by ovine farting.

16

At the point when my family was going to emigrate to New Zealand, when I was seven years old, my mother gave us, her four daughters, a very hard sell on our country-to-be. She had been brought up a strict Roman Catholic and suffered from residual guilt at the mere notion of finally finding happiness. She suffered from the, to us inexplicable, delusion that we would need persuading to relinquish the drab squalor of south London for a land of plenty with warm beaches, hot springs, exotic flowers and Maori dancers with tattoos on their chins. While she perceived the voyage out as one of unspeakable sacrifice and seasickness for her children, we saw only six weeks off school on the high seas with sun decks and a swimming pool. She was still very much in love with her painter. We couldn't wait for our new life to begin in the Garden of Eden. By the time it fell through, we had boasted about it to all our friends.

She didn't see her lover again for seventeen years and she held a candle to him for all that time. A photo of him, very bearded, sat on her bedside table. For years after our non-departure, the local children used to wind us up, asking whether we'd been to New Zealand yet. Not having been was a little, hankering deprivation. Then in 1992 I was invited by the Listener Festival to do a readings tour. I went for five weeks with Florence, my two-year-old youngest child. I travelled to just about every town of any size on the North and South Islands.

I was underwhelmed by the towns, but found the countryside really beautiful. Even the gorse (imported from England in an act of nostalgia and invading the entire country), which everyone complained about, was just a gorgeous yellow haze to my eye. I made some new friends in the Conder family who played magnificent host to my baby and me for the first and last week of our tour. It was Gail and Alan Conder who introduced me to the work of Jane Campion and Janet Frame. And it was they who showed me Auckland inside out, and the surrounding countryside; and they who took us to the black volcanic beach where we picnicked on the kind of delicacies rarely seen on a beach outside of a Victorian novel. Behind the smoky sand, thousands and thousands of calla lilies flowered in a startling waxy carpet scrunched out of shape.

There was something truly idyllic about that picnic with its wicker hampers and its game pies. We sat on rugs in a dell which was one of the few places where ten people could sit without trampling several hundred callas. I look back on the scene bathed in leaf-filtered sunlight as though at a yellowing photograph. It was like a box-camera memento with all the beribboned hats and rugs, the flowers and the half-demolished banquet – a moment captured from another era. At my feet, a young girl in a frock like an old-fashioned pinafore played in the speckled mosaic of sand and sea flowers with Florence, my toddling child. And I wonder again, as I had already many times since arriving on that North Island, what it would have been like to grow up there. What would I be like if I had lived in this sheltered Garden of Eden with its myriad lilies, its birds of paradise and hummingbirds, the soothing balm of its climate, the slight time warp of its towns (locked in the English fifties)?

I went to New Zealand with Florence, my daughter, but with almost every step I took I felt my mother there, Joanna, who had dreamed so long and hard of this place. I felt that she would have loved living here, that she might still be alive if we had made the move. People say New Zealand is too tame, too safe, too parochial. Over and over in certain wild parts of its countryside, and every time I touched its coast, I felt a desire to burrow into its rich fertile soil and stay there.

I kept being asked, 'But could you write here?', which made me think about the nature of writing and about being a writer. There were writers everywhere. When the word wasn't written, where people were mostly illiterate, there were storytellers. There always had been and there always would be people who gathered up whatever there was and shook it into a different shape. The patterns are there, everywhere, and writers (and artists) rethrow them. Maybe painters have to be somewhere they feel inspired, but writers, I think, can live anywhere because certain human emotions are universal. Love and loss are as keenly felt wherever they occur. Whether the struggle is with a totalitarian state, or gruelling poverty, decadence or the tall-poppy syndrome so talked of in New

Zealand is almost irrelevant. Writers struggle in their minds. They have to. They will struggle with whatever is there. It is a mental wrestling match with no set number of rounds: the contest is for life. The writing comes out of the tension. A writer is, intrinsically, different (all artists are). They have to be or they wouldn't do it. That difference, I believe, is that a writer has to be on the outside looking in. No matter how much a part of any society or group that writer seems to be, he or she can't see it, observe it, describe and translate that vision without standing back.

I travelled through New Zealand reading and re-reading Janet Frame's *To the Is-land* and *An Angel at my Table.* The land I saw was very much coloured by her thoughts. One of the greatest pleasures of travelling and meeting people in chance places is the reading lists, the tips, the titles of wonderful books I may not otherwise have heard about. When it comes to being parochial, nowhere is more so about writers than England. Scottish and Irish greats from the past were acceptable – they had to be or more than half of 'England's' great literary heritage would cease to be. The fact that so many giants were not actually Londoners but Irish or Scottish or (less often) Welsh was grudgingly and glancingly acknowledged. Token authors were allowed in from the Commonwealth while all the others were studiously ignored. The notion that France may have produced a man of letters after Balzac or that Gogol was not the last Russian to pick up a pen was not considered. And the extraordinary idea that outside of the French, Italian, German, Russian and Spanish languages any other country had writers at all was too absurd to give any thought to. Somewhere out there, Kafka had appeared like a homunculus, a rare and never repeated experiment. America, which we insist on calling the United States of, had a handful of interesting writers who ran out on the day that Ernest Hemingway shot himself.

England is the only country I have ever come across where, regardless of politics, the term intellectual is pejorative. I am not English, but I grew up as though I was and had to fight my way out of the insular mentality it nurtures. If Umberto Eco's *Name of the Rose* had not been published in England and proved to be a bestseller, we would probably still be locked in the kitchen-sink dramas of Hampstead Heath and the serial rites of passage on provincial English campuses. I say 'we', because I am more English than anything else, so it comes naturally to me. I was able to get published thanks to the emergence of Salman Rushdie, Timothy Mo, Kazuo Ishiguro and the Latin American bandwagon which had reached our shores. For two years previously, I had stood no chance. Writing about a foreign country was taboo. Things have changed and are still changing, but deep down there is still the ingrained conviction that British is best.

On my return from New Zealand, I went on a number of Janet Frame pilgrimages, one of which was to Norfolk, where she had lived and written for some time. I had lived in Norfolk and never come across her name. I went back and found her easier to locate in retrospect than I could have imagined. She had lived in the same tiny scatter of hamlets as I had in North Norfolk, on the edge of the Blickling Estate, by the domain of the Walpoles. She had lived, to be more precise, in a caravan at the end of the garden of my closest friends there. It was one of my sisters who placed her for me. Yes, they had all known she was there. Yes, she was a writer, a New Zealander, a recluse. I gathered more information from round about. Yes, Janet, there had been a Janet, dumpy with frizzy hair. Strange, she had been strange, she didn't talk much ... at all really. A sort of frumpy woman, you couldn't tell her age. Frizzy hair. Was she a writer? She could have been ... just about everyone said they were. The tall-poppy syndrome is everywhere.

When I arrived in Christchurch to read, there was a little package waiting for me. Janet Frame, New Zealand's most famous writer, famed almost as much for her total reclusion, had sent me a book. It was a fine, signed first-edition of hers. Maybe, the festival organisers told me, she wants to meet you. Maybe, I thought, she didn't. She had sent me a sign, she had my homage. I felt she didn't need me to tell her in person. She wouldn't have sent the book if she didn't recognize in me a kindred spirit as I had in her. What mattered was that she was out there. I had heard a lot about how she shunned contact. It seemed a mark of my respect to honour that. Maybe, the organisers said, she will feel disappointed if you don't try to contact her. I tried to explain that we were friends in spirit, fellow travellers, two hopelessly shy like-minds. Out of all the roomfuls of things I have accumulated along the way, what is dearest to me can fit into a quite small suitcase. Janet's book has a place there. She may not have made her mark while she was in Norfolk, but she has made her mark on me.

My tour of the two islands was a tour of little treasures, of magic moments and the laying of ghosts. In Hastings (the place I would have grown up in if things had been different and love had prevailed), I met the New Zealand painter my mother had loved. He had lived with us in Clapham for a year before embarking on his worldwide hike. He had been the nearest thing to a father I had ever known. He came and went, but I still remembered the comfort of holding two hands, of riding on his shoulders, of being carried to bed while half-asleep. I remembered, too, sleeping in a tiny tent with him at Pagham on the south coast and him raiding the camp store for us, sharing his looted tins of condensed milk with me inside our dim canvas shroud. During my childhood, he was the only man to make my mother happy. With him, I saw her dance. With him, her step lightened when she walked. She was beautiful, but with the painter she glowed and beamed. After he left, she lived in hope alternated with despair for nearly two years, playing Melina Mercouri's 'Never on a Sunday' on our cumbersome gramophone on the good days when his letters arrived full of wit and love. On the bad days, she cried all night in terrible muffled sobs.

When the breadth of the world finally pushed in between them as oceans and continents that would neither bring him back nor allow her to reach him, something died inside her. The light went out and a core of sadness as corrosive as pumice stone settled inside her. So when I met her ex-lover, it was with mixed feelings. He was the man I had loved, the surrogate father I had adored, and also the bastard who broke my mother's heart. I had asked beforehand for the festival organisers to track him down. He had not been hard to find, he had become a famous painter. We ate a cold lunch in the anteroom to the public library where I would be reading half an hour later. He was an old man, broken in many ways it seemed. I could not feel angry with him. We cried a lot, he more than I, which was distressing. There is always something particularly distressing in a man's tears, perhaps because we know how hard most men fight them back.

In Christchurch, I had asked for my one other New Zealand contact to be tracked down. As a penniless music student, he and his wife and baby had lived in the basement of our big house in Wimbledon for a while. Joanna had stayed friends with them, by letter, up until she died. Having dinner with such a tangible link to my past was comforting. One of the few photos of myself as a baby was on this man's shoulders. He had not proved hard to find either, having gone on to become the conductor of the New Zealand Philharmonic. I mentioned that I had seen the painter some days before and the conversation turned briefly to him. So I learnt what no one in our family knew, something that was such common knowledge out there that my hosts couldn't have realised I was unaware of it: the painter was homosexual. He was never going to marry my mother, never going to let her emigrate. All the hundreds of love letters on their onion-skin paper wrapped by year in red-ribboned bundles and stored like heirlooms in the Aunt Connie cabinet were lies. For nineteen years he had lied to her, stringing her along.

It was nineteen years because after that time, Joanna herself had tired of the charade of *la grande passion* from the far side of the world and travelled out to Hastings. It was a trip she made while I was in Venezuela. Something happened on that trip that she never told me about. She just told me something had happened. It was her one secret, the one mystery she refused to clarify, and so had rankled a little. Joanna told me all her secrets. Even as a small child she had confessed all her love and hope and, later, lust to me. Only with hindsight, only there at the dinner table in Christchurch, could I see that she had learned the truth, that not only had the painter broken her heart, he had ruined her life and destroyed her faith. Her not telling me was a woman thing, that pride that makes us deny and obliterate the most humiliating moments of love affairs, the pride that obliterates names from our memory. Women are not lying when they deny certain liaisons. We have the power to wipe them off the slate, to believe ourselves that they did not happen. It takes time to completely eliminate a day or a month or even years, to rewrite history without this or that man, but we do it.

In the side room of the library, the weeping painter had asked for my forgiveness and I had forgiven him. I thought I was easing an old man near his death from guilt at his weakness. I would not have absolved him of systematically, for nearly twenty years, lying to Joanna, of using her, of hiding his homosexuality. Had he told her, she would have understood, it would have absolved her from failure. It wasn't personal, it was a matter of gender. She could have kept her pride. She could have loved again. I was physically sick in Christchurch. When I went back home to Italy and pulled out the stacks of letters, I read them again in all their duplicity. I didn't doubt that he had, briefly, loved her and had, briefly, hoped to deny his nature. Mostly, though, he used her. It was as though he had sullied our family. Even the funny accounts of him and the man he travelled with (how we had laughed at their only having one sleeping bag between them!) took on a new meaning. He was playing a game with us, with her. Reading between the lines there was an undertow of proffered voyeurism. The love letters mocked her.

And, on a personal note, I had grown up believing we had been unable to emigrate because of my own mixed blood. Everyone, I thought, could get a visa except for me. Only in New Zealand did I discover that this could not have been the case. From the letters, I saw, we didn't take the six-week voyage because the painter, with the powers of invention of a shaman, came up with one ludicrous excuse after another as to why we had to wait, delay and keep away. The patina of guilt at having been the cause of keeping Joanna on the treadmill of London lifted. It left yet another black mark for the painter who worked the theme of my not being able to get in with crocodile tears of regret and constant reminders. And it left a grey question mark floating. After so many years, the fantasy of that antipodean love, that 'it's there if I want it', had acquired a bedrock quality for Joanna. The mimosa arrived religiously every 6 May for her birthday. The letters, blue airmail self-sealers, continued to drop through her letterbox every fifteen days or month.

Wouldn't it have been preferable not to have known, given that her discovery came so late in her life? Technically, Joanna died of cancer. It ran riot in her blood and every bone. Yet, it seemed, both at the time and later, that she died of giving up.

The last place on my map of New Zealand is almost the last place on any map of the world. It is in the far south of South Island, on the beach of Dunedin, the last inhabited place before Antarctica. The beach was bleak and windy. I arrived there with my emotions still churning for my mistreated mother and a bitter sediment brewing inside me. It was time, I knew, to use that alchemy that takes the base substance of our lives, buries the bad and distils the good, channelling it into greater energy. It was while sitting on the sand, staring out towards the pole, watching penguins flounder on and off the rocks, that I set that process in motion.

The wind and the mist wrapped themselves round me. I relaxed back into a speck of sand, there among all the other millions. It was there that I managed again 'to care and not to care' and 'to sit still'.

17

Unlike Australia, which is a hotbed of venomous snakes and insects and a land of deserts and droughts that have broken and desiccated many a traveller, New Zealand has no poisonous snakes or insects, no dangerous animals, no tropical illnesses, nothing, in fact, to endanger life but our own indefatigable need to do so. It was, therefore, the safest of places to take a small delicate child. It was, therefore, inexplicably strange that Florence contracted a virus in Auckland which nearly felled her.

As so often happens with small children's ailments, this unknown virus smote her on the eve of our departure. She had been unwell for a couple of days but broke into a violent fever just as I was preparing to take her to Hong Kong. After a night of panic, her illness appeared to subside and with only half a doctor's blessing, we flew away. It is not a flight I care to remember.

I had spent some days in Hong Kong a couple of years earlier with Robbie. It was somewhere I knew nothing about except that the name meant Port of Perfume. Had I known a little more, I would have known that it was in two parts, Kowloon and the island. Kowloon was not the place to stay or to absorb the pleasures of the Orient from. Robbie and I did stay there, though, and there was little pleasure up for grabs, just a manic centre of commerce. Had we wanted thousands of suits made up in hours only, Kowloon was the place. We ended up with a lot more suits, shirts and jackets than we really wanted, very little to eat and very sore feet trying to find it. At the end of our stay (five days so we could capture the flavour of the place) we couldn't wait to get out. It had not been possible to cross over to the island of Hong Kong proper because of a typhoon. There was some kind of religious festival which had swelled the masses into a gridlocked Malthusian nightmare. On our last day, the language problem escalated as we tried in vain to get a taxi to take us to the airport. My charade of a flight, an aeroplane, take-off, landing and fastening seat-belts was driving the taxi drivers away as though from a madwoman. No language I knew seemed to make any dent. I didn't know any Chinese. Robbie was slumped into black depression at the thought of having to spend the rest of his life in Kowloon. After a lot of running around, we eventually got to the airport with minutes to spare, strapped ourselves into our seats and determined never to return again.

However, meanwhile, cousin Mariela from Venezuela had moved to Hong Kong. I am very fond of this cousin Mariela (who is not actually my cousin, but is kin of Iseult's father), so fond that I decided to make the supreme sacrifice of braving the horrors of Hong Kong to visit her.

We were met at the airport by Mariela and her driver and

ferried into something very different from the bursting Kowloon I recalled. Mariela and her husband Robin lived in a huge thirties apartment in South Bay overlooking the South China Sea. The steep road up to it from the beach was a cascade of bougainvillea and jasmine.

The next day Florence took one look at cousin Mariela's balcony (which was, in itself, bigger than the average apartment) with its view over the sea and bright yellow sand at the bottom of the floral cliff, and another delighted look at her husband's elaborate aviary of tropical finches, and began to rally from her mysterious virus.

Mariela had recent updates on a couple of hundred members of the Terán clan, so Venezuela met the leisured Orient for our entire stay. With her I saw the other side of Hong Kong, the country club and the race track, the old town with its steep lanes lined with exquisite antique shops, the restaurants and bookshops, cafés and gardens she and her husband had found.

Between the pretty bits she showed me, there were temples of commerce. I am not usually enamoured of modern architecture, but there, rather like in New York and Chicago in the twenties and thirties, temples were being built to the greater glory of gold. No expense was spared and their designs were intended to strike awe in the eyes of the believers.

To make a change, I was not undergoing an identity crisis while I was in Hong Kong, but Hong Kong itself was, big time. It was Chinese and it was British, it was both, and it was neither. I had never been to China, but I'd seen Marlene Dietrich in *Shanghai Express* and I'd read a lot about the country. The old treaty, signed blithely by Queen Victoria, at whose expiry

Hong Kong Island and Kowloon would return to his Imperial Majesty, the Emperor of China, was about to run out. No one had envisaged Mao Tse Tung. No one had foreseen that the eventual devolution would be of the world's most intensely capitalist square mile to the world's most totalitarian communist state. The days were numbered and yet the sacrificial victim gave few signs of counting them. On the contrary, the city was in the grip of a building boom. Construction teams worked shifts 24 hours a day, throwing up luxury high-rises which would repay their cost and double the investment in 24 months despite the devolution. Behind the rather beautiful bamboo scaffolding was a hushed frenzy of work. The labourers, I noticed, were all Chinese, all scurrying, all aware, no doubt, that if they flagged there were limitless volunteers ready to take the job.

Even crossing a road in the corporate centre was a strange experience. It was so crowded and yet within that crush I have never felt less concerned about having my handbag stolen or my pocket picked. There wasn't any time for petty crime, it wasn't on the agenda. With the entire world to plunder from within the myriad offices within the magnificent towers, there were other fish to fry: big fat fish, and the fat was boiling. As a nodding concession to the Orient, among the intensely cosmopolitan troops of businessmen and bankers, some of the elite were Chinese. This was not apparent from their clothes, body language or anything other than their tell-tale eyes, hair and height.

Out in the hubbub, another category stood out noticeably: the Chinese women aged between 16 and 35 who exuded style, elegance, wealth and perfection. Some of them were strikingly beautiful, but those who weren't, who were of this class, dressed, moved and looked as though they were. They dressed in gorgeous silks with couture cuts which acknowledged their imperial origins. Some of these girls came from the great Hong Kong families whose Gatsbyesque wealth went back centuries. These were the scions of the Jardines and the Tangs. But, as my cousin pointed out, most of these were in London, New York or Paris. The princesses we were seeing were, at best, the poor relations (the real thing didn't walk, they had chauffeur-driven limos and kidnap quality). So a handful were second-cousins twice removed, some of the rest were junior or even high-flying bankers, career girls, businesswomen and accountants, and the vast majority were secretaries and personal assistants. Their wealth was all veneer, that high lacquer of China. These gorgeous butterflies fluttered around the offices of the expatriate moguls and their battalions of money-making men. The mind boggled at the temptations those hard-working gnomes were prey to at work. The wives would be hard put to compete.

This brought me to another side of island life: Hong Kong, the last bastion of English colonialism. A place where no concessions were made to the times, at least in some of the English households who were serving time out there. It wasn't the way of the families who had lived and died there for generations: the 'eggs', white on the inside, yellow in the middle. I met English women who spoke fluent Mandarin and Cantonese, English people with (a few, token) Chinese friends. And I met foreign wives who just got on with living their lives and who liked or disliked living in Hong Kong, adapting here and there as travellers must to get anything back from their host country.

For all that, there was a bizarre and clearly recognizable group of expat English women. They spent between two and ten years in Hong Kong, ignoring it in its tiny, intense entirety, never relinquishing their residency in Lala-land. These were the wives. These were the ones who had to compete with their husbands' assistants and secretaries, exquisite Chinese girls with their immaculate make-up and not one sleek black hair out of place. I say, they had to compete, of course, they didn't *have* to. I think a lot of marriages might have been salvaged from the rocks had they done so, but they didn't. They didn't compete and they didn't try, although it takes a lot of negative effort to achieve the heights of discontent and denial inherent in every thick-sandalled step of those flustered and fossilising English wives.

I don't pretend to know Hong Kong. My impressions are really just that, skimmed from a week of watching. I saw so many of the women I am about to describe that I am sure all the Englishwomen out there who were not a part of the following category will still recognize the species. I didn't stay long enough on the island to see more than broad groups. Venezuelan society, at every level, is a huge Latin American School Of Holmesian Detection. More than anywhere else I've been, everyone observes and sizes up everyone else and then from the little details (chipped nail-varnish or a crumpled blouse, or spots and stains), they reconstruct entire lives and assess their specimen's state of mind, sex life, finances and place in the jealous mosaic of life. It's mean, it's bitchy, and as often as not, it is right on the dot.

So, out with that knife! In the English shires surrounding London, what we call the Home Counties, I saw women like the wives of Hong Kong when I was a child. They lived in self-supporting groups like peas climbing up each other. Like peas, they fell down and were trampled unless supported by some kind of cane or fence. They had to be wives, they had to be married to sustain the nagging discontent. A woman on her own or in a relationship that required some effort just couldn't let herself go in that way.

By the mid-sixties, with the sexual revolution, the pill, pop music, women's liberation and television blasting into our narrow mentality, the fat floral-frocked wives of Uxbridge, Reigate and Wimbledon were pushed out of hosting parish tea parties and jumble sales and forced into life. Their repressed, anally retentive children were returning from their expensive boarding schools to throw four-letter words round the kitchen and paint their hair green. The vacuous breeding queens of the Home Counties seemed to be a breed that died out. For the next thirty years, I saw occasional traces of that tribe, but they were very rare and struggling to stay afloat, clinging on to bits and pieces of their idle past. Mostly they merged into society under other colours. They rejoiced when Laura Ashley brought frocks back into fashion and frumped into versions of them too shapely for their own taste but still comfortingly big and flowery. They gave vent to their inherent racism on the waves of dark-skinned immigrants flooding to our shores. When it felt safe to do so, they bemoaned the collapse of English society, the hippy scum, the poor quality of scones, the lack of staff, the existence of sex and the anathema of divorce. But English village life had changed for good and there was nowhere left for them to gather except in ones and twos.

Unbeknown to me, there was somewhere left for them to

flock to. They had gone underground, engendered their clones, married them off to men who could support them and who took them on their tours of duty to Hong Kong. For their husbands, it was where the money was, where the chances were. It was a way of jumping several rungs on the ladder of Mammon.

For the wives, it was hot and foreign. No matter how much money their husbands made, other women's husbands were making more. It gave those county girls many of the things their mothers had taught them should be theirs by right but which they had never had. It gave them more money, the chance to be openly racist. It gave them Chinese and Filipino servants to patronise and mistreat. It gave them a tangible stick with which to beat their husbands in their daily nagging. They could justifiably bemoan their exile, the heat, the misdemeanours of their uniformed maids and nannies. It paid for their children's school fees back in England. And it allowed them to wear their own uniform, the ones that had been hidden away but cherished as surely as the once-banned kilts of Scotland.

In the throng of uniquely trim and cared-for women, where fashion was as fine and exacting, as followed and respected as anywhere in the world, and where beautiful clothes were the cheapest on earth, these wives made their own statement. They bore several children and ran to fat which they made no real effort to curb. In a land of sophisticated cosmetics, they were bare-faced, scrubbed and proud of it. The heat turned their English-rose complexions into hot flushes. Their frocks must have been imported because their flapping tent-like cottons were in none of the local shops. They were versions of maternity smocks, a constant threat or reminder, despite there being no foetal presence underneath them, that the wearer's presence in Hong Kong was a sacrifice to her husband's career. A sacrifice neither one would be allowed to forget. They wore either sensible shoes or sandals, and bare, hairy legs. And their hair, which was often their best feature, was stubbornly hacked and combed into the unattractive home styles of fifties schoolgirls.

The only time the slick businessmen (many of whom were the chinless-wonder breed so strong in our gene pool) looked harried and harassed or lost was when they were dancing attention on their unpleasable wives. And their children, despite the lavished attention of maids and the round-the-clock presence of their mothers, or perhaps because of it, cried more than all the other children of Hong Kong and spoke with an infant version of their mother's whinge or were visibly cowed.

It is very rude to listen to other people's conversations. I do it all the time. I can sit in a tearoom or restaurant and follow four or five conversations concurrently. I didn't see many of these wives in restaurants in the evenings. It seemed their husbands were too busy to take them out. But I gleaned a lot of what did or didn't go on in their lives from listening in during the day. The only people who didn't shrug off the imminent Chinese takeover seemed to be them. They discussed it at length, imagining a pre-emptive occupation and their own lives at stake. Some of them were so horrible (particularly to their own children) that I felt I would sympathise with the Chinese if they lined a few of them up against a wall and shot them. Others, though, in another context could have been perfectly decent human beings. It was as though they had arrived unshaped, with a residue of motherly values stored somewhere in their rusty brains. They had been shown the ropes by older hands, issued with the uniform and gone to seed.

It seemed they made their husbands' lives hell. It seemed they had no real knowledge of the competition out there, or they didn't care. Their men had signed a contract, they would live it out or be ruined by alimony payments. They didn't have to try. With three or four children, they'd got their husbands by the short and curlies. It was a lesson in spirit-breaking, and one, they knew, many of them would win. Their husbands were (with or without their wives' knowledge) shagging those lovely oriental girls. It was a part of the cycle. But their husbands were corporate people only a little less racist than themselves. Few of them would have the guts, or the funds, or even want to marry one. What would people say back home?

Hong Kong was seething with commercial success, oozing wealth, literally dripping it, and in little enclaves it was also seething with discontent. The English were lording it over the Chinese. It was, for me, a lesson in colonial attitudes. I spent some wonderful days with Mariela, topped and tailed by mini-excursions to South Bay beach, but it gave me much pause for thought. I had read about colonialism, seen its dregs and met many ex-administrators. What I had never seen was the arrogance and insensitivity of colonialism red in tooth and claw. And I was seeing Hong Kong on the eve of its devolution! What must it have been like in its heyday? It was about money. On the surface, it was only about money. The Chinese bowed their heads and hurried by. Everyone hurried by. There was a big rush to make more money. The Chinese smiled a lot. They were noticeably the only ones to do that. It seemed acceptable to all and sundry that they smile. It was their place to do so. It was right that they be content with their great white masters. Many of the Asians were making money too and were probably content to be getting rich. But behind the scaffolding, behind the suit shops of Kowloon, behind the shuttered windows of the slums were all the ones who couldn't bale out when the day came to hand over power. They couldn't leave. They'd be switching one raw deal for another. It was another subject to be avoided. It was an unreal city, full of realised and unrealisable dreams.

18

After my return from Hong Kong, I began to read a great deal more about Asia. The more I read, the more ignorant I felt about that vast and varied continent I didn't know. My eight hours once spent in a stopover at Tokyo Airport and my two visits to Hong Kong accentuated this sense of having lifted the corner of a veil, peeked under it and seen enough to feel intrigued and excluded.

In 1989 Robbie, the children and I had moved to Umbria, a wooded, landlocked province of central Italy. We had bought a derelict palace, the restoration and running of which I sometimes felt was equivalent to running a small war-torn state. I had long harboured the fantasy that I would have been particularly suited for such a task. It was a novelist's delusion. In great fiction, a cast of many is followed and guided by a benign mind. Following every detail, understanding all those characters, keeping so many threads together and weaving them into a master plan on a harmonious tapestry was what novelists did.

As a teenager, I consorted with revolutionaries. While they plotted overthrows, I plotted (secretly) how to run a country. It was a delusion that lingered. Many of the skills acquired on the *hacienda* and others quietly honed went into the running of the Villa Quarata. I enjoyed the experience and was constantly expanding. Every time I came up with some new and ambitious scheme, Robbie would warn me not even to think about invading Poland. Although many of the schemes collapsed, some worked; and what I kept noticing was that the effort and organisation involved in them was probably the same as running, if not a country, then at least a small city state. In my megalomania, this gave me a sense of wasting my time, of wanting to do more. And some of that more had to be more worthwhile.

A long illness curbed not the urge but the immediate realisation of such plans. I kept things ticking over for four years, then I recovered and my first reaction to being well again was to write. Back to back, I wrote a novel based around the palace we had restored and the village we lived on the edge of, and I wrote a factual memoir of my years on the *hacienda.* By the time I had finished both, I was drained and exhausted. So much so that my grandiose philanthropic schemes went on a very low back-boiler.

One day, I shall translate the poetry of Vicente Huidobro. One day I shall start a chain of libraries in Africa and Asia. One day I'll find a way to help the disaffected adolescents our society ignores. Meanwhile, it's all dreams and talk. Meanwhile, I am no better than all the bigmouths and do-nothings I met in their exile in the Latin quarter of Paris.

I had dreamed up the libraries of Africa and Asia having

never been to either. Then I touched the fringe of Asia, then I wanted to see more. I could have just got on a plane and checked both continents out. But that is not my way. I am an incurable drifter. One with a mission, but still a drifter. With travel, wanting had always been enough. If I wanted to go somewhere, it would come up.

My first Asian tour was to Thailand, through the teak forests of the north. It was a commission out of the blue to write to the given title of 'Green Dreams'. No matter how organised things are, there is always scope for the unexpected. Mine was a truly organised trip, set up by the Swiss and therefore set up like clockwork. And everything ran according to plan with two noticeable exceptions. The first was seasonal. Teak trees and their forests are deciduous. Their big abrasive leaves drop annually and create more of a brown carpet than a green dream when one travels through them for any length of time.

The second glitch was a road already marked on a map but which hadn't been built yet. I travelled with a Norwegian photographer of note, a guide and driver. It was nineteen days of sheer traveller's bliss. On the day when our itinerary hiccoughed, we spent ten hours winding along a small bumpy road with nothing but skeletal teak trees on either side and little hope of food, drink or anywhere to stay before an incalculable number of hours brought us back to some kind of habitation. It was a hot, dreary, funny ride. Well into the night, the driver, who was exhausted, turned off onto an unlikely track to a place we could stay the night.

There, in the middle of the forest, decked with coloured fairy-lights and tinsel, was something halfway between a nightclub and a brothel. On that most sensual and luxurious tour, in which we had stayed at only the best hotels, we spent a night, each in his own corrugated-iron shack, in what is undoubtedly the worst hotel I have ever been to. It would have been disgusting by any standards. Coming as I did from the Oriental Palace Hotel in Bangkok, which is one of the world's finest, it was a gruesome shock. On arrival the driver had pointed out that it was here or the van. Within seconds of seeing where I was supposed to sleep, I opted for the van. But the driver had disappeared, as had the guide, the van was locked and the yard full of shacks was not one in which to start knocking on doors.

My room was about eight foot square. The bed was its only piece of furniture. What more, after all, did one need in a knocking shop? The bedcover was crispy with semen. The room was very dimly lit with a bare bulb too faint to highlight such attractions. I sat down for a moment, felt the residue of dozens of previous occupants and stood up again. There was no chair, nothing but the corrugated-iron walls streaked with I really didn't want to imagine what. It was an en-suite room. The bathroom like a tiny cupboard had a filthy hole in the floor and its only water was the smeary stuff in a tub with a little gourd beside it. Having touched the soiled bedspread I wanted to wash my hands, and needed to. Maybe you couldn't catch gonorrhea from lavatory seats, but I bet you can catch something nasty from rubbing other people's diseased spunk. I knew there were potentially more bacteria in the tub of water, so I had to be content with nearly rubbing the skin off my fingers against my clothes.

Having found the van locked, and retreated back into my

cabin, I pushed the bed up against the flimsy door and prepared for a night's standing vigil. Every time I dozed off from this upright position, I leant against the tin wall. I didn't know what was on it, but I could see there was a lot of whatever it was and I didn't want to touch it at all. Across one corner of the room a couple of metres of plastic washing-line was attached to the corrugated iron: it was the wardrobe. As the long night wore on slowly, with nothing to do but watch mosquitoes whirring around and wonder how long it would be before the sun rose, I wiped this clothes-line down with my cuff and held onto it.

Down and outs in England at the turn of the century could get a bed at a Salvation Army hostel for a shilling. Those too poor to afford a bed were given the additional option of the rope. This rope was slung from one end of a room to another and for a mere penny the homeless could strap themselves onto it by means of another rope round their waist and thus sleep sheltered from the wind and rain and the predatory streets. I had read about the penny rope and wondered why anyone would bother. Yet there, in northern Thailand, I longed for just such an appendage to tie round the washing-line and let me sleep.

I spent the next two nights in a five-star hotel in Nong Khai. Since prostitution has reared its head and is defacing the idyll which is Thailand, it seems fitting that it intruded on my 'hello birds, hello trees' tour.

19

Thailand began for me on a gliding ferry from the airport to Bangkok. I was a willing piece of flotsam on the river that divided the city. A smiling guide on the boat fed me and the other passengers information. The river was the Chao Phraya, the moored boats rocking in our wake were sampans and the swordfish gondolas with outboard motors that swished up and down were water-taxis. There was a lot more, but my mind wandered, snagged on the golden temple pagodas shimmering beside a jumble of ornate wooden shacks on stilts and the concrete blocks and occasional palaces on either side of us. Tamarinds and flame trees and bursts of bougainvillea cascaded over rich and poor alike, trailing confetti petals in the muddy water.

I leant over the railing of our boat and scanned the steady flow of passing debris, not wanting to miss a thing. There were scraps of paper, plastic bags, a child's thonged sandal, bamboo, a Pepsi can, fat teak logs, and the recurring tracery of lily fronds – a rosary of waste threaded on the water with the green beads of water hyacinths.

I spent two days in Bangkok, most of them watching the river. I had never confined myself to quarters before in a city, but there was so much to see from the gardens and jetty of the Oriental Palace Hotel. I was entranced and sated by the drifting clues and the little bits of the city across the bank. I had never been to the Orient proper before either, and the impressions overlapped so fast I felt punch-drunk with pleasure. There were orchids everywhere, literally thousands of them, and everywhere I walked was wrapped in the heady scent of pomelo flowers.

On the third day, my tour began with a rude awakening to the jostle of the railway station. It was packed and both porters and passengers seemed to be competing in some kind of relay race, running everywhere instead of walking, touching base, handing over packages and then running back. There were people in silk suits and people in rags, there were vendors yelling, selling everything from food to lottery tickets. The photographer Knut and I had a guide, for which I was truly grateful. There seemed to be arcane rites involved in getting a ticket and finding our platform, which also turned out to be that of about five hundred commuters, a third of whom were in crisp school uniforms and spoke to each other in semi-hysterical giggles. The noise at the station was prodigious. It and the bustle suddenly stopped as strains of music played out of loudspeakers. There was total hush; and like musical statues in reverse, no one moved until the music stopped. Then everyone resumed their activities. That, I learnt, was the national anthem, played every day to honour the king.

I knew little about Thailand before I went there. Nothing, in fact, beyond what I could glean from Yul Brynner's *The*

King and I and my sporadic patronage of a chain of restaurants called the Blue Elephant, which specialised in Thai cuisine surrounded by purple orchids with coy carp in little ponds between its tables. It was just enough, however, when our taxi driver to the station pointed out the royal palace, for me to have already known that Thailand had a king. Having used up 95 per cent of my knowledge in one go, the rest was a non-stop steep learning curve. Apparently, the palace gardens had been lit up for the delectation of its subjects by thousands of lightbulbs which kept being eaten by monkeys. The apes chomped the glass bulbs so systematically that the illuminations had to be called off.

We had a day's journey ahead of us, heading north to Chiang Mai. It was the sort of train that tickety-tacked. For the first hour or so, I cricked my neck back and forth, not wanting to miss either side of the track. It was hot and dusty and I began to feel as though my head was wobbling off, so I settled for my side and watched the paddy fields flit by, stippled brown and gold. Canals (called klongs) dissected the landscape, trickling into ochre pools splodged with lotus. Water buffalo grazed by nestling stilted shacks while intense, brash surges of bougainvillea kept rearranging the spectrum. Our compartment smelled of ginger, lemongrass and sweat. The train cut through flatlands veiled in the pink lace of a climbing weed, raggedy with palms and then sleek with paddy fields. In a field of patchwork scrub, a giant golden buddha sat stranded.

After a station called Uttaradit, the plains were studded with pointed hills. This was where the teak forests began. Skeleton trees loomed eerily over a carpet of leaves the size of kitbags. It was so hot and the train so airless with its layer of dust and the rhythm so strong I kept falling asleep, waking with the jolts and the blaring of a ghostly horn that the train blasted every time a water buffalo got on the track or we took a bend or pulled into a station. It was a very sensuous sleep in which my dreams and the languorous images outside merged until I felt drugged. When we finally reached Chiang Mai, I was in a stupor.

I felt as though I had disembarked in an intrepid middle of nowhere, but within two blocks of the station I realised that dozens of hippies had put this capital of the former kingdom of Lanna on their map somewhere in the seventies. Some of them had stayed on, gone half-native and learnt the language, but still stood out as Americans. Our hotel was on the outskirts of the city in an old Lanna palace lit entirely by lanterns. Dinner was a rather muddy fish fresh from the cobalt waters of the Ping river. I slept in an antique four-poster bed draped in watery green lace which kept the mosquitoes at bay. Having been so drowsy on the train, I thought I would sleep easily, but a cacophany of river frogs kept me company through a long vigil in which all the day's impressions re-ran through my mind, underscored by new night noises and the heat.

I started my Thai trip day-dreaming. I day-dream a lot but usually squeeze it into intervals during the day rather than use all my waking hours fantasising. I hardly slipped into real time for the weeks I was there. Sometimes I tried, particularly with our driver. Our Siamese driver was called Mr Siam. He was serene and informative and longing to chat. Each time I blinked out of my trance it was to ask him for the name of some tree. There were extraordinary trees I had never seen before. Mr Siam was very good on temples but bad on trees. Our itinerary was lots of forest and lots of temples. So many of each that they joined the kaleidoscope and became hard to separate.

A thousand metres up the steep granite outcrop of Doi Suthep, we climbed through bamboo patterns to a fourteenth-century temple. Wat Phra Tat had a golden pagoda dazzling its central courtyard of tepid stone. Dozens of gold-leaved buddhas stared out of ultramarine eyes in varying benign expressions. They seemed to be looking amusedly at the new squares of gold leaf which had been stuck over their scratches like glittering Band Aids. There was something very casual about this temple. A local man thumbed through a newspaper, girls placed lotus flowers at a shrine, bowing and giggling simultaneously. Friends strolled round in groups chatting before filing up to be blessed by an old monk as thin-boned as a lark. Everyone was barefoot. Outside, by rows of bells, a fat woman squatted cross-legged crocheting. Her strand of cotton trailed over a plastic tray with a transistor radio and pots of tiger balm.

Thailand was a jungle of flowers. Half the trees themselves were flowering in exuberant tropical blooms partially strangled by flowering creepers and then dripping with orchids on top. The air was almost constantly scented with frangipani and wild jasmine and golden showers. When I try to disentangle my memories, I pull out plants: the khaki toupees of tamarinds, white puffs of wild cotton, the fans of traveller's palms, the great rubber trees of Chiang Mai.

Somewhere on the way to Chiang Rai and the Golden Triangle, at a roadside stop, children were boiling quails' eggs in dangling baskets in a hot water spring. Somewhere else, I forced our van off the road in search of a silk factory to buy handmade silks to take back to Italy. In Chiang Mai I had bought some lemongrass at the market. It was a little bundle shorn off at the base of the stem. I kept it in wet newspaper and it grew roots. Later, it grew into a great clump, an armful in my herb garden in Umbria.

The Golden Triangle up by the Burmese frontier is Thailand's equivalent of the Eiffel Tower: everybody goes there. The street up to the little pagoda marking its centre is lined with souvenir stalls, while the pagoda itself is so full of Yao and Karen girls in costume waiting to be photographed that it was hard to get a shot that hadn't already been published in every magazine in Europe. In the end we had to pay the children to go away.

In Chiang Saen I made a brief effort to come out of the haze I was in. The Golden Triangle is so called for being the core of the world's heroin trade: opium is ferried through it. Quite a lot of people were in a haze round about. I grew up in the sixties, surrounded by drugs of all sorts, but never found the peer pressure persuasive enough to make me want to change my state of mind. I liked my mind the way it was. I was constantly retrieving things from it and I didn't want it to change. Had that not been enough reason to stay off narcotics, my mother worked with girls aged between twelve and sixteen, many of whom were on heroin, some of whom she grew very fond of, and some of whom died of overdoses, tampered cuts and dirty needles. Having lived in Latin America and seen the havoc the cocaine industry plays on the peasants forced to produce it, and in Italy, where the Sicilian Mafia controls the bulk of the world's heroin, I felt very strongly anti narcotics. So the last thing I wanted to do was to give the impression I had come to Thailand to shoot up or smoke the black-tar honey of Chiang Rai.

It didn't help not being able to speak the language or understand it in the least. Everyone I met, without exception, was extraordinarily friendly. We did a lot of joining hands as though in prayer and bowing, which is the customary greeting, but I hardly managed to get things past there. While our little crew was trying to deal with the Karen girls and take a picture that was not a cliché, I wandered around the stalls of trinkets. By hanging around a foodstall, I clocked up my only linguistic coup in Thailand. The word for special fried rice is, or sounds exactly like, cowpat. I saw several locals order cowpats. From within the indecipherable language, the sound jumped out. I had already noticed that to say two, people held up two fingers. I was now capable of ordering two special fried rice, at will, and entirely on my own, meaning I could placate my always large appetite and, I hoped, keep my blood-sugar high enough to appear more compos mentis.

I tried, but I couldn't help appearing to be in a scene from Herzog's *Aguirre, the Wrath of God* as I lay in the bottom of a thin dugout drifting through the still waters of the Maenem Kok (a tributary of the Mekong). We were travelling in a Thai gondola towards the hill villages of the Yao, Karen and Akha tribes. For hours the sun and the engine's rapid rhythm increased the dreamy sensation of stealing through a jungle. On either side the foliage trailed. In a clearing, a clump of plantains had fallen in a green crown. Fishermen on fresh bamboo rafts punted along. I closed my eyes and opened them to nothing but sun spots like scattered poppies. When they cleared nothing had changed. Later, a solitary eagle glided overhead for a few minutes and then was gone. More hours passed, punctuated only by sporadic swallows or butterflies darting over the banks.

I had come to accept that nothing could rouse me from my daze. I was drifting towards the Burmese frontier, gliding towards Mandalay. I was lost in thought and fantasy. I was lying stretched out on a mat on the floor of the gondola. I was Lopez de Aguirre's daughter trailing along the Orinoco. I was the Lanna princess who must have once slept in my bed under the green lace veils. Time became meaningless as we drifted on through tobacco fields and forest and jumbles of ferns and fallen trees.

Then Knut saw an elephant and I was up in that gondola and on my feet rocking the boat and more alert than I had been all week. My first elephant! Of course, I had seen them in zoos, and in a circus, and even once at Sestri Levante being led through the street by the station to advertise some event. But a real elephant in the wild was something else. Knut did not share my excitement, nor did the boatman or our guide. They had seen lots of them at other times. I hadn't registered that there were to be elephants in Thailand. Casting back, of course, there had been elephants in *The King and I.* If one started believing everything Hollywood put in its films, though, no one would want LSD or science fiction. The rather small brown beast stared nonchalantly into the river as we floated by. Behind it was a backdrop of hills shaped like Akha hill-tribe hats, adorned with streaks of silver beads. After the elephant was lost to our sight, I lay back down. It was boatman's orders. From the bottom of his long-tailed boat, the hills behind and the wading fishermen casting gossamer nets were invisible again. The pace of the river reclaimed me in its soothing, exciting tropical massage. For long hours, if I rallied, it was only to compile my own mental thesaurus: water, and all the words to describe it.

I don't know if we glided past villages. I really couldn't see anything but leaves and grass. I didn't notice us mooring either. It seemed that out of nowhere a small Karen boy was standing over me proffering a single wilted flower: a squashed yellow trumpet.

Somewhere in my luggage there was a seventeen-page itinerary. Had I read it, I would have known that this arrival at an elephant village was pre-planned. Since I wasn't in charge of getting myself anywhere, I liked the surprise of a magical mystery tour. On such a trip, I could be truly passive and just go along with whatever came my way. Apart from knowing Thailand equals silk and wanting to acquire some, I was a willing hostage to others.

The village was a huddle of bamboo huts staked round a dozen muddy cracked-flanked elephants with wistful long-lashed eyes and translucent speckled ears. I edged past them to accept a cup of water and was then invited to mount a high platform. From there a Karen mahout looked on fiercely while I clambered onto a sort of vegetable crate mounted on a waiting elephant's back.

I was on, with my bare feet on the elephant's rough neck. Four of us lurched off in convoy through the flowers of the forest. I was face to face with thatches of dendrobian orchids, ducking the rasping, rough-tongued teak leaves, touching all the rare blooms at will. I felt absurdly happy on that elephant. I had learnt to love the tropics in a guarded garden, inhaling it through a filter of dos and don'ts. I was never allowed to touch the plants at Kew. Out there, I could touch everything to my heart's content.

The first few minutes of my ride had involved a conflict of feelings. The Karen mahout controlled his elephant by means of clonking it sharply with a small iron hammer on its bony forehead. Having been on the beast for all of five minutes, I felt it was *my* elephant whom this rather savage-looking young man was hurting. It was all I could do to keep myself from remonstrating with his cruelty. However, the elephant really didn't seem to mind other than to straighten his course, and the mahout showed other signs of affection to what was patently *his* elephant so I soon lost myself in the jungle idyll. We moved at a leisurely pace. I was number three in our swaying convoy. The elephants picked out our route along a pounded trail of red dust with occasional digressions to uproot a tender banana palm or to rip up a hummock of bamboo. After a couple of hours, my elephant sensed a wild female somewhere down a ravine and charged after her. From my vegetable-crate saddle atop, it was an exhilarating roller-coaster ride, stopped midway by the angry mahout and his ice-pick hammer. The thought of illicit sex was clonked out of my mount, and we returned with some difficulty to our trail. My elephant hadn't got his thrill, but I had. The rest of the trek was uneventful. We arrived at another Karen village as night was falling and I dismounted feeling as though I had been riding elephants all my life, watching the world through the blurred screen of their ears.

The rest of my Thai travels were by car and train. We snaked along the Thai side of the Mekong river. It was silted up and turned into a thousand market gardens. It is a riverbed of salad beds. We stopped somewhere and ate a picnic surrounded by hundreds of baskets of tomatoes. It was an avenue of loaded baskets waiting to be collected. There were more than I had ever seen in Italy. When the river flooded, it would swallow the allotments, reclaiming them as the waters swelled to take their rightful place en route to Vietnam and Cambodia. For now it was a quilt of greens dappled red like a Tuscan meadow stippled with poppies. I kept the analogy to myself since poppy thoughts were unpopular up there.

20

One of the side-effects of being in love was wanting to settle down: a conscious desire not to keep moving on. Venice was our first choice simply because it was so staggeringly beautiful and the most romantic city in the world. We bought an apartment on the Rio della Guerra, halfway between St Mark's and Santa Maria Formosa. I have written so much about Venice – a place that was not lacking in accolades – that I shall limit our sojourn there to the reasons why we left. We all loved Venice, but Robbie found it so aesthetically overawing he was unable to paint there. Allie, a four-year-old footballer, discovered that soccer is literally a hit-and-run affair in La Serenissima, (as Venetians proudly called their city). Gangs of small boys gathered and kicked their footballs against the walls of palaces until some irate inhabitant inevitably chased them away. Whereupon the children would run off and find another peeling façade to thump, and the process would repeat itself. For born Venetians, this was what one had to do. For Allie, who had been used to a garden, it was a poor substitute. For me, the lack of that garden was a festering wound. Everywhere I had lived I had spent hours a day gardening. On the Riviera, I had tended my extensive balconies as though they were acres of land, buying up ridiculous quantities of plants and stuffing them into pots.

The foreman's wife on the *hacienda* had had a beautiful garden in used milk tins. In the absence of land, I determined to have as good as Zara. My roof terrace was awash with pots of hibiscus and mimosa, bougainvillea and plumeria, orange and lemon trees and big floppy cinerarias. No matter how many I bought, there were never enough. Every spring, I scattered handfuls of morning-glory seeds so that every summer would be filled with blue trumpets. It was more than a hobby and only a shade away from an addiction.

In Venice, our apartment overlooked a convent garden from which we were separated by five large barred windows. I had hoped that this proximity to the nuns' banks of splendid oleanders would placate my plant lust if I kept my hand in with windowboxes on our eight large window-ledges. It was not to be. I probably spent more money at the two local florists than anyone else in Venice during that time. Every week I restocked those boxes, and every week straggly, diseased pigeons chose our formerly empty ledges to roost on. Twice they even went so far as to lay eggs there.

I loved Venice, but I wanted a garden. The other serious obstacle to living in that gorgeous museum was that so many other people loved Venice too. From March to September it was so packed with tourists we could barely get out of our very grand front door. Those Venetians not involved in fleecing the incoming hordes solved the problem by migrating to the countryside on what they called their annual *villaggiatura*. Since we aspired to imitate our hosts, we decided to do likewise and seek out a country cottage for ourselves.

Had we come from one of the great Venetian families of the Golden Book we would, no doubt, have inherited some lovely villa in the flat malarial plains of the Veneto. That not being the case, we had no family ties to that visually rather dull region and decided to look further afield.

We were looking for a summer place, so it could be quite basic. It could be a cottage but it would have to be a very big one, and we would have preferred some kind of folly. An Australian entrepreneur had been trying to sell me a ruined castle in Umbria for some years. He claimed that it had a small habitable wing and a lot of interesting ruins. Since he had refused to send me any proper photographs of the place, I had tucked his letters away in a trunk and forgotten about them. However, while unpacking in Venice, the letters resurfaced. Perhaps, we thought, this (suspiciously cheap) castle would do. And perhaps we should take the trouble to see it before settling on something less appealing to our shared dreams of grandeur. On that Umbrian foray we came across the Villa Quarata, which was about the least suitable or sensible summer house we could have possibly imagined. It was love at first sight. Common sense played no part in our contract. Within seconds of seeing it we decided to buy, and within an hour we had bought it.

To keep myself on the straight and narrow, before setting off for Umbria I had compiled a checklist. Whatever we bought had to have arches, a wisteria, big windows, water, beautiful views, be near a village and have enough room for all of us, and it had to have a garden. The Australian's castle we saw scored one out of eight: it had an arch. The Villa Quarata scored full marks. If I were making such a list again, I'd keep all the original criteria but add some new ones, like it had to have a roof, floor, doors, drains, electricity and bathrooms. Instead of 'land for' a garden I'd like it to have a garden already there for me to restore and add to. Quarata had a lot of bumpy hills and fields with a mass of wisteria strangling a coppice of young oaks on an escarpment.

The villa had been empty since just before the turn of the century. In England we call the ambitious follies of eccentric country-house lovers dream houses. Ours was the dream house of an Umbrian architect called Giovan Battista Nicasi. He inherited a set of hills dotted with property, among which was the compact rectangular villa at Quarata. He took this seventeenth-century stone core and designed an L-shaped extension three times its size around it. His plans were grandiose, his taste catholic. The villa was to be in the style of a sixteenth-century Florentine palace, yet it was the first domestic building in Italy to be built with iron girders. The terracotta – several thousand tons of it – was hand-finished in Siena and dragged by ox-carts to the remote hills. Having no water to mix the mortar, the visionary builder swapped a barrel of his wine for every barrel of water the willing *contadini* dragged up to the site. The extra-long beams required to bridge the great ballroom were imported Baltic pine from Sweden. Giovan Battista was building a monument to himself. Had he just got on with it, he would have lived to see it completed in all its glory. Alas, Giovan Battista was a stubborn man. When the edifice reached the second of its five floors he became dissatisfied and demolished the new wing back down to the ground. It was facing the wrong way. The master bedroom suite with its terracotta balustraded balcony didn't look out over the bulk of his lands. It didn't look down the Morra valley and across to Muccignano. He would rise in the morning and not see his vast estate. Undeterred, he swung the villa round, rose it to the fifth floor, mounted its terracotta frieze and some of its many roofs, and then died.

There is an advertisement on English television for a telephone company which asks, if you want to talk one-to-one with someone from the past, who would it be and what would you say? For all the years I have lived at Quarata, laboriously finishing the architect's task, I have wanted to raise Giovan Battista Nicasi from the dead and point out to him that he didn't have to demolish half the villa, it would have been enough to change the site of his bedroom. That way, the floors, doors and windows would have been in by the time we saw it. That way, we wouldn't have had to keep trying to read his decomposing mind to work out where exactly all the precious terracotta not yet mounted was supposed to go. That way, he might have got round to planting out the garden, maybe even putting up a gate.

Until some, at least, of the villa became habitable and mirrored inside some of the grace it promised on its façade, I used to have days when I loathed Giovan Battista and his rashness. It was impossible to dislike him for long, though, because every day meant traipsing up and down the four floors of turning cantilevered staircase, treading its wide marble steps and marvelling at the sheer extravagance of the man.

Within two years, over half of the villa was finished. We

had a hall with a pink marble floor and fourteen windows. It was big enough for four hundred people to dance in. We had twenty-five rooms which were bliss in summer and gruesome in the winter. It took much longer to beat the garden into shape. This was an endeavour never helped by the marauding in-roads of our neighbour's pigs (in just one year, they ate fourteen thousand lily bulbs), the microclimate of that part of northern Umbria, or the poor quality of the first lorryloads of trees and shrubs we planted. Now I can walk around a beautiful garden divided into lawns and terraces with a rose garden, shrubberies, herbaceous borders, herb and vegetable gardens, full of the statues, fountains, urns and steps I would have liked to find there in the first place. It took six years for the garden to emerge, seven for it to thrive. Before that, it was like a hologram that no one but Robbie and I could see. Apart from the four front lawns and their central fountain, made ready for Iseult's first marriage, the rest was an act of faith. I could tell, as I walked our many visitors around the various other bits in the making, that they feared a little for my sanity.

Our house was as two-faced as Sestri Levante. It was extraordinarily grand at the front and derelict behind. We grew fond of its half-finished pillars and the stacks of sculpted terracotta waiting to adorn the ruined loggia on the *piano nobile*. We held parties in the ruined ballroom, and regularly cooked barbecues on the crumbling loggia with candles stuck into the stone niches and the scent of jasmine and wisteria which had already reached the roof. They were among the first things we planted, standing by for the day we would want them to wrap around the six balconies-to-be.

Although at the time we bought it the Villa Quarata was not the ideal summer house we were looking for, we loved it enough to move there full-time and to restore it. When we bought it, so long as our plans stopped short somewhere of turning it into an Umbrian Villa d'Este, we were in a position to bring it back into shape. We knew it would require sacrificing my shooting lodge in Scotland and, if need be, the Venetian apartment. Meanwhile, we set about its restoration, floor by floor, with the help of a team of very fine local builders and craftsmen.

Several days before the final completion of the purchase of the villa, my stack of financial dominoes had begun to fall down. The first ones were pretty well spaced and were able to absorb the shock. I had been rather counting on a one-off payment on my very slow *Slow Train to Milan* which was due to be filmed. I was to get my money on the first day of principal shooting. This was to have been seven days before completion on the house. It fell through. We cracked open our piggy banks and scraped everything up to cover the deal, then immediately put my Scottish property, Loch Dhu Lodge, on the market. There would have to be a few lean months in the interim, then all would be well.

They say in the Andes that every day a fool sets off to the market. I was that fool. The sale of Loch Dhu went better than I could have possibly expected. It was in the hands of Knight, Frank and Rutley, a big estate agency, and the response to their advertisement was overwhelming. Their switchboard jammed. The national press took up the news that I was selling Loch Dhu and printed a number of large articles about it, each with a photograph of the lovely lodge and each completely free. The newspapers claimed I had written my books there, which was untrue, and published 'interviews' with me in which I waxed lyrical about the shooting lodge, its private loch and surrounding Caithness. I didn't give those interviews, but they brought in a lot of interest. The lodge could not fail but sell and we in Umbria would be home and hosed.

My dominoes had regrouped a bit closer when, through that sale (conducted by an Edinburgh legal firm of note and good standing and the household-name estate agents), I was the victim of a criminal fraud. Italy by no means has the monopoly on corruption. It has been a pioneer and it probably still is the *capo di tutti i capi* when it comes to organised crime. Yet other places, like genteel Edinburgh, were also bustling with the spirit of free enterprise. A fairly complicated trap was set up by a buyer and a lawyer and I was stitched up like a prize turkey. Six years further along an embattled line, I still didn't have the purchase price of my lodge, I no longer had the lodge itself, but I did have debts run up by the erstwhile buyer in various banks which I was supposed to settle, and the tab of mortgage on the lodge which I had outstanding with my own friendly high-street bank was being squeezed out of me with 33 per cent interest. All in all, it wasn't the right moment to embark on stage five of the restoration, which is why the ballroom is still a derelict beauty skulking at the back of the villa.

From the day the Loch Dhu sale messed up, I began to juggle. It was lawyers with one hand, and life with the other. The thing about juggling, if you keep your pace and introduce each new ball in rhythm, is that you can end up juggling a lot of balls. I have juggled so many for so many years that I sometimes just let them drop for no other reason than loss of interest. I know I could leave them there and walk away, but they are not all my balls and for a long time I have been the only juggler my children have, so I keep all those balls up in the air, more for them than for me.

Adults used to warn me when I was a child that daydreaming was the curse that would ruin my life. I have found it a blessing. That ability to switch in and out of any situation at will has enabled me to harvest enjoyment from what might otherwise have been gruelling stretches of time.

There *is* life after debt, and there was a lot of living during it. I trod a new path in Umbria, a new kind of travel that went round in small circles on a treadmill of legal battles. Every day, no matter what, I also travelled around my garden. Nothing has ever killed that pleasure. The trips I have made far away from Quarata (far enough away to avoid, albeit temporarily, the legal summonses and their losses – because win or lose you always have to pay your lawyers) have had the sweet bonus of escape. It felt like playing truant all over again. My only regret was that I wasn't writing. Yet that in itself carried its own comfort, because I knew that in the long run I would change my life in such a way that writing came back into it. It had to. I knew it would. So whatever tripwires I was jumping or missing were a phase, a challenge I rose to as best I could.

21

In 1994 I was invited by the BBC to travel to Brazil and Bolivia to present a television programme there. I was just coming up for air after a long illness. It was winter at Quarata with all the struggles living in palatial splendour entails. I was tired of the cold and couldn't think of anything I'd like better than to tour the equatorial south of Brazil the following February. Things had been getting a little tense at Quarata and a month of holiday might do Robbie's and my relationship a lot of good. Being the 'sue me' target of the year might have been character-forming for me but it wasn't particularly romantic.

I was to write and present an hour-long documentary for a series called *Great Railway Journeys of the World.* My episode was to be one of six. The programme was to be made by the BBC but paid for by PBS, an American television station with lots of money who were putting up one hundred thousand pounds per episode. All six budgets were the same, and each presenter had one month in which to complete his or her journey. Mine was called 'Santos to Santa Cruz'. We had to travel from the Atlantic Ocean to the foothills of the Bolivian Altiplano. The journey was to begin in the once-famous coffee town of Santos and end in the newly famous drug city of Santa Cruz de la Sierra. Unlike most of the other programmes, whose journeys could have been made several times over within their allotted month, ours would take a minimum of twenty-seven days. This meant we had no room for mistakes. It did not, alas, mean we were to make none.

Before we set out, the director, producer and I watched – with growing alarm – the one programme that had already been completed, on Pakistan. It was perfect: beautifully filmed, brilliantly presented, with a witty, knowledgeable and seamless script. The trains themselves were fabulous old steam trains that instantly conjured up the magic of rail travel. Both my director and producer had been on a recce for our trip and apparently the trains were plug-ugly and a big chunk of our journey would be through hundreds of miles of flat monotonous scrub. Since this was to be my presenting debut, I was a bit worried by their gloom.

That same evening, my cup overflowed when the executive producer, an American, met us for drinks and quizzed me on what he obviously assumed to be my expertise on southern Brazil (having supposedly lived there for seven years farming sugar). It was the eve of our departure and I was more than keen to go, so I skirted around that bit of my life, limiting our conversation to sugar itself. Sugar, I told myself, had to be much the same everywhere. The meeting ended, we shook hands and his parting shot was to thank God I was bilingual in Portuguese. I am bilingual, but in Spanish. I speak some

Portuguese, or rather I had, five years before. I didn't know if I still did. Iseult used to speak Spanish and yet she hadn't a word of it left. My own Russian had slipped irretrievably into the fourth dimension. The only bit I remembered was how to say 'I do not understand or speak Russian'. In the taxi home, I tried to remember some Portuguese phrases but not a single one came to mind.

It had been explained to me that one had to get an official permit to film in Brazil and that this by itself would swallow up nearly half of our budget so we were going in undercover. We would then tour the south with an eleven-man crew in two landcruisers and by train, and under no circumstances was I to admit to what we were doing. Our sixty-nine pieces of equipment all had to be passed off as the stuff of home movies.

I was so looking forward to going that had I been asked to present the whole programme while standing on my head, I would probably have given it a go.

We started our journey proper at Santos on the coast, with me learning the ropes as I went along. By the end of our third day I could see that what was required of me was a running commentary of verbal diarrhoea, a lot of patience and a sense of humour. With some jostling for position, it also seemed that the key men in our team were the director (an erudite Englishman and a stickler for schedules), the cameraman (an old BBC hand who'd been in Brazil for years), the soundman (a giant Dutch Adonis), the producer (an English theatre producer) and the fixer (an Anglo-Indian son of a de-frocked vicar). The latter lived in a *favela* in Rio de Janeiro and also happened to be the godfather of my grandson. The other members of the crew didn't get much of a look-in.

Technically, I was supposed to be the prima donna and the one who threw all the tantrums. Actually, there was some debate as to whether I could get an extra credit as set therapist. I was lucky in that I had been able to leave my problems behind. Apart from missing my children, the entire month felt like a holiday. Others were pursued by their problems, some imaginary and some very real. Under the circumstances, which veered from the sublime to the ridiculous, we were a pretty good team.

Filming out of sequence, we spent our three days in São Paulo, which is such a dump I wasn't sure I could rise to the challenge of saying anything nice or interesting about it. The BBC had carefully set up a lot of 'chance' meetings for me for the whole of the trip. São Paulo's included watching a friendly football match with the Corinthians, a team set up by British railway workers. From their museum of medals I could see they were a famous team. Football is huge in Brazil and Pele was the king of the sport. I love Pele, but I hate football. I tried not to look bored out of my mind as I was filmed watching the match under a punishing sun on the terraces. Studiously ignoring the game, I could take in a good atmosphere on the hot concrete terrace.

I knew in advance that I didn't like São Paulo. I'd been there very briefly before and hadn't been able to get out quickly enough. Within the set route of the programme it wasn't possible to skip it altogether. I made it clear beforehand that when I talked about São Paulo, it would be about its *favelas*, its child prostitution, its police brutality. None of them easy subjects to slip into a light-hearted hour of aesthetic musings. It was supposed to be about my impressions of each place and I would have had to be blind, deaf and stupid to have entered that city and not been aware of its plight.

All in all, it was a horribly depressing couple of days, filming street children sniffing red glue from plastic bags that looked like Jubbly ice-lollies, cruising through shanty towns and Aids shelters, visiting a charity providing places for the homeless to wash in. We didn't do any soup kitchens because, apparently, that is the one thing São Paulo doesn't need. There is so much wasted food from the city's rich inhabitants that the two million homeless can eat their fill from leftovers. It was all there: the good, the bad and the ugly. The good was the people working both inside the government and without it who were actually solving some of the problems. The rest was a dossier of distress. São Paulo used to be the city with the world's biggest growth rate, an avalanching slum. En masse, that most Catholic of places had renounced the Pope and his religion over his intransigent stance on birth control. The city had given up Catholicism for Spiritism and the birthrate had dropped to zero per cent.

A hundred, even fifty years ago, parts of Italy were also in dire poverty. Four million starving Italians had emigrated in just thirty years at the turn of the century in what they call the Great Exodus. The Italians grasped spontaneously that birth control was the best way out of poverty. Although they didn't renounce the Pope, they completely ignored his edicts. Italy's birthrate is also zero per cent and condoms are sold on every sweet-shop counter.

The one bit of the journey I didn't enjoy was São Paulo: I felt like a patronising voyeur offering (with my television crew behind me) the hope of something I knew I couldn't deliver. There would be a few minutes on São Paulo in the programme, but every mention of pollution and poverty would have to be fought for. This was my first time round, I didn't have the clout to have my way. I knew my script would have to be approved by a whole slew of producers. Television was about ratings and our slot was more about entertainment than social realism, more about railways than people.

I said goodbye to that urban labour camp with mixed feelings. Then I sat on the train and talked to myself loudly in the first of many hundreds of soundbites which did wonders for clearing other, worried passengers away.

22

For the next twenty-seven days, we stopped and started, embarked and disembarked from endless dilapidated, peeling silver trains. We were travelling along the state-owned federal railway network (RFFSA). Much of the way we were escorted by Gilmar Ruiz, a railway official and expert on the history of the track. The three days in São Paulo were like one trip, the rest of the month entirely another. The dividing line was an afternoon on Santos beach, bloated with coconut water and roasting under 38°C, lulled to sleep by a warring hum of radio stations.

Everywhere we went, there was music playing: everything from sambas to lullabies, folksongs to salsa. One of the more surreal elements of our programme was that it was filmed over many hundreds of hours in places that literally throbbed with music. There wasn't a hut or a train, a shop or bar that wasn't playing something feisty and entirely natural as we arrived. However, it had been decided by the powers that be that the programme would be set to a sombre piece of music composed by Villa Lobos on a train. It was a little funereal, but not unattractive. Its main disadvantage was that as we went looking for the heart of Brazil, much of which lies in its spontaneity and music, two people went ten paces ahead like a Sound Gestapo, killing all the music. So we'd arrive and every little platform would be jumping; then, within minutes, it was muted, the people, stopped sometimes mid-dance, stilted and bewildered. It seemed like a form of cultural homicide, although imposed to air Brazilian Culture with a capital C. For me, that was the single worst mistake, not least because the vibrant, exciting culture that has surged out of Brazil is of the people and from the people. The great writers like Jorge Amado capture that. We didn't even try. We cut it out.

On Santos beach a lot of the men looked heavily pregnant, their well-gestated paunches bulging over mini nylon trunks. Cinnamon-skinned women glistened, their tanga-traumatised buttocks parading along the sands. Coconut vendors appraised the flesh. They slumped in plastic chairs on the pavement, rallying only at the best and the worst of the passing arses. I gravitate towards coconuts and their vendors wherever I happen to be in the tropics. The water of green coconuts is my delight. Thanks to this penchant, I gleaned a lot of miscellaneous facts from the vendors, who shared not only a common trade but also languorously smiling eyes, appalling dentistry and mutating skin afflictions.

Having once run a dispensary from the Big House on the *hacienda* and become overly familiar with skin diseases, I cannot help taking a semi-professional interest in the likes of impetigo and petiligo, ezcema and scrofula. I would rather not see them, but they just jump out. I didn't have my little doctor's bag of fungicide and antibiotic creams or any sulphur with which to treat the endemic mange, so I just noticed all those scabs and flakes and moved on. The one bit of medical knowledge which did stand me in good stead was having read fairly extensively on amputations. A sugar-cane plantation is always full of amputees, more than elsewhere, because of the honed machetes used to cut the cane and the voracious rollers through which the cut cane is then stuffed to squeeze out its juice. The men who load the rollers lose a thumb if they're lucky, a hand or an arm if they're not. It is hard hot work and the slightest loss of concentration is the immediate loss of flesh and bone.

Since I was, by default, the stand-in doctor on the *hacienda*, and since so many of the workers were already missing bits of themselves, I felt I had to prepare for the day when I would be called upon to sort out such an accident. I studied, and felt pretty confident that I had perfected an off-above-the-knee job, and a thumb cut, both above the first and above the second joint. The books and papers I read for this were most insistent about correct flaps (having sealed the appropriate arteries and sorted out tendons etc.). Dependent on how and where that flap was stitched was the patient's being able to get on with his or her life without suffering unnecessary pain or irritation. A prosthetic limb, for instance, would rub and hurt if the flap was in the wrong place or the amputation incorrectly performed. My role was more that of a nurse really. I used to lower fevers, administer drips and drugs, dress and clean wounds, stitch and bandage. There were snakes, but I never had to use any of the serums I kept refrigerated. There were poisonous insects and they made up for the lazy snakes. Mostly, there were fights and fevers and babies being born.

Every time my mother came out to visit me in Venezuela, I got her to bring me more medical books. At night, I pored over *Gray's Anatomy* and prayed that I wouldn't ever be asked to deal with mutilation. I never was. Which is probably just as well because no matter how prepared I felt or how often I memorised the steps and stages of such an operation, the reality of it would have been too much. I know that having pushed back a woman's prolapsed womb, I felt sick for weeks. Had I been a man and had to do that, I think I would still be celibate.

Years had passed and all that study seemed to have been in vain – until I went to Brazil, riddled with amputees, and found knowledgeable discussion of those flaps a doorway to conversation. It took a few days for my Portuguese to come back, but return it did, and I made a few stumpy friends along the way.

The journey we made *was* a great railway journey. The irony was that no one after us could ever make it again. Some bits of the line closed behind us. Some, far more worryingly for the programme, closed ahead. These were to be treats in store for us in the Mato Grosso do Sul. In the beginning, the director said, 'Let there be trains': and there were trains. And they ran, not always on time, but they did run, though in one noticeable case they were pulled.

Behind Santos, the battered silver train climbed through the rich verdure the rainy season had renewed. The sky was kinetic with magpies. On the highest ground, hamlets huddled back to back and belly to belly, jutting out on their outcrops with narrow hems of faded hydrangeas, spindly pawpaws and washing-lines trickling T-shirts into the swallowing undergrowth. The slopes were awash with wild lilies so fragrant we could hardly catch our breath.

We were passing through one of the last pockets of the Atlantic rainforest. Ninety-five per cent of it had been destroyed. I have a thing about lilies. The thousands became millions and covered every expanse along the tracks and under the trees. Damp humus blended with their scent. I also have a thing about morning-glory creepers, the sight of their blue trumpets gladdens my heart. They did wrapped round the door of the police station in Clapham, they did in the Andes, they do in Italy, and they grew like the weeds they are in a tangle all over Brazil. Above the lilies and the trellising blue, a tree with startling purple and white flowers predominated. It was called the quaresmeira, the Lenten tree, blooming for Lent.

The rainforest presented a uniform ceiling of dozens of species of tropical and subtropical trees. Anything growing over its height became smothered by lichen and strangled by orchids. Apart from an occasional daring palm tree, the only trunks to pierce the high mottled ceiling died from the top down and stood out in skeletal pallor, victims of the tall-poppy syndrome. They were the perches of hawks and vultures and were white-washed with guano.

I liked being on that railway and the railway staff all liked having us on board. I was bombarded by facts and details and pride in the daring engineering of each line. This one, in particular, was almost unique. It was an anglophile stretch, built by the British who left a trail of memorabilia behind. The railways had brought work, mobility, stability, cinema, football and a simplified version of cricket to the area, so anything to do with trains or England was regarded with affection. It was a plus to be English there, so, ready to wear whatever hat fits, English I was. Later, it was a plus to be Latin American, so I pulled out that hat and dragged my paternal great-grandfather from Belem in northern Brazil out of his coffin to keep me company. The only hat I was not allowed to wear was the huge-brimmed straw one I had bought specially for the trip. Hats, apparently, got between the presenter and the viewer, so despite kicking off at 38°C and graduating to a staggering 47°C in the Mato Grosso, I had to frazzle.

In 1848, the British built a winding gear to haul trains up the precipitous incline from Santos to Paranapiacaba, which means the place from which you can see the sea. Once there, I was assured, you could see the sea before eleven o'clock in the morning. After that, it was swallowed by mist so dense the station buildings seemed to hover over the edge of the world. To venture beyond was an act of faith. Paranapiacaba also meant several dozen out-takes while I tried to wrap my tongue round its correct pronunciation. We stood for ages at the end of a moody, mysterious platform while I kept getting it wrong and the local, intensely anglophile midges devoured us.

We were just beginning, we had two thousand miles to go. The station was in a ghostly time warp with antique carriages and the Emperor Pedro II's private compartment. We weren't going to get any local music, but we would get the national theme song: time is a different concept in Latin America.

There is nothing urgent about time. It flows. It stops. It doesn't rule anything. It didn't rule trains. They all had timetables, as the director pointed out to the station-master, but they were suggestions rather than facts. During pre-production, we had had a few arguments about this. If we were due to arrive somewhere in the jungly swamp at 15.15, it was unrealistic to pin our itinerary on leaving that same station at the projected 17.30 the BBC researchers had so efficiently discovered from London. My point was that the 15.15 would almost certainly be late. It would be a cold day in hell if a train that ran only twice a week actually left on time. We would have to allow for such vagaries, stopping over, if need be, for days. This view was unacceptable. At the two crucial changes in the Mato Grosso, I had stuck to my guns. No, I had never been to southern Brazil, but, yes, I was sure they did things the Latin way there and we would come a cropper if we counted on timetables English style. It became apparent on that midge-ridden platform as the train we were due to leave on failed to materialise that if we wanted to cross Brazil we would all have to chill.

On the trains themselves Robbie was with me in fact but not on film. He had to sit behind me or across the way and our conversations were endlessly interrupted. The filming was supposed to be very natural and spontaneous. I had to chat other passengers up to throw in local colour. Being shy, I am the least appropriate person imaginable to be called upon to play the opening gambit. However, in the spirit of the thing, I accosted people and we had some good talks. Unfortunately, I had to pump them for potential and then report back to the director which ones I would then re-interview on film.

This meant that I had to repeat what I had just said, which, of course, the locals found totally baffling. When a rogue transistor radio or some other such intrusion meant a re-take, I would then ask the same questions to the same person all over again. Despite having explained that this was how television worked, the concept rarely sunk in. Irate or frustrated interviewees kept saying things like, 'For the love of God, madam, I've just told you that three times.' Or, 'You look so intelligent, but really you're not!' Often these encounters would end with my victim in tears, thumping the plastic seats or leaving the carriage. All their gems, wit and social commentary went overboard.

We got our programme and most of what one sees is real. Some of it is fake, all of it is posed. I had much more fun on that trip than I am seen to have had. It was a wonderful, touching, ludicrous noisy shambles. Every time I came off camera, Robbie and I lounged around in the heat, taking in the local music, the dancing, the swarms of children and that feeling Brazil gives you of sheer pleasure in being alive. And we laughed, a lot, not least because the locals all the way along the line, no matter how dire their poverty, saw the funny side of life and the funny side of us. So long as I didn't corner them one-to-one on camera, that is.

There was a national referendum coming up on the monarchy. It was a constant topic of debate. A lot of the workers I met said they were going to vote for a king on the grounds that one corrupt leader had to be better than hundreds of them. Others, on hearing I came from England, wanted to know exactly what our king was like, warts and all. Whenever I told them we had a queen, they were a bit disconcerted.

Brazil is macho, but also philosophical: 'Oh well, in Bahia they want to elect an African king . . . black, female – keep it human!'

The train stopped and started, jogging along at about twenty kilometres an hour through the flat dull plain I had been warned about in London. I didn't find it particularly dull, but apparently for the screen it was a big no-no. Apart from the twelve of us and our sixty-nine pieces of equipment and our luggage, our compartment was fairly empty. Two wagons behind us, though, the train was packed. I went absent without leave for half an hour to talk to the labourers and the homeless who were squashed into the two compartments at the end of the train which the government reserved for the very poor to travel free of charge.

'They used to travel on the roof,' someone told me.

It doesn't make wonderful television, but the way Brazilians constantly give and gather names is a striking phenomenon. It is more than elsewhere, it stands out, strangers volunteer their names, run up and give them, shout them from the side of the tracks. Before asking for money, before anything, and often as the sole item of intercourse I am asked my name. I suppose a name, in a country with a population of 148 million people of whom 25 million live in *favelas* and 12 million are abandoned children, is one of the few things everybody owns. I sense genuine pleasure at the receipt of my name each time I tell it, and an act of generosity in those given to me. In São Paulo and Rio, street children risk their lives to graffiti their names on walls. If they get caught the police as often as not shoot them. The children keep doing it. Names matter.

There used to be several million Indians in Brazil, most of

whom were wiped out by successive acts of genocide. Among the few tribes left, anthropologists have noted that names are uniquely important. Yet whereas their compatriots broadcast and volunteer their names, tribes like the Amazonian Wa Wa guard names more jealously secret than anything else. Not even their closest friends can know their name. It is given and never used. To say it is taboo. To say it is the deepest insult. To tell someone else's name is also insulting, frightening and terribly wrong.

In the rest of the world, shaking hands, rubbing noses or bowing and then giving one's name is a customary introduction. For all the violent traders and slavemongers who have approached the tribes of Brazil, there have also been travellers, missionaries and scholars who genuinely wanted to be friends. What irony that they should have approached the naked Indians shouting their own names and demanding to know theirs. Even with interpreters, there was never a chance. They were asking to despoil the other's soul, to steal their very person, while burdening them with their own sullied, because spoken, names. What was meant as a friendly overture was perceived as hostile, as abuse.

I wondered if there was a connection between these two diametrically opposed stances, the primitive and the modern meaning of names.

23

I had a schedule, laboriously worked out by BBC researchers in London. Some of the stops I would have gladly missed. The ecological nightmare at the edge of the rainforest vomiting out toxic waste, for example. Others, like the Confederate cemetery outside Americana, I would have missed on my own but was glad to have seen. Americana was the last stronghold of the Confederate Army. After they lost the civil war, a group of them went there to plant cotton and then to die. I bumped along an interminably dusty red road in a jeep. It was so far, I kept wondering who could have had the stamina to carry the Confederate coffins. I had noticed other cemeteries from the train. They were full of blue crosses. There is a lot of blue in Brazil: glass, shutters, tombstones, houses, lorries, even the weeds seemed to be blue. This one was plain stone and had all the moodiness one looks for in a graveyard. For once, I didn't have to be directed to look 'lost in thought'.

We made a big stop in Bauru. It is a boom town, closely modelled on American ways, achieving the shape without the essence. Our hotel was a fifties monster. Robbie and I had a big plastic suite on the fifth floor. The air-conditioning had broken down making it into a sauna full of grotesque bulging armchairs and sofas. The plastic coverings were too hot to sit on. Of all the towns I have been to in Brazil, it is the one I would least like to visit again. It was brash and ugly and fiendishly hot. Its specialities seemed to be fried-egg sandwiches and a miniature horsefly which inflicted a bite that turned into a suppurating sore that stayed for several months.

It had once been a major railway junction, but had spurned trains for landcruisers and buses. Just about everyone in Brazil travelled by bus. The railways were dying. Most of the veins and capillaries were already dead. Even main arteries like the Bauru line where the trains changed gauge were neglected relics. In the few weeks between the recce for the trip and the trip itself there had been a series of derailments. As a result, all passenger services to Campo Grande had been suspended indefinitely. Bauru was sinister by night and depressing by day. The food was uniformly revolting and, something which is most unlike Brazil, the people were mostly unfriendly. We spent a panicky day at the thought of being stranded there, not finishing the programme, not getting to see the beautiful Pantanal swamp, not getting to Bolivia, having to eat a lot of mushy meals stewed in dirty dishwater, having to bear the glaring heat and getting chewed putrid by the Bauru biters.

When salvation came in the guise of an old engine driver called Ovideo, I loved him. I hung on his every word, laughed at all his jokes and virtually kissed the old 1904 steam engine he called his wife. I had set my heart on crossing the Mato

Grosso; I was determined to finish my chosen route, programme or no programme. It was personal. For the passenger line to have closed down after over a hundred years of use just as I was arriving was something I took very badly. And the goods trains shunting away to Campo Grande and Corumbá seemed to personally affront me too. Sometimes it pays to be stubborn.

Ovideo was eighty-four and unwell. He was due to travel to Campo Grande on a freight train, escorting four carriages of antique rolling stock to be restored further along the line. Being so ancient, these carriages were the only ones physically capable of embracing the gauge of the freight line. Ovideo smiled like a boy: 'Of course you can come with me. We'll have a party. Buy in some ice for the drinks, bring your own cook and we'll talk trains for a few days!'

So even Bauru, a city any tourist would be hard put to remember fondly, has a gold star on my map. Ovideo's wagons were lovely by any standards. For a train-lover, being able to travel and sleep in those museum pieces was like winning the lottery of life.

I had never yet seen a railway museum which I hadn't felt tempted to hide in after closing time, just to squat in the splendour of its lovely old carriages. I could have travelled on the Orient Express, but that seemed to me like faking something and I wanted the real thing. The train from Moscow had been stately with its blue silks. I had made a fairly disastrous trip to Mexico, lured more than anything by the thought of its Tapatio, a chance to ride from Mexico City to Guadalajara in the luxury of its original turn-of-the-century rolling stock. The Tapatio itself didn't disappoint, but I try to erase the ensuing three months in Jalisco. I don't want Jalisco on my memory map. Ovideo's train, though, was splendid and it was all for us.

For the purposes of the camera, I had to pretend to write at a mahogany table in the dark wood-panelled sitting room with stained-blue glass windows and brass lights. From pretending, I actually wrote for the first time in two years. It was the beginning of a short story which progressed with me all the way to the frontier at Corumbá and on into Bolivia.

Everyone was celebrating on that, our first night aboard. Ovideo held court. He had worked on the railways since he was a boy. He recalled how wild cats used to wait at lonely stations to maul alighting passengers to death. He recalled how the steam trains from Campo Grande to Corumbá used to have to keep stopping in the swamp so that stokers and passengers alike could get out and gather scrub to fuel the engine. He remembered the fights there used to be, the cowboys and the travelling bandits. He spoke nostalgically of the days before buses, of the camaraderie of the line, spilling his memories as the train swayed through the night. Twice, he ferried me out to the yellow striped verandah to 'absorb the bush', but the mosquitoes drove me back in.

Ovideo was enormously tall and powerfully built, the network of veins under his weathered parchment skin threatening to burst every time he laughed. He had a huge laugh which rocked on and on. Some of his stories made him laugh so much, I feared for him. The following tickled him the most. For the rest of the journey it was enough to point two gun-like fingers at the window and pull an imaginary trigger for him to burst out chuckling. It was the one story we could all share. Since Ovideo only spoke Portuguese, it was too much like hard work to translate everything.

'One of my friends was a ticket collector on this line . . . it must be forty years ago. One day, there was a big man, a cowboy with his hat and boots – he was big though, bigger than me. My colleague asked him for his ticket. The cowboy gave him a mean look, took out his knife, took out his ticket, stabbed it, and handed it to my friend like that at knife point. So my friend was very calm, he took out his gun, took the ticket off the knife, shot a hole in it and handed it back.'

Early the next day we stopped at Araçatuba, touring around our itinerary of things that would be interesting for me to see. Some of these things I had chosen myself, like a sugar plantation; some were chosen for me. I was so moved by the sight of the cane fields and the lines of cane-cutters I was tempted to lie down on the red earth and wallow in nostalgia. But it was rife with snakes and 42°C so I settled for skulking under a thorn tree and having my picture taken by Robbie.

Another bone-shaking stop was at Taveros. It had an old station house and a dead line. I was sent backwards and forwards about thirty times to knock on the door of the station house and enquire about a train. There weren't any trains there any more, which made my request doubly confusing to the family living inside in jumbled squalor. An old black man with blind, pale blue eyes sat like a corpse in the little entrance hall by what must once have been a ticket office. Taveros was the place where I sowed the greatest confusion. The old woman who kept answering and then not answering the door perceived me as a visiting witch. While walking up and down the little garden to her house, past a mango tree with burgundy leaves, I thought up another short story, 'Dom Leopoldo': a ghost story about a railway line and lost love.

Despite the moodiness of the story that came out of Taveros, the tiny village itself was a cluster of bars, one of which was a thatched tree. Here crew and a dozen villagers gathered for drinks and a knees-up, with an old man singing rhyming couplets to another's guitar. It was one of the nicest interludes of the entire tour and a magical place. I really don't know why, in the story I wrote, I made it either deserted or sinister. All I know is that it cast a spell.

Later that night Ovideo the magician was waiting as planned with his beautiful Wild West train which rattled us off to Campo Grande, a Latin Dallas-cum-pioneer-outpost. From there on, everything slowed down. There was no bustle, no rush, hardly any people and few signs of modern times beyond the ubiquitous transistor radios. There would be days now between each train. We broke our journey a couple of times but there were to be no more Dodge Cities. At Miranda, we parted company with Ovideo. He took his museum piece onto the Bolivian frontier while we paused for three days of wildlife. From there on, a train still ran twice weekly.

Acknowledging my Italian connections (and probably hoping to sell the programme to Italy too), we made a bizarre visit to an Italian alligator farmer in which we got to see a few more Cayman alligators than we really wanted to. Despite the blasé quality of the much-edited snippet in our film, six of us were chased screaming by a giant male across a tongue of land between two lakes full of his brethren. The equipment went flying, and it was every man for himself. It took quite a while before any of us felt ready to go back down and watch the suave Italian chuck cow's shins into the waiting jaws, and for me to be filmed asking him pertinent questions.

By the end of the afternoon I had learnt that the alligators were like Hollywood films: they were gentle, but savage; safe, but dangerous. They were fast, but slow. Good, because they ate the piranhas, and bad because they'd eat you. They also made gorgeous fashion accessories, went down well in Japan and had the bland taste of chicken.

The next stop was Miranda, a dusty sleepy place nestling like a sloth in the swamplands. Doves cooed in the waiting-room rafters. The station-master's small son was half naked and so round and sleek compared to the handful of other locals that I surmised his dad had the best job in town. It was a long wait for the town's three horse-drawn taxis, the only taxis there were. I stood by our sixty-nine pieces of equipment and our pile of luggage.

My own brown-leather suitcase, which had been a favourite before the trip, had fallen out of favour. It was so heavy it was stretching my arm. Every time we arrived or left, there were little shots of me and my suitcase getting on or off a train. These got shot and reshot and each time I had to lug my twenty-five kilos myself. Each time, someone ran and got it for me to take it back to the starting line, but for all the long shots it was me and it. Without thinking ahead, I had bought a massive rawhide lasso in Campo Grande which added another four kilos. We were short of space in the two jeeps. The deal for Robbie coming with me was that I would have to fit everything into one bag.

I wasn't at all satisfied with the film. I felt I could have done it differently and shown the Brazil I really saw, which I believed was much better. Despite my own misgivings, it got good reviews and a lot of appreciative fanmail. The one consistent complaint was the apparent fakeness of my luggage: how could I have such an array of outfits in that one case? It was pure stoicism. The suitcase nearly killed me and every item I wore on screen was inside it. As we approached the Bolivian frontier, the items in that case got thinner and faded. For the sake of continuity, my entire wardrobe had to be ready on a daily basis. Each evening, it was someone's job to whisk it all away and get it starched and laundered. The wear and tear began to tell. Had the filming gone on for another fortnight, I would have been in rags.

Robbie and I liked Miranda. We almost liked it best of anywhere. We spent three nights there: long enough to get our bearings, and long enough to idle under a palm roof sipping drinks and listening to the tree frogs and cicadas. We hadn't spent much time together on our trip. My twice-daily sessions with the soundman, when he strapped and unstrapped the microphone in my cleavage, securing it with surgical tape to my bare skin, was a lot more than my husband's jealous temperament would stand for. Also, neither of us had realised quite how many times a day Robbie would be asked to move away. This latter so irritated him that he had resorted to avoiding me as much as possible. Since an average day of filming was between twelve and fifteen hours long, the honeymoon part of the trip just wasn't happening. We had a truce in Miranda.

24

The Pantanal is a swamp, an enormous swamp. Larger than Britain, it spreads across the Mato Grosso do Sul and the Bolivian and Paraguayan frontiers. It was relatively dry when I visited it – but for the floodplains full of water hyacinth, it didn't really look like a swamp at all.

From Miranda we explored on a daily basis. We spent two days traipsing round a nature reserve where I became far more athletic than is my wont. I rode a stubborn Pantanal horse across a fraction of the vast Klabim estate, observing the Jabiru storks which are the symbol of the Pantanal. They are as big as goats and make nests the size of mattresses. Their necks have orange and yellow pouches the size of shopping bags. A series of guides bombarded me with facts, most of which just didn't sink in. So the names of most of the birds and beasts I saw there have gone, except for the ambling herds of capybara, a gigantic rat which we were invited to watch. We watched and the small herd of big rodents did nothing. We waited; they waited; we got very bored and they didn't move.

The dominant male was the size of a small sheep. I have never been fond of rodents, big or small, so I gave the capybara a big thumbs-down.

Just as I began asking quite how big the Klabim estate was and quite how much of it we were going to observe, the rarest of all the birds in the Pantanal flew overhead, dropping a brilliant blue feather into my lap. It was a hyacinth macaw with brilliant blue and scarlet plumage. They are virtually extinct, but were nesting still at Klabim. The sight of the macaw and its precious feather gave me a new burst of energy. Which was just as well because we had a long evening ahead of us to get back to Miranda and our hotel.

En route we were caught in a thunderstorm so violent the road became impassable. We took refuge at a fisherman's lodge in the middle of nowhere, bunking into cabins. The rain beat down for hours. It was torrential, tropical rain, pounding on the tin roof, drowning out any hope of talk or travel as it rudely messed up the schedule. A rain shot was therefore pencilled in and set up. It took so long to orchestrate (what with the storm, makeshift facilities and the growing confusion), that as the camera rolled, the rain stopped, as suddenly as it had started. Undeterred, the scene of 'sheltering from the storm' was recreated courtesy of a number of small boys standing on the tin roof with powerful hoses. The handful of locals found this so entertaining that we were the toast of the evening. Why, they asked over and over again, hadn't the rain been filmed while it was raining?

Since the roads were still heavily flooded, we had no choice but to stay on, becoming so pally with the fishermen that they invited us to buy the lodge. Even a man who had been bitten by a piranha fish and had sat nursing his torn bandaged hand cheered up in the light of our eccentricities. They came at us from all angles on the sale of the place, leaving us no choice but to pull out the strawberry filter and for me to conduct a number of fake interviews about the forthcoming sale.

The strawberry filter is a very useful device. It got us through hours of officialdom. Every time a shot was taken without any film in the camera, it was a 'strawberry filter'. Without wasting any of the previous film, minutes and even hours of footage could appear to be included, turning all recalcitrants into potential TV stars. It got us through lots of tricky situations and it eventually got us through the Bolivian frontier. With hindsight, it's a shame that we didn't actually use any of our film on some of those encounters, because no one was ever as forthcoming as those government officials making what they thought were their television debuts. Very few people believed we were making a train documentary. Most people were convinced we were shooting a soap opera and a lot of them wanted to be in it.

Everywhere I went in the Pantanal I got the impression I had just interrupted a siesta. It had a dozy, languorous feel. It was overwhelmingly hospitable. There were token settlements of Tereno Indians, token signs of habitation, but mostly it was an animal world. Up until Corumbá, it felt like a place where time had stood still, a beautiful serene slice of nature immune to all the ills of urban decline.

As though to augur change, the railway line from Miranda to Corumbá curves endlessly. Its British builders were paid per mile of track and so made it as long as possible. I got the sensation I was travelling from innocence into evil. Of course, such thoughts were helped by heading out of somewhere referred to as a terrestrial paradise into an area whose railway is called the Line of Death. One thing we really weren't supposed to do, by mutual consent, was get ourselves killed by any of the drug barons or their armies who ruled from Corumbá to Santa Cruz. It was cocaine country we were entering, and Corumbá was a laboratory for organised crime. I had heard bad things about Corumbá: it had the reputation of Sodom and Gomorrah rolled into one.

So I was surprised to see that once-grand inland port with its riverside architecture showing the remains of what might have been foreign embassies. It had elegance and charm that disguised much of what it had become. Looking one way, fishermen could be seen casting their nets in the great dividing Paraná river. Looking another, there were ostentatious signs of wealth with chic shops and restaurants. Then there were Pantanal souvenirs: stuffed piranha fish and Tereno feather necklaces. Tourists went there for both the wildlife and the cocaine. The streets were full of guides, many of whom seemed more willing than experienced. And, as if somehow to give credence to all the malign rumours that hovered over its head, Corumbá had a phenomenal number of pharmacies: tiny shops with disproportionately large laboratories above them.

I don't know why that pretty faded town surprised me, or why I was expecting it to have cloven hoofprints in the pavements. After all, I live in Italy and love it with a passion, and yet I know (as most of the millions of tourists who visit it each year must know) that Italy is riddled with Mafia and is a hotbed of drugs and corruption which we don't really see at all. We go for the frescoes and the architecture, the pasta and the wines.

I suppose I saw everything on that tour differently, because I was so dossiered up, so briefed.

I had been given folders of background information to look at on Bolivia. I made a point of not reading it until the day before, which had worked fine in Brazil: being there for three and a half weeks my knowledge accumulated. Bolivia, on the other hand, was all shoved into four days at the end of the trip. The irregularity of the trains left us no choice. Our month was up. To camera, I pontificated about the country like the expert I wasn't. In private, it was much too much to take in.

On top of that, there was a train strike between San José de Chiquitos and Santa Cruz. I made the last fourteen hours of my Great Railway Journey squeezed like a sardine into a tiny maintenance car with six other people and the essential equipment. We literally couldn't move more than a few inches and then only by complicated contortion. It was one of those little carts you see in Western movies designed to take two in the front and two in the back. It shuddered along the track. We hadn't eaten all day and the thought of that long night ahead with no food was more than any of us could take, so we made a picnic of what we could get. This turned out to be a packet of incredibly sickly pink wafer biscuits, some mini tins of condensed milk, a packet of crackers and a jar of olives. For the first few hours, nobody wanted to eat the rations, but eventually, dividing the food five ways, we developed a taste for it, olives and all. We left one tin of condensed milk in case we got stuck in the bush.

It didn't feel as if it could get any worse, but it did. In the small hours, our driver yelled out, 'Shit, that's an express train!' We were on a single-line track through the jungle. There was a national train strike, so all trains had been cancelled. The express train shouldn't have been on the track. If the strike had suddenly been called off, and there was a train coming, then that train, which our driver said he could hear shuddering the rails, was about to obliterate us. When the driver ran out and abandoned us on the track, we were all locked into the maintenance car. The driver had stopped by a little hut with a lantern outside it and had run to it like a man possessed. He hammered on the door, threw himself in as it opened and then disappeared. We sat and waited. We had become friends during the month's journey, the director, the cameraman, the soundman and myself, but what we had most in common at that moment was a reluctance to die.

Since we could barely move, we couldn't get any of the tiny windows to break. The car was made of iron. I thought of my three children, of the books I hadn't yet written and the things I hadn't done. I thought of Robbie driving through the jungle on a mud road twenty-seven hours long through which few vehicles made it in the rains. And (I am ashamed to recall) I thought of the tin of condensed milk we hadn't eaten but could have done, under the circumstances.

It was a bad fifteen minutes in which we prepared to die, found hope, began to feel less vulnerable and eventually saw the silly side of our predicament. The driver returned, unabashed, and drove on, keeping up his ten-mile-an-hour marathon. We had already decided that whatever vibrations he had felt or heard must have come from inside his own trousers. We speculated on the woman who must have been in the hut and what powers she must have had to make him run so.

I don't know Bolivia. I know Santa Cruz de la Sierra a bit and I know every inch of the inside of that tiny maintenance cab. I know what it feels like to be in the middle of the jungle with a bursting bladder and fear in my heart. Mostly, though, what I feel about Bolivia is distilled into the Jesuit mission town of San José de Chiquitos.

Until I went to Bolivia, I'd always thought of the Jesuits as the baddies. At San José de Chiquitos and in a circle of other mission towns, the Jesuits built churches the size of cathedrals. They built them out of mud and stone and fortified them against attack. Slave traders hunted and kidnapped the local Indians. It was the Jesuits who protected them, building adobe villages for the Indians within the compounds of the Church Militant and defending them with force against all comers.

The mission of San José de Chiquitos was founded by Father José de Arce in 1698. The road to it and the other missions was beaten by the Church Militant and its indoctrinated Indian followers. Those roads closed over long ago, hiding the self-sufficient Indians in their land-locked Atlantis. When the railroad was completed in 1951, the Bolivian government took it over. It is the only way in or out of San José in the rains, the only safe way ever. After the Jesuits were expelled from Brazil in the eighteenth century, the jungle swallowed up their compounds.

The sleepy village of San José is dwarfed by the mission with its fortified gateway, its campanile and its high walls. In the evening, some hundred and fifty men, women and children attended the weekday mass: almost the entire population of

San José. The congregation was all dressed up. They were all Indians. Their hair was sleeked with water or plaited into waist-length braids. Despite being abandoned for over a century, the Chiquitanos retained their religious fervour. They made their responses in Spanish, the language of their saviours.

There was one hotel: a cluster of rooms round a courtyard. The candle and matches by my bed seemed like a charming touch until I realised there was no electricity in San José at night.

The church was undergoing restoration by the Indians themselves, newly trained in the old crafts. Mass was held amid the scaffolding. One of the project overseers had a lorry. Against his better judgement, he agreed to bale out Robbie and the crew, who had still not arrived. They eventually reached Santa Cruz caked in dirt. It took them thirty-five hours, many of which were spent wading through mud and pushing the lorry.

The clearing in the jungle had red-bricked streets and an ice-cream parlour in somebody's back room. We ate chicken and rice in a backyard while the girls of the family washed their hair. The ice cream was home-made and had an undertow of rancid butter.

In the morning, a horse-drawn cart delivered fresh milk in pails. There were no cars. There was nowhere to go. It was a railway town, but few people ever caught the train. It was isolation that had preserved them, and isolation they treasured. Only supplies and occasional visitors came by rail. From the state of the shop, not much came in either, except beer, condensed milk and the sickly strawberry wafers that seemed to be the culinary mainstay of San José.

25

If someone were to ask me what is the most beautiful place on earth, I would tell them it is in north central Sulawesi, in Torajaland, on one of the thousands of islands that are the archipelago of Indonesia. It is best viewed from the edge of a ravine, looking down a thousand feet over paddy fields terraced thousands of years ago. From the valley bed, man and nature merge, then the landscape rises up slow slopes to highland forests in a mosaic of greens, a symphony of greens, scented by wild jasmine trellising the gigantic trees. I looked down from the high ledge of winding road on to something so perfect, so ethereal, it was hard to believe.

The Toraja people live in time past and time present in a dream world that holds no thought or care for the future. If one looks at a map of Sulawesi (which on my atlas is still called the Celebes), one sees a raggedy man dancing. His body, arms and legs are all there, but his head is strange. Instead of a head there is a cloud floating out of his body. I had often noticed that shape. In Torajaland I seemed to find the embodiment of that island: a floating-head-in-the-cloud tribe with their feet on the ground and their craniums exploding with dreams.

Everything those people do and make is a conscious continuity of their past. They weave their history hieroglyphically and cryptically into every cloth and braid they make. And they carve it into every object and utensil. They paint their history, the myth of their migration, on their houses, their shutters, their rice barns and their tools. They use only four pigments: red, black, yellow and white, all symbolic, and all repeated. What appear to be patterns is their preserved history, constantly updated. Their culture is a never-ending visual ballad.

They are a tribe of artisans who farm. The women do the farming, plant the rice, harvest it and tend the other crops. The men, from their earliest childhood, have a mission: to carve, paint and weave. The sheer quantity and the intricacy of those carvings is proof of their unflagging dedication.

They came from the north (probably from Vietnam) over a thousand years before. They came by boat across the sea and then down river. They found refuge in the empty, fertile, enchanted enclave of the Celebes. They pulled their boats ashore (probably living in them at first) and they stayed, with their imprinted memories. From that time, their every breath has been a celebration of their exodus, their odyssey and their survival.

If ever there was a tribe deserving of the name 'boat people', this is it. Their boats were ornate canoes with deep sides and high curling sterns and prows. They too were carved with their history. That shape, redolent of bull's horns, is recreated daily. The stilted houses are boat-shaped, as are the ornate rice barns, their carts, boxes and even their coffins. Every inch of every surface is carved, repeating over and over the symbols of the bull and the cockerel.

The Torajans never took to the sea again. Even their fish are kept in ponds in the paddy fields, but they have never forgotten their link to it. The land they chose to settle in is rich. It yielded all a tribe could need. They never needed to go hungry. The fruits of the forest could feed them. Rice thrived, their barns filled and they prospered. But Torajans measure their wealth only in oxen. Each life is spent either carving or accruing the big, placid, white beasts. The events of every day are added to their recycled history in carved bulletins. Everything gets to go in: acts of heroism and foolish mistakes, births and betrothals, purchases, and, above all, deaths.

It is all about honouring ancestors. It's the apex of ancestor worship. The dead are buried in chambers chipped out of the rock. The tools used for carving and those for rock chipping are much the same. They have beautiful ornate handles and pretty useless blades. It can take thirty years to chisel a new tomb.

The Torajans not only share with the ancient Egyptians a use of hieroglyphs but also the custom of burying the dead with all their earthly chattels. Where they exceed is in the extravagance of their funeral celebrations. Anyone who has had to foot a funeral bill knows that death is a costly business. All over the world, the poor save up for a decent burial. In many societies, a death is marked by extravagant entertainment and display. But the Torajan people are the only ones I know who sacrifice their family's entire wealth and livelihood: who cripple the future to honour the past.

When a Torajan man dies, *all* his oxen are slaughtered. Since a man's standing equates to how many oxen he owns or can muster, uncles, cousins, and brothers all slay *their* oxen too. They don't sell them, they eat them. The entire community gluts on beef. Funeral parties can, and do, last for months. Sometimes hundreds of head of cattle are killed. Which raises the question, how much beef can anyone eat?

Once the embalmed corpse has been ceremoniously carried to its resting place (standing up in the rock), an effigy is placed outside the tomb on a ledge and the cycle of life goes on. No matter how rich a family was, after a funeral it will be poor. The Torajans hurl themselves off the wheel of fortune, and the impoverished heirs knuckle down to paying off the debt. They live in hock, forever reaccumulating oxen and keeping up instalments on the last lot that have been bought, slain and eaten as a mark of respect for whoever has been fortunate enough to join the adored ancestors.

One would think that a tribe bound to a never-ending hire-purchase agreement, doomed to pace the treadmill of certain loss, and who valued death over life, might have an air of gloom about them. One might imagine a general lack of incentive there.

Yet they seem to live in complete harmony, united in purpose. Everything that happens is good: it is fodder for the chronicle. They are the chosen people, they have chosen themselves. What could be simpler? They don't make a song and dance about it, they paint, carve and weave it instead, remaking the boats that will never see water, and heaping all their riches on their dead.

The Torajans seem to live in true harmony. Everything is decided communally. They help each other and share as though their idyllic lands were still a refugee camp. They are all dreamers, all artists, sculptors and carvers. From their sculpture, past and present, they are clearly gifted. Yet no one seemed to feel the urge to do their own thing: to carve different images, to let the bulls and the cockerels alone and introduce new symbols. No one designed new thatch shapes. No one had altered a prow. No one moved on.

Through an interpreter, I had a long talk with an old Torajan who tried to explain what it meant to be one of the chosen people. They were unique: survivors of their flight. They were links in a chain, and the chain was eternal. It was rooted in the past. Rooted in rock, in the core of the earth. It was a chain they were forging, carving: carrying the past forward into the future.

Within the legislation of Sulawesi, the Toraja people own their lands and are allowed to live their lives according to their custom. Their rice barns fill and then empty to buy oxen. Traders come in to buy their beautiful carvings and see them for the pretty things they are rather than for their symbolism. Life goes on quietly waiting for death in Torajaland.

The Torajans are no threat to anyone or anything, except, of course, to oxen. I haven't had a lot to do with cattle, but I noticed the Torajan beasts had an anxious look in their eyes. They seemed to follow people with their gaze with the concern of pet dogs who look after their masters. It must be worrying for a Torajan ox to see one of the tribe flag or falter. The death of just one Torajan leads straight to the slaughter of generations of oxen with no equivalent chance of any bovine ancestor worship for them. Well might their slow gaze hover!

26

I went to Indonesia as a travel journalist, spending three weeks there with the photographer Simon Upton, who was also my close friend. Thanks to the help of the Indonesian Tourist Board, our trip flowed seamlessly. We kicked off in Jakarta which I rather enjoyed despite the appalling traffic and the pollution. This was thanks, in part, to my refinding some Dutch friends there and managing to get across the gridlocked city to spend an evening with them.

John Weduwe was the head of the lighting company, Philips, out in Asia. He and his wife Astride had been living in Jakarta for some years. We ate supper in their house with two of Robbie's paintings hanging on the walls. Although several of Robbie's paintings had sold abroad, I had never seen any of them hanging outside of Europe. So to be in that Asian capital among friends, with a painting of Iseult hanging in the dining room while we discussed the webs of our mutual friends, was a treat. We also discussed where in the great scatter of islands we should go, and what we should see, and what we shouldn't miss.

Indonesia is composed of thousands of islands. The Dutch had colonised them and then left, leaving hardly a trace of their long administration. Of all those diverse lands, we were visiting only three: Java, Sulawesi and Bali. It was my first visit to a Muslim country and I had arrived armed with a great many preconceptions and general prejudice collected subliminally while growing up in England and more recently from the reported rise of Islamic fundamentalism. Fanaticism, under any guise and for whatever cause, was anathema to me. Since Indonesia had the largest Muslim population in the world, I had imagined it would also have the largest proportion of religious fanatics. It was a prejudice that began to disperse within hours of arrival: there is something very gentle, friendly and hospitable about your average Javanese. So much so that Simon and I began to wonder whether these charming, open sweet-hearted people were being laid on for us along the way by the local tourist board. It was, therefore, reassuring to talk things over with friends who lived there.

During the three weeks we travelled around the three islands, so much was miraculous that it became hard to sift out what to write about, what to photograph and even what to do. I kept wanting to stay where I was. Particularly in Sulawesi. Simon knew Bali well and, rightly, urged us along. Looking back, the most unique piece of timing was our arrival after a long ride at Yogyakarta. We had spent the afternoon visiting the temple of Borobudur, which, if one were to make the wonders of the world eight instead of seven, would have to take next place on the list. We were feeling tired but inspired as our taxi limped into the city, hard put to get through the crowds which had spilled all over the road. As we approached a bridge, we had to stop because the crowd was solid. Everyone was staring in the same direction, looking up in wonder.

I was reminded of scenes from Waterloo Station where the noticeboards never seem to function adequately and where platform numbers are given out to the general public on a need-to-know basis with the general assumption being that nobody needs to know until seconds before any given train departs. At rush hours, this means that hundreds of anxious commuters stare up at the empty boards waiting to see what platform they have to run to. From the outside, it always looks like a crowd in the throes of adoration: disciples waiting for an angel to descend or a miracle to occur. It almost is a miracle if an English train runs on time and isn't cancelled, so that breath-held atmosphere is very real.

Out there, in Yogyakarta, a miracle of nature was occurring before our eyes. Mount Merapi, the local unfriendly volcano, was erupting. Out of its mouth a jet of flame was shooting into the night sky with a halo of orange sparks some fifty metres high.

Simon knew me well enough to know I always want to linger and that I am always falling in love with places. In that, we were kindred spirits, though he was less of a bigmouth and more of a doer in the travel department, having settled, albeit temporarily, over half the globe. I loved our tour of Java but I didn't really want to stay there, even for six months. Half a year, that was my timespan for fickle immigration. Italy was my base, but I kept an eye open for places where the family and I could migrate for half a year (the winter half). There had been lots of candidates, lots of possibilities on my mental list. Salvador do Bahia was one, Miranda in the sleepy swamp was another. But it was more the idea of knowing I would or could enjoy six months somewhere than any real intention of doing it.

Things changed in Sulawesi. I wanted to come and winter near the head of the dreaming man of the Celebes, somewhere on the fringe of Torajaland. On my return to Italy, I began to make plans. Robbie took some persuading but not nearly as much as I had feared. We had reached a point where I did most of my travel journalism and readings without him. It was the only way he could get on with his painting and we had found it didn't help our relationship to travel together with me in the limelight. However, I so loved Indonesia and so did Simon that Robbie wanted to see its wonders for himself.

Our projected tropical escape had to be cancelled when the forest fires blew so much smog over certain islands of the archipelago that to have gone there would have involved the constant use of gas masks. We cancelled our tickets and spent a rather disappointed winter in our terracotta fridge, as the Villa Quarata was sometimes called. The winter before I had arranged to spend two months in northern Goa with my children and one of my sisters and had had to cancel it because of an outbreak of pneumonic plague in neighbouring Rajastan, so I felt a little cheated. Therefore, when a chance visit took Robbie and me to St Kitts and Nevis and we both fell in love with the sister islands, I made short work of renting a house and organising while we were still there for us to return, *en famille*, the following November.

27

I had been to the Caribbean many times before. I had been to Trinidad and Tobago, Barbados, Curaçao, Margarita and Aruba. Iseult had spent two months on Grenada with my father when she was a little girl. He had a house there outside the capital, St George's. It was an old colonial house with a swimming pool in the middle and a garden full of tropical fruits. That house had been shelled by the Americans when they briefly invaded Grenada, ousting and killing Prime Minister Morris Bishop. My own planned holidays lost in that coup were nothing compared to the civilian casualties, but I still missed them.

When I went to St Kitts–Nevis in May 1998, I hadn't been to the Caribbean for twenty years. On our way to our first hotel, I didn't just think I was going to come back and live there, I decided it. It wouldn't be for ever. It would be for six months. I was writing an article for an English magazine, but I knew I would not be short of things to say, and I knew that

I would have to find a house to rent before Robbie and I left, which gave me exactly five days.

I would have taken anywhere: a shack on the beach, a hut on the hill, really anything so long as it had a roof and a minimum of three rooms. I was even prepared to waive a proper bathroom so long as it had running water. From that humble start, we ended up on the site of what was once the finest house on Nevis, when Nevis was the Queen of the Caribbee.

Montpelier House was a set of four West Indian pavilions on the ruins of the much older house where Horatio Nelson married the Nevisian heiress Fanny Nisbett in 1787. There was a plaque to that effect on the big stone gatepost. Across the garden was a little gingerbread house called the Villa Emma, in homage to Lady Emma Hamilton, Nelson's beloved mistress. It had two tiny rooms and two tiny verandahs, and a bathroom with a frog in the lavatory tank. It was the guest house where many of our visitors stayed. When we didn't have visitors, Florence used it as a Wendy house. She had seen photographs of Villa Emma and had set her heart on using it as her bedroom suite. To compensate for the rigours of the journey out, I kept her company there on our first night. We both found it so frightening she never wanted to sleep there again, which was just as well, because it was too far away from the main house to be properly safe.

There are a lot of things that don't sink in on a cursory visit somewhere. Our five days in the summer had been spent wining and dining and being whisked around by the tourist board to see the two islands' finest points. From the luxury of our hotel rooms we had been aware of donkeys braying, just as touring round the bumpy island roads we had remarked on the many stray donkeys wandering around. It was only when we took up residence that we realised that donkeys are the bane of Nevis. Twelve years before there had been only two cars on the island; now it was a place of many jeeps. Whereas people used to go around on donkeys and moved things on their backs, cars had been found to be quicker and less temperamental. Almost to a man, the locals had let their donkeys go and the beasts had multiplied. The sound of two donkeys mating is a memorable affront. Every night, herds of stray grey beasts roamed the countryside, barging through fences and demolishing gardens.

The groundsman who was to take care of Montpelier House during our rental had dropped some fairly heavy hints about violent break-ins. The house had been empty for a while before we came. I woke in the night to hear whispering outside our window. The window was just a flimsy wooden shutter with a hurricane bar. Florence was asleep beside me. I heard footsteps, and twigs breaking in the grass; then more whispering. I took the iron bar from the window and crept outside. It was pitch dark. I let my sixth sense guide me to the presence I felt but could not see. A dim bulb in the main courtyard about 80 metres away threw a shaft of light ahead of me. There was nothing in it, but something shuffled to my left. I clutched my bar and remembered how I'd learnt in Venezuela to fight dirty and hard. From within the silence something shifted, barely audibly, but it was there. I took a step in that direction and was about to take another, bar poised, when I came eyeball to eyeball with someone. The eyeball was the size of a tangerine. I'd been ready for burglers, muggers, drunks or kids, but not giants. I cried out, all hell broke loose and four donkeys charged me. I moved, they missed and stampeded through the gate, smashing through shrubs and flowerbeds as they went.

It was a rare night when they didn't return. Sometimes they threw parties. Sometimes they held orgies. Sometimes it was just one, lost and lonesome. Our sleep had to learn to absorb their demented braying. For all those people who, like us, had come here for a visit and stayed on – and there were several dozen – the donkeys were inexhaustible food for conversation. When you live on an island six miles by six, most of which is taken up by a volcano, topics grow threadbare. The only good thing I can say about the brutes was that they sustained flagging conversations.

Nevis used to be the centre of the sugar trade, producing the finest cane sugar in the world, and it used to be the centre of the British slave trade. All slaves were sold through Charleston, the capital. More recently, the European Common Market and the general influx of beet sugar put an end to the sugar that made these Leeward Islands great; and which made both them and Britain rich. Some of the old plantations have become hotels and all of the island of Nevis lives from tourism. It is a rich man's playground. The likes of Bill Gates, Giorgio Armani and Princess Diana have frolicked on her shores.

I knew about the sugar before I came. I had read about its rise and decline. And I had noticed that the hotels we stayed in were pretty pricey, but they were also good, and I imagined that the bottom end of the market was tucked away somewhere. There isn't a bottom end of the market, though. Nevis caters for millionaires, it doesn't want any backpackers. Tourists without bottomless wallets who happen to sail ashore don't make the same mistake twice. And that, like the donkeys, was something I didn't like. I had wanted to live on an island with a life of its own. Somewhere with a mix. Somewhere with less social discrepancy than Nevis turned out to have. There were a few more things I didn't like on Nevis, but they were never quite enough to spoil the lovely, often idyllic time we spent truanting on her shores.

I had four acres of garden, half of which was thorny scrub with a few rogue fruit trees, and half of which was studded with volcanic rocks. The discernible shape of the once vast Montpelier House traversed the grounds in low walls and foundations. We were 33 metres up and overlooking the sea. There were mangoes, star fruit, guavas and pomegranates. There were terraces of allamanda bushes with big yellow trumpets. The front of the buildings were draped with a purple flowering creeper which crept through the slatted unglazed windows and cascaded over one of the bathrooms. This was a roofless shower, like bathing in the jungle.

The dining room was an almost wall-less pavilion with a dangling glass candle-holder on a pulley. There was no other light and the shade was very deep. It looked lovely and was very romantic. Every night, when whoever lit it burnt their fingers, the big clump of aloe vera growing just outside was used to treat the burns.

Robbie made a studio out of a wooden toolshed some way across the garden and installed himself in it. It rained so hard for the first six weeks that he had to use duckboards to get to it. Had the island not been so extraordinarily beautiful, that unseasonal monsoon might have soured our trip. It rained inside the house and out. The dining room (having no walls to speak of) was often unusable despite its view of the sea and the jasmine that straggled beside it. Since the tourist board had been all over us like a rash when we visited in May and had appeared to love the idea of our coming out to live there, it was a rude shock to find myself shunned and boycotted by them. Their complete volte-face puzzled and hurt me, until I had stayed there long enough to see that the last thing they wanted was a journalist in house. There was a fabric of lies and recent myths on Nevis which had to be jealously maintained.

I went to live on that island because I felt it spoke to me. It stirred something in my blood. It still does. It is just as beautiful, just as warm, as fascinating and historic as it ever was. Knowing it hasn't changed any of that. You just start to notice things, like the primary schools, supposed to be the fifth-best in the world in which everyone can read and write and yet in reality have illiteracy problems that get swept under the carpet in the interests of keeping the UN tag. The real population is a tad larger than the official one; the crime rate ('safest resort in the Caribbean') is low because crime is ignored, unreported and even covered up. Theft happens, though probably less than on other islands, but rape is a real risk, for foreign women and Nevisian girls alike. That was the single shameful fact that was being most actively hidden, I think. It was why our groundsman didn't want eight-year-old Florence to sleep alone. Even little children ran a risk. At least one multiple-rapist was known and allowed to roam unprosecuted. The police just didn't want to follow cases up.

It was an uncomfortable subject and it may be seen as treacherous to discuss it. But it won't go away by pretending it isn't there, and sooner or later it will not be possible to gag the victims. None of us was attacked and nor were our visitors, but friends we made on the island had been. They brought others to tell their tales and urged me, if I wrote again of Nevis, to acknowledge them. I wouldn't walk down the street at night in any city in Europe and feel safe. Most women wouldn't. Nevis was no different; the tourist board just claimed it was. It is a lot closer to paradise than London or Brussels, but it isn't a reincarnated Garden of Eden. Not for its safety value – and certainly not for its fruit. A real danger of living on Nevis was the risk of getting scurvy. There was such a lack of fruit that vitamin-C deficiency was a problem.

It was ironic because this was Admiral Nelson's chosen island, and scurvy had been the scourge of the British Navy. Fresh things, fruit and salads and vegetables, were in really short supply. Once a fortnight a boat came in from neighbouring Dominica laden with produce. We housekeepers used to go and fight over bananas and mangoes, carrots and yams. The rest of the time, the market consisted of about five stalls with five miserable little huddles of tomatoes, potatoes, grapefruits, onions and four or five other shrivelled-up things. With a houseful of guests, I could buy it out and close it down for the day. The prices were like Fortnum and Mason's, the most exclusive shop in London; the quality was not.

I was in there haggling and grabbing for the first six weeks, but I had been tipped off the previous summer. Part of what I took out in my luggage were packets of seeds. I kept my own little vegetable garden for all the time I was there and smugly picked lettuces and rocket, green beans and dill, parsley and basil and big fat tomatoes which were my pride and joy. I even got a little traffic going, giving seeds to any one of the locals who would care to try them, together with little lectures in our kitchen to anyone who would listen. My best recruit was the telephone-repair man, who came by several times a week to deal with our delinquent fax machine and phone line.

28

Although the tourist boom was the main factor in killing off the market gardens that had once flourished on Nevis, the recent hurricane had delivered the *coup de grâce.*

I had fondly imagined living off tropical fruit, coconut water and fish. The hurricane had stripped the island of fresh fruit and coconuts. Even the ubiquitous mango trees were barren for that year. To add insult to injury, the eastern Caribbean was fished out. Without friends in low places, fish was off. The lavish exotic displays offered by the hotels were airlifted from Miami. As a resident, scavenging was the order of the day. On the beach and in the dilapidated capital, people lean out of their jeeps and spread the news of available foodstuffs. 'If you see it, buy it' is the shoppers' motto. It might not seem like an exciting headline to outsiders, but when a neighbour yelled, 'Quick, they've got butter' – or cabbages or anything else – 'at Superfoods,' it was a source of joy. All the too-cool-for-school waiters assured me for the entire six months that the fruit juice was fresh. But fresh on Nevis means fresh from the tin.

If housekeeping was a challenge, it was a minor one, and welcome to spice up the languor of that exotic setting. I had got stuck in a groove; being there was my jumping off. I was up for anything that came. It was what I wanted, to engage in a different life.

On the eve of our departure I had settled, once and for all, three court cases, one of which had been like a running sore for years. Lighter in my pockets, but also lighter in my mind, I was glad to be away from Italy for a while. I had tired of being dunned for other people's bills and needed a break so as not to transfer to the country I loved the frustration I felt at what its legal system was doing to my family. Then, too, after six years of a ludicrous legal farce, the small inheritance Allie was due after his father George Macbeth died in Ireland had finally been secured. The hassle was immense and the legal fees came to more than the sum, but it was all Allie had coming to him so I had fought his battle on a weekly basis, flogging backwards and forwards to the Court of Minors in Perugia. Like a concurrent sentence, the gruesome saga of Iseult's divorce was running like a bad B-movie in its fourth year. But that too was distanced, as they say in Italy, *per forza.*

Other than the obvious perks of missing what turned out to be the coldest winter in Italy in living memory, and having an extended holiday in the Caribbean, I had made the move, more than anything, to write. It was four, nearly five years since I had finished my last book. I had another in the pipeline which was an increasingly reluctant hostage inside my head. It wasn't writer's block so much as a writer blocking. Mine was a case of wouldn't write rather than couldn't write.

I had finished my last book, *The Hacienda*, under such

unfavourable domestic conditions that I had promised myself (and to bind me, my mother) that I would not embark on another novel until I had cleared my decks. In short, the juggling had to stop. If getting out of debt meant selling the palace and moving to a cheap shack in the tropics, then so be it. On Nevis, I was testing the waters. It was also supposed to be the honeymoon Robbie and I had never had. We renounced ours to nurse his dying father and then got caught up in strife.

On Nevis, I was out of range of all legal canons. I was free to write on my own terms. This was what I'd been telling myself I wanted. I knew what the next novel would be – I had been thinking it out for six years. Yet somehow I couldn't get down to it, inventing, as writers do, urgent distractions.

Thus the first six weeks of my stolen time was frittered away in lazy days spent by the beach or exploring the island and the rainforest. There were also all the chores like leasing a jeep and a telephone, opening bank accounts, transferring water bills, joining the library, checking out schools, and then making friends.

During those early weeks, the rain kept us company with its monotonous drum beat on our red tin roofs.

We flew into St Kitts via Antigua. The plane to Nevis is a little eight-seater. We had made friends with the owners of a plantation hotel on St Kitts and arranged for our first night to be spent there in luxury before getting into the pioneer spirit on our own. I had a fantasy that within minutes of arriving I'd be at my typewriter banging out Chapter One of my opus. With that sense of missing a day, I did a warm-up, starting a diary. As the lazy pace of Nevis beguiled me, I kept the diary up for six weeks, abandoning it when I finally started my novel. I had never written a diary before for more than two days. There are lots of them somewhere in the billiard room at the villa, all with entries for December 26 and December 27 of given years, dutifully using someone's well-meant Christmas present.

I remember sitting on the beach and in the garden at Nevis, jotting; and that there was an element of 'Whoops, I'm a writer!' about it. I was trying to convince myself as much as anyone else. Dipping into my diary three years later gives my first impressions without any hindsight. Rain, luggage and a certain sadness colour it.

We arrived very laden: 90 kilos overweight. The hurricane had blown the roof off the left-luggage deposit at the airport so our entrée to the Rawlins Plantation Inn was a mess. Since Robbie and I had last taken the winding road up to St Paul's parish the island had been battered and smashed. There were corrugated iron roofs stuck in trees, the palms were bedraggled or blown down and there were piles of debris everywhere.

> 8th Nov. At the turn-off to Rawlins, by the side of the sandy track, there are little clumps of pink-tasselled grass. It is the capin melado of the Hacienda. A good omen. Florence is vaguely impressed for which I am pathetically grateful.
>
> All along the road I have tried to describe 'paradise' through our route across this tropical, idyllic island. The hurricane-battered shacks and mauled woods blown over with debris, peppered with litter, are not really doing it

for her eight-year-old eyes. She is trying hard. This is our dream.

As soon as we turn into Rawlins, Eden moves back onto the horizon. Paul's garden has been beaten, but it has survived.

Both Paul and Claire manage not to get distressed by our distressing amount of luggage. From hot, sweaty, dirty and done-in, we scrub down to a family half human and begin to wonder what dinner will be ...

Sweet potato, soup, prawns, rucola, avocado and lettuce salad.

sleep

I seem to have reverted to my adolescence: sleep stirs in with the menu and I nod off several times during the sorbet ...

9th Nov. Breakfast and bananaquits and Cuban finches dart onto our table ...

A run-in by phone with the St Kitts tourist office. It seems all my faxes have been ignored there because we will be staying on Nevis: as near to mortal sin as a tourist can get. Curiously, if someone attacked me with an axe, I would gladly tackle them barehanded, confident (probably foolishly) that I would win. But if anyone is rude to me unexpectedly, my solution is still dissolution – I cry. So, 'tired and emotional' I retire to the verandah rummaging for my shades to try and hide my ridiculous tears – I am 45!

It is hard to stay serious bundled into the Nevis Express – ten people including the pilot, shut your own doors and hand-luggage clutched to your lap. It is so hot,

I have to laugh. A sauna gone mad. It is 7½ minutes – a survivable torture. It flies so low over the sea you can see the reefs and even the bigger fishes . . .

Customs is relaxed, the golf bag with the photographic tripod and the other extras will arrive within 24 hours.

Maybe.

I scribbled away en route, recording the trivia of what was, for us, a momentous time. The next bit was added later that night:

Nevis is greener than I remembered. It has suffered less than St Kitts. When I first saw it, it was May, and scorched, now it is rich and tropical, still trellised, as before, by the ubiquitous pink bee flower. The same quick-stick that was draped over Thailand.

Montpelier House looks as lovely as I remembered it.

The sea is grey.

A carpenter is working in the open air, finishing (starting?) huge doors to replace those battered by the hurricane. I fall asleep to the sound of his sawing.

Florence wakes me to meet Bernard, the factotum of this house. He explains lights, generators, water etc., but I am too zonked with jet lag to take in a thing. He looks a bit like Robert Johnson. He crawls into the stone generator shed and crouches beside the beast. It half-chokes him with black smoke.

'OK?'

I say OK but I have no idea how he did it and he really doesn't look OK.

As Bernard leaves, night falls. A tropical dusk you could miss if you blinked. Montpelier is plunged in darkness. I wake up Robbie and together we play hunt the light switch for a while. Managing to light two rooms, a closet and the guest bathroom before Robbie cuts open his toe on a stub in the sitting room. While he bleeds into the basin, I play hunt the sticking plasters in our luggage.

Sutured and limping, he leads us to the Montpelier Plantation Inn. The barman, Edison, is also an electrician. I wonder if he was the fantasist who hid our light switches.

Flurries of rain beat on the roof and the bamboo outside amplifies the wind.

Dream of the sea.

Donkeys.

One of the things I planned to do on Nevis was research a book about sugar. To this end, I needed access to several archives. The tourist board could help. I went in for a couple of masochistic attempts at meetings.

Let them go. Their 'go to jail, go directly to jail, do not pass go' message is loud and clear. They don't want me here. Half the problem is sheer pettiness. Kittitians and Nevisians dislike and distrust each other. My sugar letters had been sent to St Kitts. Finished!

17th Nov. A cockroach three inches long lives in our bathroom.

18th Nov. Up at dawn then early to Ouallie beach. Not a single visit to a single office. Not one piece of luggage. Miles of cream-coloured sand. Brown pelicans diving. Every time Bob Marley comes on the radio – which is often – everyone begins to twitch and sing along. It presses invisible buttons. At Ouallie we start our collection of conch and cockle shells.

Early again and back to Ouallie beach to swim in the shallows, then over to Sunshine's Bar. I had planned to take the ferry to Basseterre but the Sea Hustler doesn't go today. Tomorrow.

I have my first successful linguistic encounter:

'How you doin?' passing Nevisian.

'Good,' me.

'OK,' him.

This is a feat.

It took a couple of weeks to decipher what anyone was saying up in the parishes, and months for us to adapt our accents and vocabularies enough for them to grasp we were speaking the same language.

Before we arrived, a herd of goats had strayed into the airing and open Montpelier House. They shat over the entire house. After ten days the lingering smell was gradually fading.

Because of the Nelson connection, the house is full of books on Nelson. I am going in for full immersion. As I read in the sitting room at night, a lurid green and yellow lizard climbs up the ceramic lamp base and sits under the bulb catching mosquitoes and midges and watching me. The edge of its jaw is scarlet tinged.

20th Nov. A massive half rainbow sits over the sea.

To Basseterre on the 7.30 ferry. Or not. Robbie's watch is slow. Waiting for the 8.30 Sea Hustler has its by-now familiar element of tension and mystery. No one will say for sure which boat it is, or isn't, and where, exactly, it will arrive. We make two abortive attempts to board cargo boats to other islands before embarking on the Sea Hustler. On board, for the full hour of the crossing, an unintelligible chanting blares out of the radio. It is religious, it's catchy, but I really don't know what it is. On deck, the view of the island is stunning. The sea is a beaten silver sheet. But Florence and I stay under the blue awning because she is badly sunburnt after hours of swimming and shell collecting at Pinney's and Ouallie beach yesterday.

21st Nov. Swam again. Am reading 'Nelson in the Americas'.

22nd Nov. To a deserted beach approx half a mile from Nelson's Spring. We walked along the hot sand to the edge of this pool. The hurricane had blown the thousands of water lilies off its surface, so egrets and moorhens no longer step across them as they did in May. We take shade under a cluster of young palm trees. Our picnic is indifferent – the exquisite tropical hamper hasn't quite happened yet.

Saw a sandpiper and demoiselles hovering over the beach.

23rd Nov. To Basseterre on the Caribbee Queen. This ferry is a lot less funky than the Sea Hustler and you can't sit on the deck. We come to do battle with the customs. Then lunch at Rawlins. The thought of the one shall sustain me through the other as I release our air cargo from Rome. Meanwhile it is 8.30 and we are in Piccadilly Circus, St Kitts style.

Some of the women here have backsides so wide they defy gravity. While I'm bitching, there is a hairstyle here which is obviously catching on. It could be influenced by the Sun King's court. At its best, it adds up to half a metre onto the height of the wearer. It is unisex. It is elaborate, it is persuaded to stay upright with anything from nylon stocking bandaged around it, to external and internal combs.

I arrived here feeling (and looking) rather raddled, and overweight, and with my nerves frazzled. I haven't written for four years.

24th Nov. Home all day and loved it. I started a herb garden and walked all over the garden (except for about half an acre of impenetrable jungle). Two more gum trees: red-orange bark so smooth it explains the difficulty of being 'stuck up a gum tree'. An orchard of sorts and thorny acacia. And everywhere more ruins of the old house (of the family, Herbert). The stone is purply-red volcanic rock, or maybe just red sandstone. The house looks out to sea and it feels good to me. Called Iseult. 'Mamma, you've abandoned me!' A lot of lizards and butterflies.

25th. Collected shells on Pinney's beach. Met up again with Buckey, a dark Harry Belafonte cum Chicago gangster with an enormous smile and a laugh that brays like a donkey. Also Alex: American, New Yorker, an old hand on the island – she could be a friend.

26th. Waited in all day for a fax machine to be fitted. I like being here more than going out.

Walked Florence up to Montpelier Inn for a homemade ice cream.

27th. The fax arrived, brought by Ward. We talked about growing herbs and salads. He says everyone here is asleep, meaning no one will do anything for themselves anymore. He may become the lettuce king of Nevis. He may bring me some aubergines. He may show me the old sugar ruins.

28th. Reading a dreadful Patricia Highsmith, then a very silly American novel, then, 'The Ultimate Good Luck' by Richard Ford. So good I had to keep stopping.

Florence met a little girl called Pearl who lives on a yacht and in the rainforest in the 'Monkey House'. We are invited up. On the way out, we pranged their car. Will the invitation still stand?

29th. Buckey called and invited us to dinner with him and Alex.

I've set up my typewriter in the big sitting room. A short story? Wrote, 'A little Bit Wild'.

30th Nov. I feel sad today. What can I say? Saw this, saw that. Did this, did that, and . . . ?

1st Dec. Last night we went with Alex and Buckey to the opening of a new restaurant at Cliff Dwellers. Our car was almost washed off the road by a flash flood. We spent a very exciting two hours wading through torrents. Soaked and relieved, we ended up eating pasties in a roadside shack, waiting for the storm to recede.

2nd Dec. Rain, power cuts. One telephone blasted out by lightning, no fax. I snatch moments to garden. Reading Norman Lewis's autobiography. We visit Sunshine's but my heart isn't in it. I would rather be at Montpelier gazing out to a grey sea than on that most lovely beach. Sad at heart still.

The sitting room has fifteen slatted windows painted pastel green. It feels very West Indian and I feel very West Indian too.

3rd Dec. We return to the opening. This time we get there.

Buckey is so stretched and lonely inside, scarred by failure. He's scared of the future in ways I remember and recognise in myself. He switches from laughter to tears when he's really relaxed. The foiled despot in me wants to lift him out of that despair.

6th Dec. It has rained and rained. The garden (yard) has large areas of swamp. Mildew is forming on our clothes. The money in my wallet is wet. All our thousand envelopes have stuck themselves down. Inside, it rains most in our bedroom and the kitchen. Moving from one pavilion to the next is a drenching experience. Each day, for a few minutes, the sun comes out and we go down to Sunshine's for a swim. Every day there are rainbows. My hair has been braided by Sweet Pea. I am reading up plantation records and accounts.

29

We had been told on St Kitts that the heart of Nevis was a beach bar called Sunshine's. Indeed, such is the grudging rivalry between the islands, we had been told it was the only place of any note there. It took us a while to find it because the hurricane had blown down the sign where you had to turn off Island Road. Island Road, skirting the base of the volcano along the coast, was the only road on Nevis. The sign hadn't been replaced because 'everyone knew where Sunshine's was'.

It was a West Indian *favela*, a botch job of a shack made to be repeatedly blown down and thrown back together. It was owned and run by Sunshine himself, a broad-faced, jet-black Kittitian with a disarmingly sweet smile. He served two drinks: killer bees and beers. The killer bee was, he claimed, a secret recipe whispered to him by his grandmother on her deathbed. Not having been privy to that long-winded encounter, I couldn't be sure, but I reckoned the secret recipe was a lot of rum, a little passionfruit juice, lime, angostura bitters and thin Nevisian honey. Whatever the recipe, it was a delicious, near lethal concoction. Sunshine blithely offered a prize to anyone capable of drinking fourteen killer bees. No one could. We personally saw two contenders pass out cold from their palm-trunk stools while trying, and another, a grossly fat sailor, had to be strapped to a stretcher and taken to hospital. I almost said 'rushed'. But nothing was rushed on the island, not even disaster.

When Florence was a baby, I had suffered a kidney failure, part of my long illness. I didn't touch alcohol for six years. By the time we reached Nevis, I had graduated to an occasional sip of white wine. Carried away by the Christmas spirit and the arrival of all my children, I got leglessly drunk at Sunshine's one day. The aftermath was so dire to my system I have never touched alcohol again. To have thus been stung by the killer bee gave me a certain cachet locally. Apparently I drank eleven, just three short of a T-shirt. However, that one and only lapse in Florence's entire lifetime has stuck in her memory and recurs regularly as she regurgitates all the unsavoury details of that last fling. I'm the sort of drunk who dances on tables. I have paid for that wildness many times over in shame as the 'Do you remember that night you were really drunk . . . ?' resurfaces before strangers, teachers and clergymen.

Although technically a squatter, Sunshine raked it in, because his bar was the only thing between the remote and elite Four Seasons Hotel and distant Charlestown. Pinney's beach was long and deserted, hot and beautiful. Any guests who strayed from the hotel could not help tripping over Sunshine's with its cold drinks, fresh lobster and grilled fish. Every morning his pick-up truck bumped over the sand, packed with his staff (who were all his own nephews) and all the ice, salad, water and everything else he needed to run his bar. Last but not least, the ghetto blaster and box of CDs were unloaded and set up to croon reggae and blues.

Behind his makeshift bar was a collection of votive offerings to his heroes: Martin Luther King, Malcolm X, Nelson Mandela, Taj Mahal and Robert Johnson, to blues musicians in general and to the growing cult of himself. A pack of tawny mongrel Ridgeback dogs lounged around in the sand and were his pride and joy, supplying a conveyor belt of mongrel puppies, many of which found homes in the United States. It is hard to resist Sunshine when he presses a small puppy into your arms as a very special gift. I was adamant we would not accept one. Most weeks, I pressed such a puppy back after he had solemnly presented Florence with it.

Iseult has a habit of adopting stray dogs and then leaving them with me and Robbie. Her heart is moved by dogs. We had many difficult experiences of this kind on her many visits to Umbria. Since we were due to leave Nevis in the spring, we were forearmed for that particular brand of Sunshine's always boundless generosity. However, during the week when I was unwell in the middle of January, on the eve of her departure, Iseult snuck two puppies up to Montpelier House. Naples and Jane Bond, as the children called them, were two emaciated, sickly, six-week-old curs whom somebody had abandoned at Sunshine's Bar. They needed feeding in the night and a lot of attention. I really didn't want a menagerie, but was too unwell to prevail. Jane Bond turned out to be a vicious brute intent on tearing Naples's throat out. After about a week, I managed to get her adopted by an unsuspecting

American tourist in search of one of Sunshine's legendary pack. Naples, on the other hand, whom I had disliked on sight, became a great favourite and was later adopted back as Sunshine's special house dog to live in residence with him and his fiancée Maria.

By the end of January, Florence waited at the driftwood tables for huge tips, Robbie became such a regular he was awarded a staff T-shirt, and the image that beams out of Sunshine's website (he thinks big for 'an island boy') is of himself and Florence cheek to cheek.

From having been a skeleton nuclear family, we grew to a full quota.

> 11th Dec. Iseult, Allie, Felix and Cinzia are to arrive tonight from London.

The day before, Francesco, an Italian friend of Iseult's from her teenage disco days, had flown in from Guadaloupe. To all of us, he is like family. Cinzia Rosello, who was arriving with the children, was my closest friend, invited to stay for five months of our six-month sojourn.

> Great excitement at the tiny, dusty airport. In the night sky we could see the plane cresting over Mt Liamuga on St Kitts, then beetling over the straits to Nevis. There are eight passengers on the tarmac but none of them ours. Florence is in tears. Robbie and Alex head off to a bar. I push Florence's distress up to the counter and beg for our party. They are stuck on St Kitts. The Nevis Express pilot

kindly turns right around and goes to get them. 30 minutes later, they arrive.

We are a close family. We live like a clan. We make our plans jointly and spend as much time together as possible. Iseult's and my friends are mostly the same. Alexander is equally close to both his sisters. Florence and Felix, though aunt and nephew, are the same age and best friends.

> 12/13th Dec. Like characters in a black and white film, family drift in and out of rooms in varying degrees of jet lag; passing out under mosquito nets, on the grass, at the table and on sofas.
>
> 6 am is the best time to catch up on news and get some sense of what has been happening while we've been here.
>
> Iseult is terrified at the idea of monkeys.
>
> Felix is in heaven, and Florence so thankful for his coming.

The telephone hardly worked at all. The fax worked between 2 and 6 o'clock in the morning. It all looked very hi-tech but as soon as more than a handful of people on Nevis dialled or received a call at the same time, Cable and Wireless lost the ability to keep the island in contact with the rest of the world. The post seemed to be an entity in name only. We received under a dozen letters in the six months we were there. Of the 180 Christmas cards I sent out (at the cost of over $600), I think four made it to their destinations. With no television, and only the newspapers cadged from incoming tourists, we were cut off on our five-star island.

Much as I enjoyed most elements of our escapist isolation, I missed my children. The six weeks of Iseult's and Alexander's visit was, therefore, my happiest time (barring the bad day).

15th Dec. Getting 8 people into our jeep is a challenge we rise to several times a day.

I needed the children around me. I see the island more clearly for their presence, picking out sights for them, the treats, the languorous calm of Pinney's beach.

16th. The days begin to gravitate towards afternoons at Sunshine's. Allie has made friends with Zoo, Sunshine's nephew. Iseult sunbathes and reads as though in a state of suspended animation: in love. Florence and Felix are both so happy. Cinzia unwinds. Robbie is happy at Sunshine's. I feel like wallowing in this rare moment of family harmony, and so pleased we all came.

One should not mock the Gods.

Troubles between me and the children almost invariably come from the outside. We hardly ever fall out or fall foul of each other, either en masse or individually. Discord has come in the guise of either illness or attack. Iseult has had the lion's share of both. Alexander has had his moments, but Florence, apart from her brief virus in New Zealand, had lived a charmed life. That is, until she was eight, and poisoned by a food colorant that nearly killed her. We were on holiday in southern Puglia, in the toe of Italy, when it happened. For six days we had lived with the certainty that angelic Florence was going to die; for another ten days, we lived with the fear that she had something irreversibly wrong with her brain. When we left the hospital in Lecce and carried her home in 43°C heat to the villa we had rented for our family gathering, we did so with fear. For five weeks, we were in and out of hospital as each successive attack (of what looked to the doctors like a cross between strychnine poisoning and a brain tumour, but was neither) enveloped her. Only nine weeks later was the mystery solved. F113 is a red colorant, innocuous unless consumed when the outside temperature is over 32°C. This rarely occurs. When it does, the victim tends to die, days later, with no apparent connection to the red colorant. It happened the summer before we left for Nevis, whose gentle embrace had finally rid us of the fear.

We hadn't bargained for an aftershock. One came, though, on Sunshine's beach. In front of all the family, Florence passed out in the sea. Someone snorkelling bobs on the water. Florence was standing in the shallows watching tropical fish through her mask, while Cinzia sat only metres away watching her from a deckchair. It was early January and after two months on the island Florence had made several friends. The mother of one had come up to the bar where I was reading and asked if she could take Florence for a swim. Having been so ill in the summer, Florence was a chick to my mother hen and I only allowed her in the water with an adult.

She is a good swimmer. She went out fairly deep with two other little girls and the mother, but was somehow separated. Feeling strange, she waved for help and called to her friends, who waved back. She swam for the shore and was just reaching it when she lost consciousness. Part of the closeness I have with my children is the ability to feel them telepathically. Robbie and I both had our backs turned to the sea. As I read, I heard her call inside my head: 'Mamma!'

Although the distance was not great, it was just too far for me to reach her in time. I pulled her out unconscious and was unable to bring her round or resuscitate her. Robbie, seeing me hurl down my book and run, had run after me. When my ER skills failed, we ran for our jeep and the hospital. Robbie was so distressed his body was jerking. Carrying her, his arm jerked into her ribcage, whacking her hard with his elbow. She coughed up water and came round.

That was our one nightmare on Nevis, the bad day, the one disaster none of us could laugh away. It could have happened in the bath. But it happened there, in the sea. Within a few days, Florence was back swimming to her heart's content, but I didn't swim again for months in unnoticed protest.

That incident jolted me out of my lull. Cinzia sorted out Florence's formal education. Teaching was something Cinzia had never done before, but was fully qualified to do. Together they did morning lessons. Robbie painted in his toolshed and I started to write, day by day, on a roll. Sometimes it was just the four of us; sometimes we were bursting with guests who had flown out from Italy or England to stay. I kept on writing, claiming every morning for myself. Without Cinzia there, it wouldn't have worked, because Florence didn't know me as a writer. She had never seen me thinking with a look of intense concentration and a vacant stare into the middle distance that would cut out everything else, even her. The time factor was not a problem. She was a child who never felt bored. She was used to making up games, talking to herself, and chose to spend hours a day drawing. What upset her was my expression as I sought a lost word or image, searching like a mobile-telephone network temporarily out of range. Each time she saw the look, she got worried and asked if I was in pain. What was it? She had never seen me look that way.

And each time it brought home to me what a gap there had been in my writing that a child of mine could know me so well and yet know me without my 'thinking face'. Both Iseult and Alexander had known it from their babyhood. When Iseult used to ask me things, she'd say, 'Are you listening with your head?', knowing I spent so much of my life on automatic pilot: there but not there, speaking, answering, but not listening properly. Iseult likes 100 per cent attention and learnt quickly how to get it. Click, and she'd switch off my dreaming and searching, and then click me on to her wavelength. Alexander was much the same, although he found putting his face very close up to mine and saying, 'It's me,' broke through the screen. Only Florence saw my writing as something alien: an insidious rival which scooped out the inside of my head, leaving an empty, half-witted stare.

In the immediate run-up to my starting a novel, there are a lot of those empty gazes. And the new novel was, I hoped, the big one, the real thing, the one, like Iseult's beloved, I had been waiting for all my life but began to despair of finding. I rose before dawn to work on it, and I nursed it through the night. I shut myself off in the big be-windowed sitting room with the tame lizard and worked on it every morning, all morning. I had started on it just after Christmas and it was going well.

The accident with Florence on the beach put it away. But a week later, it was out again.

Every afternoon, having made a picnic lunch with Cinzia which we ate in the open dining room, 'we three girls', as Florence called us, spent time together. We lay in our garden, talking, we walked around the parish. We ate ice creams at the hotel and we went shopping. We drove (Cinzia drove) to all the different beaches and coves on Nevis. We gathered shells. We went to the ruined Bath House and the hot springs for which Nevis was once famous. We soaked in the hot sulphury water for hours. We climbed over the ruins of once-great sugar plantations and their factories and grand houses. We spent a lot of time on Sunshine's beach, from which Robbie had become almost immovable. Once a week, we went to Basseterre on St Kitts. Cinzia made new friends and introduced them, linking them in with Alex and Buckey and Sunshine.

About once a month, Captain Lennox took us out on his catamaran to the reefs. And about once a month a couple we had met and who had befriended us on St Kitts on our first fleeting visit came over in their old steam yacht, the Tiger. Every time they took us out on it, around the islands, it felt as though we had tacked straight out of Joseph Conrad. Philip, who owned and had restored the Tiger (he called it the other woman in his life) was completely enamoured of his task. Kate Spencer, his wife, was a painter who had trained in Florence, and together in rare marital bliss they lived in what I think must be the most beautiful house in the Caribbean. Philip had been the last white planter on St Kitts, and was now the Caribbean's most romantic sailor. Although perhaps romantic is not the best word to describe a man with a booming public-school voice who found being caught in a hurricane on the high seas 'most amusing'.

Thanks to the Tiger, Robbie sailed off with Philip and Kate to the classic Yacht Race in Antigua, saw the famous T-boats race again together for the first time in decades and developed an interest in all things nautical. Despite our having drifted a little further apart, we both adored our Caribbean escapade. On our return, he would have his first proper big exhibition in London. He had been taken on by the Francis Kyle Gallery, and was being so well looked after by the Kyles that they had come out to Nevis to see how he was getting on, and showed every confidence in his future success. I no longer needed to sustain his career – it was taken care of. All I had to do was be with the children and finish my book. Almost every day on Nevis had felt like a holiday to me. All the chores were lesser than those at Quarata: the house, the garden, entertaining, shopping – it had all downscaled. Six lawyerless months had also done wonders.

I flew back to Europe ready to take on the world. Which was just as well since, unknown to me, I was about to walk into a maelstrom.

30

I was writing a novel about a series of misunderstandings that led to a quiet, studious boy being catapulted into the international arena, and turned a gentle man into a feared revolutionary and a legend. One after another, these misunderstandings pushed him into the limelight of political upheavals. I was writing it from three angles: what he felt and thought, what he actually did, and what the media, the public and his enemies made of it. It took place in four continents over seventy years and had a cast of hundreds. It was the most complex book I had ever tackled. Given the density and weight of the material, the political background and sometimes harrowing details, I decided to write it as a kind of black-comedy-cum-confession.

I got the idea for the style from Jorge Ibarrengoitia's *The Lightning of August*, a Mexican novel about a revolutionary general recalled from the wilderness to serve the new president who is his old comrade in arms. On the train to Mexico City, the general accuses a fellow passenger of stealing his pistol and roundly insults him. As the train pulls in, it becomes apparent the president-to-be has died before ratifying any new appointments. The scenario goes from bad to worse, stirred by mistaken identities, misunderstandings and runs of bad luck. The voice is one of recurrent denial and a setting straight of the record.

I got the subject matter from my best friend, Osvaldo Barreto, code name Otto, whose revolutionary past jumped many times from the sublime to the ridiculous. Every summer for years Otto had been coming to Umbria to be with me. Bit by bit, the story he told me of his life accumulated into such an extraordinary testament that I wanted to write his biography, to save his memories of events of historical significance. Otto had been one of Fidel Castro's chief advisers, and he had played a role in the Algerian battles for independence, in the coup in Chile, in Uruguay and Iran, in France and above all in Venezuela.

From my own years in the latter country and my many Venezuelan friends, I had heard endless stories of what Otto had done. Only in Umbria did I realise that his reputation bore little resemblance to the truth. I broached the idea of a biography to a few publishers who all told me they would love it if it were a novel. It didn't take shape as one for another couple of years but then, thanks to Ibarrengoitia (who happened to have been a close friend of Otto's), I saw how to write it, and I began to work on it in my head. A couple of years after that, I felt ready to start. It was then that the four fallow years occurred.

I didn't see Otto at all while we were on Nevis, but he was with me every day as I crawled around his mind, taking liberties with his life and generally tampering with his character for the purposes of fiction. I hasten to say that I did this with his full approval and blessing.

We flew back to Italy via London to see Iseult. We arrived on the last day of April, and might perhaps have seen it as an omen of things to come that no sooner had we sat down in Iseult's London flat than we were evacuated by the police in a bomb scare. We spent our first day hanging around in cafés waiting to get back in past the security cordon. And we noted that the little stall on the corner of Queensway had more tropical fruits to sell than all the ones we'd seen on the island.

When we got back to the Villa Quarata, Trouble with a big T was waiting for me. It escalated rapidly and cloned, then it came so thick and fast and from so many directions, most of the following year is a blur.

I have had so many dealings with lawyers that I sometimes feel like a character out of *Bleak House.* So many that Robbie says if I ever write a full autobiography I should call it *A Hundred Years Of Solicitors.* They have mostly been such dull cases; I fear it would make an even duller book. Just as *la signora* Nadalina and *la signora* Berta on the landing in Bologna had little labels on everything they owned, I think I had a label stamped on my back for a while saying, 'Sue me'. If anyone ever wanted proof of how much I love Italy, it is there in my continuing to live in the country through a five-year storm of court cases of Kafkaesque complexity. On our return from Nevis, this became a deluge.

It was a classic case of life imitating art. I was writing a novel about misunderstandings taking over and wrecking someone's life, and now petty errors were snowballing and taking over mine. Week by week, the screws turned, while from the sidelines the slings and arrows also found their mark.

People say, and Otto has confirmed, that torture victims crave the approval and even love of their torturers. Considering I got diced up into little pieces by both lawyers and bankers, perhaps it is a bit perverse that among my close friends now, post-trauma, are precisely that: lawyers and bankers. In the days mid-crisis when I needed a lot of legal advice I could not afford to pay for any more, I acquired, in Otto, my oldest friend, my own, free of charge, personal attorney, who re-emerged from my past to bail me out. Since I was a teenager, I have known Otto in many lights and guises, but, not until recently, as a lawyer. And yet he is one and not only a good one, but versed and qualified to deal with the Napoleonic Code. He helped keep me from drowning. And out of the blue a banker appeared, to guide me out of the minefield. Without them, I would have probably combusted all by myself.

From within the blur of that year, two things shine out: these new friends, and Mali.

Life went on, because it does, with or without one. Florence went to school in the village, Alexander went to school in England, Robbie kept painting but was worried sick. Iseult and Nick and Felix set up house in Notting Hill. And I put my novel away, lost two stone through stress, and missed a great deal of sleep. I did a little bit of journalism and a lot of worrying, a lot of apologising, and a lot of travelling. Most of my trips were around either northern Italy or northern Europe. Most of them had a built-in clause that I was supposed to be in two different countries at the same time. I got so tired, I no longer knew what I was doing. There seemed to be no one else to take my place, so I kept going.

It was a far cry from Nevis. When Otto insisted I meet him in Mali, it was about the last thing I wanted to do. However, I owed him a great many favours. He had to go there to interview some oil people and he asked me to come too. He called me from Trinidad.

'Can you come to Mali?'

'Where?'

'Bamako.'

'Could you please spell it?'

He gave me his new mobile number and rang off. After I put the phone down, the Mali rather than Bali registered. I loved Bali (even if it was a difficult time for me to go) but I didn't know where Mali was. I looked on our atlas and couldn't find it. The atlas is from 1911. It calls Sulawesi The Celebes, Sri Lanka Ceylon, and has all the British Empire shaded in pink. I called back and asked where Mali was. I'd interrupted a meeting. He said, 'French Sudan,' and hung up.

I called a few friends and asked them what they knew about Mali. Two had never heard of it, one said it was the armpit of the earth. He said when he'd been there there'd been a lot of soldiers in the street, curfews and things, and that it was dangerous. I knew Otto had a business trip to Trinidad and had probably called me from there. The last time I'd been there in a convoluted route via Houston, it hadn't exactly been the highlight of my life. Airport immigration tried to deport five-year-old Allie as opposed to allowing him to transit with me and Iseult through their lounge. Yet whatever courage I may have once possessed had long since died, so Caracas and Trinidad suddenly seemed like attractive alternatives to an armpit. I called Otto back and suggested it. He told me it was Mali or nothing. 'It's hot,' he said, 'you'll like it,' and since it was his shout, I packed a bag.

The worst of the Trouble was over. There was even a glimmer of hope of getting a life again and writing that book. I would go to Bamako for a long weekend, but there was no way I was going to go unprepared.

When I set sail for Venezuela, my mother prepared me as though I were going to darkest Africa. She packed me a trunk of emergency supplies that presupposed a combination of dire need and the age of Stanley and Dr Livingstone. Despite it only being for a long weekend, I now was going to that darkest Africa and I packed accordingly with all sorts of explorer's supplies: a first-aid kit fit for a field hospital, hard rations, a torch, two packets of batteries and several cans of mosquito spray.

My last-minute fact-finding phone calls upped my trepidation: don't get malaria, don't go out, don't get mugged, don't carry a handbag because it will get stolen and don't go!

Otto had fewer don'ts: don't forget to get a visa, and don't be so silly!

I had never been to Africa, north, south, east or west. A part of me was excited about going to a new continent, but another side of me was afraid. I had reached a point in my life where I was afraid of most things, including my own shadow. My nerves were as strung out as they had ever been. I had contracted debtitis, a condition in which everything I touched turned to debt, and every move I made seemed to increase them. Every time I juggled to sort things out, a new lawsuit swung in and hit me.

I was newly emerged from these shadows when the invitation to Mali came up. Like an amputee feeling pain in a limb no longer there, the fear lingered long after the danger was gone. I have never been entirely free from paranoia, but in those days, it galloped through my veins.

31

Sitting on the plane from Brussels to Bamako, I felt as though I were flying into the lion's den. The pilot announced that our flying time would be five hours. Five hours was nothing! It took almost that to reach an airport from Quarata. I was travelling to the end of the earth and I felt cheated by the short duration of the journey there. I was too nervous to read my book, too nervous to sleep, so I read the in-flight magazine. It had a photograph of a citadel in the desert: Tomboctou, in French, an ancient city in the north of Mali. I hadn't realised it existed. To me it was a familiar name but a mythical place. Whenever Joanna didn't know where something was, when our things slipped into the fourth dimension, she would say, 'I don't know where it is, it's probably in Timbuktu by now.' The sinking feeling I had carried with me onto the plane lifted a little with the resonance of that name and I felt a flicker of excitement.

From the moment we landed, that excitement grew. I was bombarded by impressions new and outlandish, but beautiful to my eye. Only the airport staff wore clothes as I knew them, everyone else was in robes, gorgeous bright robes on which wealth could be measured by the fineness of embroidery. The women wore headdresses like origami creations of stiff cotton in the shape of fruit, parrots and swans. The women were tall, often taller than me, and so erect and graceful I was constantly straightening my curved shoulders, wanting some of their extraordinary poise to rub off on me. I had never seen so many truly beautiful girls as the ones in Bamako. Swathed in the coloured sheen of their wraps were the daughters of many different tribes and ethnic groups, from jet black women, to pale Arabs, Tuaregs from the desert, Peuls, Dogons and a mix of every shade from black to beige with intervening hues of cinnamon and even grey.

A first impression, later confirmed, was of many apparently prosperous but skeletally thin men. It was a male thing; the women were often slender, sometimes plump and occasionally obese, but a lot of men looked as though they were ravaged by parasites. There was a thin look which was more than wasted flesh: thin high foreheads, thin chiselled noses, long high cheeks, shoulders carrying crisp, calf-length robes as a coat hanger might.

It was a world dusted with red: the earth, the roads (even in the city centre) were pulverised terracotta, and a fine powder became ingrained into everything. When a breeze rose in the dry heat, red dust enveloped everyone and everything. If the wind blew down from the Sahara, everyone dived for cover and wrapped their heads in cloth as a sandstorm beat the town.

I was expecting to be met by my friend. He wasn't there. As

I stepped into the heat haze on the forecourt, looking for him, someone grabbed my arm and began to pull me to the barrier. I had been worrying about abduction but hadn't expected it to occur in my first two minutes. I clung to the metal railings while a strange black man with a powerful grip hissed to me in French that I had to go with him. I wasn't ready to make a big scene, but I wasn't ready to be dragged off either. My brain raced through scenes of rape, Aids, imprisonment, to my children, the unfinished book, unplanted flowerbeds, Robbie, the village, the forthcoming Umbria Film Festival I was supposed to be presenting, and Otto. Where was he? If I held on long enough, he would come and save me. Then it seemed he was almost there. I heard his name, several times, but took a moment to come out of my panic to realise that the man who was pulling me was saying it. He'd been sent to do so as my driver, Otto was caught in transit and wouldn't be in till later that night.

Feeling incredibly stupid, I climbed into a scabby car, which looked as though someone had taken large bites out of its seats, and was driven down the long road into Bamako. Out of the bright red earth, thorn trees and flamboyant date and traveller's palms, stood proud of clumps of low, dusty shrubs. The huts and houses were curious shapes, different from anywhere else, except Barcelona. They curved and toppled, peaked and bulged like Gaudí's architecture. The further we went, the more struck I became that he must have seen these things. Later, seeing more varied villages, the Dogan houses, and pictures of Timbuktu itself, the influence seemed overwhelming. Rising as they did from the dry russet earth or from sand, seeming to grow out of the ground rather than to have been built on it, the shapes were more beautiful than their Catalan versions.

By the side of the road, mud compounds were hidden behind red mud walls. Outside them were enormous bundles of furze and sticks, and beside them, in varying numbers, were sheep, so clean I had to look twice to see that was what they were. The sheep in Mali are washed and groomed. The currency is mostly ovine.

The driver was friendly but wary. He obviously wasn't used to passengers who behaved as I had at the airport. Much of the ride took place in a silence interrupted by the taxi's radio which blared on and then died at irregular intervals. The snatches of music played were intriguing but took turns with a monotone of what sounded like Arabic and seemed like praying. As we approached the town, there were mosques and a couple of streets of peeling mansions. In what appeared to be the centre, some dilapidated government offices squatted in the shade of their gardens. Vendors sold mangoes in neat pyramids, girls wrapped in metres of patterned cotton carried baskets of carrots on their heads. These were stacked so high, and were so big, the girls' heads looked as small as necks and the baskets themselves like heads by Arcimboldo. There were a lot of people milling about the town. Many of the women carried babies strapped to their lower backs, the bare lolling heads of their infants just above their behinds. Many of the women carried calabashes on their crowns and could run and even trip without spilling them. Men, women and children wore elegant robes in a palette of colours, most of whose glare had been softened to pastel. The variety beat even the coloured stones of Patagonia. Pigments, it seemed, were big in Bamako.

Cotton is Mali's main export. The market is full of stalls stacked with bales in every colour under the sun. The finest is marked along its edge 'Africa 1'. This, supposedly, is the best cotton in the world. Mali was awash with it. We drove past a roundabout scattered with Californian poppies. We drove past huddles of men, solitary Tuaregs in inky-blue costume with their heads and faces covered in cloth and their curved swords strapped across their chests. We went past dozens of little stalls selling anything from matches to bags of rolls, bananas, peanuts, Kleenex and strings of small fried fish. There were not many cars; those there were had beggar children running after them, holding up their hands for alms, for a quick sale of a mango or a bag of five peanuts in the pods. The road surface was full of potholes and bumps. It was made of pounded earth.

Bamako is a capital city, but a small town. Its streets were full of sleek sheep and scrawny chickens; the taxi had to stop for a herd of goats to cross in front of it. The air was full of voices, calling from stall to stall and across the street, chattering in a language called Bambara. Mali had French as its official language, but French was the language of officials and taxi drivers, waiters and the upper class. The poor spoke Bambara and a number of other more local dialects. Most of the Malien are poor. Greetings were in Arabic, giving the lie that everyone spoke that language. They don't; it is a Muslim country, conquered by the Peuls who came from north Africa, who converted the conquered to Islam. Many of the schools are Koranic. Having learnt to repeat the Koran, verbatim, for seven years, seven months, seven weeks and seven days, a scholar could know the entire holy book off by heart and still know what none of it meant. Only the elaborate greetings were universally understood, so the streets resounded to what sounded like everything Allah: bismillah and Allah akhbar and inshallah. Arabic is not my forte, neither was Bambara. I got a few Allahs going, mumbling most of them, and I learnt to say 'En y chey', which is thank you in Bambara.

There was something so run down and primitive about most of the buildings that I prayed the room at my hotel would have a door, and the door a lock, and that somewhere there would be a bathroom with running water. My hotel took me completely by surprise. It had high gates and railings, four stars, Parisian prices, several receptionists, fleets of porters and bell boys and waiters in smart uniforms. It also had a lobby full of French and Belgian visitors waiting to check in. Rather than tourists, as such, Bamako has businessmen, engineers, geologists and technical advisers of various sorts who come out to help develop the developing nation and to help stick their hands in the honey pot. Mali has important minerals in its northern desert, hydroelectric power and a great many exploitable resources. Visitors tend to pass through Bamako en route to the hinterlands.

It was swelteringly hot and the air was peppered with hovering mosquitoes. My room, booked for me, was beyond a cavernous restaurant with a vaulted thatched roof, through gardens of hibiscus, crotus and strelitzia. The sun bore down in a steady glare, bouncing off the white path. On either side, cushions of moss-like lawn were spiked with exotic flowers. I saw a lizard half a metre long with a bright orange head, then another that was blue. They looked as convincing as cheap plastic until they scuttled away, jumping over the hummocks of grass.

Somewhere in the distance, a muezzin called to prayer. The peripheral noise stopped, and two men in the swimming pool with gleaming black backs turned towards Mecca.

I had decided to wait in for Otto to call. I had a television in my room. It showed tribal dancing and cookery programmes for the intellectually challenged. News seemed to come exclusively from school playgrounds or the large stuffed armchairs of people's sitting rooms. It was partly in French and partly in Bambara. Some of the cadence of the French was so chopped and changed it took a while to realise it wasn't all in tribal dialect. After two hours, Mali TV went grainy and came off the air with a buzzing only slightly less loud than the anarchic choirs of tree frogs outside my window and the swarms of mosquitoes within. I would find out that every day the television was the same: two hours of tribal dancing and chicken stew.

My initial disappointment at not getting a good old black and white movie to while away my evening disappeared when, subsequently, it became clear what a blessing that complete lack of contact with American or Anglo-Saxon culture had been. Mali is a country turned in on itself. Its own culture and customs are almost intact. Its traditions, dialects, commerce and outlook have not been swallowed up by the American Way, or even the French Way. Apart from the few dozen mansions, the odd school and mission, a smattering of its language and quite a say in the cuisine, it was as though the French had never been there.

So much of everything I saw was itself, undiluted by any outside influence since the eighteenth-century conquest by the Peuls. I could not call it a lost world; it seemed to have more heart and centre than anywhere else I had been. I felt drawn in by it. I felt a cultural osmosis. I began to see things their way, to re-evaluate my perceptions through their eyes. Visually, the novel shapes and the barrage of colours awoke a hitherto virgin part of my brain. I found Mali exciting. It was like a shot of adrenaline straight through my sternum and into my heart.

I had left very precise instructions at the reception desk about my expected phone call. Otto was due to arrive, I would be in my room, waiting for his call. Nothing happened.

Eventually, I fell asleep to the hum of air-conditioning and insects. Next morning I awoke late to the sound of voices outside my room. It sounded as though two men in the corridor were about to fight but kept backing down as one cajoled and coaxed the other to be reasonable. I waited for it to end before exploring breakfast possibilities. Then, since it was obviously going to be a protracted affair, I ventured out. A teenage boy in a very new, very crisp beige uniform was talking to a vacuum cleaner in two voices. What had sounded like scuffling was him switching his machine on and then almost immediately switching it off again. He held the beringed plastic hose as though handling a giant python, and seemed to be both addressing and threatening the body of the machine itself as though it were a captured lion that kept behaving with unwonted savagery. Every morning this monologue was repeated, with a little more hoovering and a little less admonition.

After I had befriended one of the waiters, he told me the boy was new. Working at the hotel was like winning the lottery and a huge help to his entire family. The boy would be desperately proud of his new position as a cleaner at the prestigious establishment. But having been brought in from the bush he had never come across the likes of plumbing and electricity and had certainly never seen a vacuum cleaner before. He would have been given cursory instructions on how to use it, and was now going through the process of taming it in his own way, bringing to bear his tribal and huntsman's skills as all African boys possessed from their initiation ceremonies.

'You can't explain things like that Hoover,' the waiter said. 'It's too big a jump. He'll have to work it out for himself, get used to it all by himself. We all had to when we started. This is another world for us. If you notice, in the evening, when the cleaner knocks off work, some of the children hanging onto the railings are his family who come to see their hero. We don't make much money by your standards, but that boy is probably keeping about twenty people out of what he earns. We have big families here, with all the wives, and there isn't much work about.'

I waited in all day, enjoying myself even though I was only commuting from the restaurant to my room and back, and from the restaurant to the main reception to ask about my visitor. Every time I transited the restaurant, at least one of the waiters stopped me for a chat. It was there that I learnt of the West African phenomenon called random drop. You dial a number, any number, and at random and for no apparent reason, the line disconnects. If, by some miracle, you do get through, it drops mid-conversation. This made it virtually impossible to communicate by either phone or fax with the outside world. That was why I couldn't get through on the telephone in my room, and, by general consent, the chances of anyone getting through to me were slim.

Spread out across the many rooms, the small flurry of guests who had arrived with me were scarcely visible. The place seemed empty, ticking over with a vast staff standing by with no one to serve. I was encouraged, invited and then begged to come to the restaurant and eat something. Apart from some rolls and guava jam and a pot of weak coffee, I'd rather been avoiding the food options. Hungry as I get, I am a squeamish eater. I had brought several kilos of hard rations with me in the guise of biscuits and chocolate and was rather hoping I wouldn't have to eat locally until my friend and food taster arrived. However, the kitchen and dining-room staff were just too sweet and insistent, so I braced myself to deal with the food with fortitude, determined to eat whatever it was so long as it did not originate in the intestines or head of any beast. Elsewhere I had dealt with crocodile meat (very good) and snake (nothing to write home about) and ants (sour, crispy and not worth the fuss), but I am no fan of snails and I had heard they ate snails in West Africa the size of my fist.

In fact, the menu was in French, and so was the cuisine. I ate grilled fish with sautéed potatoes and haricots verts, topped off with a delicious lemon meringue pie. The one concession to Africa on the entire menu was a choice of rice or aloko instead of potatoes. Aloko was the humble plantain.

By the middle of the next day, there was still no word from my errant friend. Then, in the afternoon, a very large Arab gentleman came into my room. It was locked; he had knocked. I was expecting one of the waiters to bring me up some more water, so I opened it and he was there, fully robed in pale blue cotton with fine embroidery around the neck. Etiquette is very different in Mali. There is a complete lack of shyness. And although there is a baffling amount of ceremony, the ceremonies we usually stand on elsewhere, like strange men not barging into a lady's room, do not exist. Taken aback, I was relieved to hear he brought me news: Otto was still stuck in transit. Air Afrique, the purveyor of incoming connecting flights, kept cancelling his. He had now flown to several airports, hoping to beat the system, but kept being foiled. He would not join me for two more days. His message was to change my return ticket and wait for him. The one question that leapt to mind was how did this man know this? Telephones didn't work. The telephones and the random drop were for the likes of me; he had a satellite phone, a massive contraption with a satellite dish which sometimes, not always, worked. It was called an Inmar Sat (or rather it sounded as though that was what it was called. I had been informed several times that my only hope of getting through to anyone was with such a thing, but the name had hitherto been incomprehensible).

Having delivered his message, he turned to leave without more ado. I asked him if I could use his magic satellite, at least to call home. Alas, he said, he was '*désolé*', he was on his way to the airport as we spoke. If only I had asked him earlier, the chunky phone would have been at my disposal.

So I ate and drank wishy-washy coffee, fresh fruit juice and cups of mint tea, sitting doused in mosquito repellent in the restaurant. I talked to the next shift of waiters and spent time in my room, reading whenever the light allowed it. The hotel was prey to powercuts. I felt pretty silly to have come to this astonishing country, to have been so taken with it, and not to have set foot outside the hotel gates.

By this time, the restaurant staff had seen photographs of all my children, and I had been ferried brothers and sisters, daughters and sons to say hello to through the railings. At supper, one of the waiters told me that since I was a writer, there was a young man who would like to speak to me, and could I be introduced. The young man was a medical student from the Cameroon, and a well-read, softly spoken person. I ended up asking him for a reading list of African writers; he ended up asking me what a writer was doing cloistered in her room. What indeed! I made my way back through the hibiscus beds determined to change my ticket and get out to explore Bamako.

Next day, at breakfast, there was a book waiting for me: a well-read paperback by a Malien writer called Amidou Hampaté-Bâ, *L'Histoire d'un Enfant Peul*. By the end of the first chapter, I was hooked. For the first time in years, I was also glad I had paused in my own novel. Here was something new, both the rhythm of the prose, and the way of weaving through a story. It was a very exciting breakfast time. I went back to my room and read more of Hampaté-Bâ's song to Mali. Under all the history and detail, it was a song. It was one I could carry in my head and transpose back into my own style. This was not an intended plagiarism. I felt inspired by the author's use of language. My head was buzzing.

Mid-morning, I asked for a safe taxi at the hotel reception and prepared to arrange a later flight. We bounced along in a battered yellow taxi in a red, powdery cloud. The gentle look of so many of his compatriots was not upon my driver. He was very big, very young and his eyes were alarmingly red. He drove me to the nearby Sabena office and within fifteen minutes I was booked onto a later flight. In fact, six days later: that was the first available date.

'Where now?' the driver asked in French that was barely decipherable. I had no idea, but suggested a museum or market would interest me.

Living in Italy, one gets used to seeing men of all ages grabbing their genitals in public. It is like a nervous twitch; they touch them for luck, checking, it seems, to make sure they are still there. So I wasn't one to get unduly prudish about a man scratching his balls, even if he was sitting next to me in an old jalopy in Bamako. But my driver seemed to be doing a lot more than scratching, and each time I glimpsed his bloodshot eyes, they seemed to exude sexual voracity. Maybe, I thought, having him rub up against me in a crowded market was not such a good idea.

As he manouevred through the potholes he was as friendly and chatty as everyone else I had met in Bamako but most of what he said seemed to be about sex. I was too new to the city to know if this was the usual banter of a driver–passenger relationship, or an overdirectness due to his poor French, or the straight come-on it appeared to be. His taxi was all over the road, avoiding ditches and ruts, but his line of questioning was very direct. Had I ever had an African lover, and did I know what incredible studs they were? I told myself I was out to see the city, not to get paranoid; that the man was an official, authorised taxi driver, obviously known and trusted by my hotel. What was needed, I thought, was a little time apart for me to calm down and him to come up with another topic of conversation.

As luck would have it, no sooner had I come up with this plan than we passed a board for the Bamako Botanical Garden. Nothing, it seemed, could be safer or more sedate. In broken French we discussed the fact that this was not a market and I could not buy any gold or leather goods inside. Eventually, having spoken a little more sharply than I meant, we drove through its gates. By now the driver looked aggrieved and sulky. There would, of course, have been kickbacks at the market from every stall I bought from. Once out of his smelly car, I felt I had been imagining any ill-intention on the driver's part. He was probably a nice, decent man who just happened to look potentially very violent. With the dust at Bamako, it was not so remarkable that he had scarlet eyes. The miracle was that everyone else did not. He mumbled something about getting a better guide than he was, and ambled off to a clump of palm trees, clutching his testicles firmly.

Behind the palm trees, a man was hacking at something with a machete. My driver greeted him in Bambara and pointed to me and smiled. Then they turned away and I felt sure they were laughing. I was halfway between being in the garden and day-dreaming Hampaté-Bâ. The small man in khaki and his machete were to be my guides. He introduced himself and I bade goodbye to the driver, instructing him to wait for me there. First: palms and bamboo. He began to throw out names, pointing at each new specimen with his machete. Both his commentary and walking pace were fast. I found myself trotting to keep up. Behind me, in silence and about five metres back, the taxi driver followed. The bamboos were an important collection. They were seemingly endless and liked it in Bamako so much they were trying to swallow up the path. Their feathery leaves swished in my face and their jointed canes tripped me up. Each time it happened, both men apologised as though it were they who had hindered me. I found this very English. I had already noticed it from the hotel. West Africans apologise when they hurt you and when you hurt yourself, and even when you hurt them. The English do it too. You tread on someone's foot, and they say sorry. As we delved on and on into the woods, the only sounds were of birdsong and the chorus of 'sorries'.

The garden was laid out *au naturel* with massive slabs of red sandstone interspersed with vegetation over a substantial hill. It was 34°C and the sedate stroll I had envisaged was turning into a mountaineering expedition. We seemed to be straying too far. I kept suggesting we turn back, but the guide insisted we carry on. It was imperative, he told me, that we reach a certain point. If I turned back without the guide, I'd be in the middle of the bush with my red-eyed panting driver and his itchy balls, so I kept clambering onwards and upwards.

I don't recall ever feeling so hot. I notice when it's hot and like it to be so, but I rarely suffer from heat. The cold is my bugbear. I was very unsuitably dressed that day, in a high-necked jumper, trousers and stiletto-heeled boots. I'd chosen it as a look that was smart and wouldn't offend the Muslims. The heels were hell on the rocks and slow work on the flat bits too, aerating the earth as I walked. The bare stone slabs were scorching through the soles of my boots and the sun beat down with glaring white heat. Without a hat, I was getting dizzy. I am the least athletic person anyone could meet. The one sport I practise is shove-ha'penny, an old English bar game requiring the minimal exertion of half-moving one finger against a ha'penny coin. We played it a lot in Italy. That was my kind of game. This was not my kind of walk. I would have sat down on a rock and rested but the rock was too hot. I caught up with the armed guide and told him firmly that this was just too far.

'I am taking you back by another way,' he said, striding ahead again.

At which point, it occurred to me that the two men could be partners in crime, leading me up that mountain the better to murder me with the machete that never left the guide's hand or my field of vision. If their intentions were bad, I had come too far to safely turn back. I felt my only hope was to talk my way out of the situation. The ball-carrier behind me seemed to be waiting for me to drop or run. The guide, on the other hand, who may or may not have been a guide but who did know most of the plants, was older, the whites of his eyes were white and he didn't keep yanking his groin.

I tottered along beside him, cursing my heels. I made it clear that this had not been an impulse visit to the gardens, that I had told not only the hotel staff of it but also my influential friends. I told him I had foolishly come out without any money and hoped he would buy me a drink back at the base. I laboured both points to make them think that if they killed me they would not only get no money they would get caught as well. The machete kept swinging and the sun kept beating down.

We were approaching a stone plateau. The guide turned to me and smiled. 'We have a surprise for you.' He hauled himself up and then grabbed my wrist to pull me to him.

'*Et voilà!*' he said, pointing to a big stain on the rock.

Blinded by the increased glare, I tried to see what it was. A cave painting perhaps? Or a bas-relief, or maybe some rare, tropical lichen? As I focused, I saw to my dismay that it was a wide circle of congealed blood.

'Look,' he shouted, pointing at it with his machete. The guide ran up behind me. 'Look!' he repeated almost gleefully. 'Guess what it's from.'

He released my arm and I stared down, pretending not to recognise the lumpy black craquelure with its red streaks. It was speckled with flies. It smelt bad. My gorge rose.

'Go on, guess what it's from.'

'I don't know,' I lied, taking a couple of steps back.

'It's from killing,' he announced.

I said nothing.

'We kill here.'

I hoped he wasn't going to drag everything out with a question-and-answer session. It would be bad enough to get hacked to death without having to go through a primary-school exam before it happened.

'We kill here and chop up the bones.'

It was so hot, I just wished he'd get on with it. It was so hot that all those last thoughts and memories, wishes and regrets that generally flash through the mind on the brink of death failed to materialise.

'That's a good surprise, isn't it?'

I felt like telling him it was pretty good but a bit predictable – they had been doing it all over Kenya for years.

'Come,' the driver said, pulling me bodily towards an iron fence.

'Do you see them?' he asked, pointing towards a shallow

cave. I didn't know what I was looking for. If it was dismembered body parts hanging from the thorn trees *à la* Mary Kingsley, the answer was no.

'Look closer, down there,' he whispered conspiratorially. 'There they are – lions. If you had turned back, you would have missed the lions, and they have a cub. Come and see. You will be happy to see the cub.'

I was ecstatic. Strolling from another direction, two women with extravagant headdresses had come to see the lions too.

We recrossed the sacrificial altar and began our descent by a different, gentler route through a small zoo. We walked the gauntlet between caged apes, chimpanzees and orangutans who looked bored, tired and depressed. Beside their cages, three small boys were tickling fetid mud for frogs. A turquoise humming-bird hovered over them, darting in and out of a straggling pink hibiscus. There were a few women sitting on the concrete edges of the cages, sucking mangoes and throwing down the stones. Underfoot was bumpy with half-eaten mangoes.

At the far end of the row, an outsized orangutan was reaching through his bars, gathering up the mango stones and flinging them aimlessly. As we approached, he began to shriek and direct the furry missiles at us.

'He likes you,' the driver said.

'How do you know?'

'He finds you attractive.'

A parchment-coloured missile hit my well-armoured shin.

'You've made him excited.'

Another mango stone whizzed past my head. I picked my way across the muddy path, heels sticking in the slime, and put some distance between me and the orangutan. Passing his cage sent him into a frenzy. He rattled the bars with one hand and masturbated with the other. By now all the other visitors were watching the simian antics, marvelling at his excitement and laughing. The guide found it so funny it brought tears to his eyes, while the driver found in it an opportunity to discuss an abridged version of Darwin's theory of evolution. It was so abridged he skipped everything except 'like ape, like man'. Long after the flying mango stones had stopped hitting me, I could hear the ribald laughter behind my back.

Across a long stretch of shrubs, I could finally see the entrance gates. We passed a big painted sign on a white-walled enclosure saying 'Manatees'. The driver joined us to contemplate it.

'What are they?' he asked.

'There aren't any,' the guide announced proudly.

'But what are they?' the driver insisted.

They slipped out of French and into Bambara. Without any translation, I understood the guide tell him: 'Big ugly things with enormous breasts.' There was as much mime as language. The driver looked impressed. All the way back to the hotel compound he kept up a breathless commentary on big breasts, little breasts, pointing up, down and sagging. Sagging, he announced as we pulled up to the main door, were sad. As I paid him (a pittance by the hour), he told me he'd had a lovely afternoon which we should repeat tomorrow. His robe was tented by the size of his erection which he did nothing to conceal but rather displayed as an extra inducement to a re-run. I hobbled back to my room and removed my boots. My feet were so hot and sore I doubted I would ever walk again. If I did, it would be in the market, and my criteria for my next driver were that he be very small and old.

By the next morning, my crushed feet had recovered. I explained to the receptionist that I wanted a tiny driver.

'How tiny?'

'A lot smaller than me!'

Three minutes later, I got Moussa. I spent the next five days happily by his side.

32

Otto's two days' delay turned into five. He eventually arrived overland caked in dust. He had sand in his hair, in his clothes, in his eyes and ears; red sand ingrained in his face and as thick as a tie round his neck. He had travelled for over a day across the desert bumping along in an unsprung truck with the windows closed against the dust and the sun turning the cabin into an oven. He hated Bamako, hated the dust, the small-town feel, the powercuts, the lazy pace, the heat, the flies, the dead telephones and the impossibility of following what was going on at his newspaper back in Caracas.

Exhausted by the trip, he took to his bed and slept for sixteen hours. He apologised profusely for having lured me there. I tried to convince him how much I loved it; something he refused to believe. I told him about my day in Koulikoro, a fortified port on the Niger with its sleepy market selling only fish, baskets and calabashes. I told him how Moussa had taken me on a pirogue to the sandbanks that striated the wide river with beaches. I told him how we had eaten chicken under a tamarind tree while the men of Koulikoro played *pétanque* (another legacy of the French). He was having none of it; the place was a dump and we both had to get out as quickly as possible. I think the only moment he enjoyed of his trip was checking through immigration on his way out.

I left with sadness, determined to return and spend more time in the fissured plains of Bamako Province with its desert-in-the-making. Although I had never heard of it before, I now wanted to know everything about Mali. I knew it was a desert through which the Niger river flowed. As though despairing of such aridity, the great river fragments in the north. On a map, it looks like shattered blue glass with hundreds of shards criss-crossing the sands.

I took a foolish trip to the lion hill; I took six hours to send a fax through to Quarata to explain my delay; I never did manage to make a telephone call, and I ate some green slime at Moussa's brother's house which I don't ever want to see, smell or taste again. Yet all those things were minor. What mattered was that for me, the sub-Sahara was a revelation: a well from which I drank and was replenished.

I flew home with Mali music in my head, laden with tapes of Ali Farka Toure and the blues-like strum of a Malien guitar with its long handle and its small gourd at the end. I was laden with calabashes from Koulikoro, and swathes of cotton damask in a small hand-painted trunk. The villa is studded now with royal blue, peach, rose madder and bottle green and the raw sienna and maroon of Malien dyes.

Under Moussa's diminutive wing I felt entirely at my ease. It wasn't the old 'I belong'; it was a marvelling at a foreign court. In the months since then, I have been back again to absorb more, picking up the sweet, gentle strains of friendships made in the dust.

33

When after many years Thesiger, the intrepid explorer, went back to Arabia, he was disgusted by the way people now saw the desert from landcruisers and planes. There are probably many wonderful things about riding camelback for weeks on end in semi-starvation, fever and thirst towards an almost certain death, but I can't think of a single one. I rode a camel in Djerba in Tunisia and rocked and wobbled on the lumpy saddle with my legs splayed wider than seemed either polite or humanly possible, and it was an interesting way to see the dunes for an hour or two at the most but untempting as a profession or even a hobby. Despite that, I do feel fascinated by deserts.

An unexpected bonus while flying one time to Bamako via Ouagadougou was a low, entirely cloudless flight over the Sahara. For over an hour I watched the skeleton-leaf patterns in the sand: giant grey lines endlessly repeating on a beige base. It looked as though trees struck by lightning were lying flat. It looked as though the Tree of Life, transposed from the floors and walls of any number of Italian churches, was sketched in charcoal, stripped of all trimmings and of any peripheral life but its basic shape, and repeated over and over like a ghostly engraving. Another recurring theme was the giant imprint of an old woman's hand. This was criss-crossed rock, but it kept appearing. It was a landscape of smudged grey fingerprints, of etched trees, of leaf veins and handprints. It was, paradoxically, full of the signs and symbols of life lived and burgeoning despite the vast, barren impossibility of it on its arid plains and dunes.

There was nothing heroic about watching the sands from the comfort of my aeroplane seat, but it was beautiful and also comforting to see familiar patterns and shapes recur even in a land banished from most of life's cycle. Even the Sahara is in on it: carrying a sameness for all its difference. And only lazy travellers like me would see the signs because they emerge only on a grand scale and aerially. Across time and place certain themes, dreams and ideas repeat themselves spontaneously, just as, on a much wider scale, certain shapes and patterns recur in nature. As a species we have never been as far away from nature as we now are, nor more aware of our intrinsic links: not far genetically from the fruit fly, and with the spiral of our DNA identical in shape to the spiral inside thousands of shells.

Antonio Moreno, the foreman on the *hacienda*, was always remonstrating with me for reading and thinking too much. He used to insist that thinking was very bad for you, that it damaged the brain. He had a theory that if you looked at things in a certain way, you would understand them. He was already an old man when he told me this, and although he could neither read or write, he was wiser than I could ever hope to be. I heard recently that he is still alive, aged 107, and has thus survived almost every vagary and calamity that man and nature can combine to contrive. If he could see me now, I expect he'd still shake his grizzled head at me for my reading and writing, but at least after a quarter of a century I have begun to find my way into stillness. In the days since I have heard of him again, I feel myself inside his head, staring out through his cataracts to the green slopes of Tempé, behind the sugar mill of the *hacienda*.

During the months between my first and second trip to Mali, I came across a handful of people who had been there too: mostly on business, mostly against their will, and most of them sided with the armpit theory. Their verdict in no way altered mine. Outside of the circuit of five-star hotels, how many businessmen have eyes for the intrinsic charm of most places? Anywhere that hinders or encumbers the smooth running of their affairs is a no-no. Bamako, with its dust and turmoil, was off their scale. For travellers, however, like myself, it was a slice of something very rare. I gleaned a lot from a couple of old Mali Hands, neither of whom shared my enthusiasm for Bamako town but were full of tips on faraway Mopti and Timbuktu. One of these travellers challenged me to define the charm of Bamako. So here goes.

I have a fondness for Bamako, both its town and its province. I found it dynamic and anatomical: a bloodstream pumping round and round; not going anywhere but back on itself, its sole purpose maintaining life. It is busy with a steady circular rush. It is sensuous because life is sensuous. It is cheerful and squalid in the way places tend to be in direct proportion to their proximity to the equator. It gave the impression that everyone from infants to ancients knew exactly where they were going and why, which made for harmony under the apparent disorder – an order behind a façade of chaos.

First impressions came thick and fast. Bamako seemed to have been built between and around thousands of flamboyant trees. Life evolved under the shadow fingers of their leaves. In places the trees became woods and the city disappeared altogether, emerging again in straggling scabs which broke open into trickles of urban life. Stamped into every layer of it, with the tenacity of tribal scars, were the hallmarks of the villagers that filled it. The rural immigrants never really let it become a city. They injected flocks of sheep, herds of cattle and batches of hens. Then they studded it with stacks of firewood and reeds. Then they overran it with mud compounds like rabbit warrens tunnelling out in dry hummocks behind the cluttered, tumbledown streets.

Every city in the world has its quota of refugee villagers who are marginalised and then, eventually, swallowed by the metropolitan cog. Bamako seemed to work the other way round: the village system held sway; its grip was not loosened. Mud huts outnumbered houses, and temporary shacks outnumbered huts. Sheep were the centre of attention. Traffic seemed incidental. The few, new, grand buildings of banks and airline offices stood in splendid isolation. They appeared to be ignored. The action was all down on the fruit stalls and the markets, in the narrow backstreets and dead-end alleyways.

Bamako lives in a dust cloud, a pink haze. It silts over as the roseate sand persists in reclaiming this unseasonal and unruly flower. The jumble of colours never ceased. It was a blossoming framed by clusters of huts which began and ended with a field of blues, greens, pinks and reds, flecked with charcoal grey. From a distance, these fields, large as a tennis court or small as a truck, were thick with billowing blooms. In a land of dry stalks and burnt savannahs, where arable farming was funnelled into small tended allotments, there was abandon in those patches sewn not with plants but with plastic bags which having been dumped had planted themselves in the sand. Where other garbage was eventually disposed of, the plastic remained. They were seen, it seemed, not as a blight on the landscape, but as a record of all the deals done, the produce sold, bought and bartered.

By the banks of the Niger, pyramids of millet sat in a long row, giving way to a tented line of wicker cubby holes and baskets of big grey river fish. Some of the fish were still gasping and seemed to be the only living creatures to acknowledge the heat. Further into the shambling city, every street was a market and every square metre of dust a stall.

A single-track railway ran through the city. Bits of it were lined with vendors, much of it was lined with sheep. Huddles and flocks of gleaming animals who walk on straw and are constantly washed and groomed. From within the dustbowl, only the sheep and the glistening exotic cottons of the native robes are pristine. And only the sheep are idle. They are the pampered ones, the symbols of prosperity. Their fodder sits in high mounds of weedy wreaths. While children hurry on errands, lug loads, man stalls, and dodge across the streets selling things, the sheep take it easy, munching lazily under their shimmering fleeces, safe in the knowledge that they are everybody's goal.

At the end of Ramadan, a Malien will sell everything except his immortal soul to buy a ram for his family. In a place as bulging with poverty as Bamako, everyone has to chip in to make ends meet. The extended families are big. Moussa, who has gone from taxi driver to my constant companion and guide, has thirty-two people to feed out of his meagre salary. Despite the Islamic custom, he has only one wife and five children, but his brother has several wives, many offspring and no work. It is a vicious circle but one that Maliens are used to running round.

It would seem that poverty is the law Maliens rejoice in cheating, claiming little gains at every turn. As stubborn as the sheep they adore, the women sit in regal splendour in the dust in the doorways of hovels, selling handfuls of whatever forlorn product they have against all the odds on a glutted market, sticking at it until another filthy, tattered Cefa note takes its place. The money itself is the most worn and battered I have ever seen.

There is a baby boom in Bamako. It is swarming with toddlers and half the women have babies strapped to their backs, heads lolling over the fine cotton. Even the babies seem to know they are in a get-on-with-life environment. They hardly cry: not for the sun beating down on their mostly bald heads, not for the long hours they wait unattended, nor for the rising red dust. When they are hungry, their mothers swing them around inside their loose cotton wraps and suckle them without missing a beat of whatever commerce they are engaged in. Toddlers get strapped onto the backs of slightly older children, and the older children are on the make, wheeling and dealing whatever there is, with fruit as the common denominator.

*

Early one morning Moussa drove me for twenty minutes out of town along the road to the old airport. A new Bamako is in the making there with building under construction. In ten years' time the hubbub of the present centre could well become a teeming suburb. It is too entrenched ever to be cleared, too haphazard to respond to any kind of urban planning. As Mali reaches into the future, it is clear that Bamako is planning to decamp.

Several miles beyond the building sites and beyond the statutory field of half-planted plastic bags (on which a herd of speckled ceibu cattle are grazing), Moussa bumps his sky-blue Peugeot into a rutted expanse of dust. On either side, low mud compounds squat, lined by vendors hopefully offering token wares.

The car whips up a red cloud through which we swerve into the open gates of a compound a little larger than the rest. Moussa's brood swarms round the car, greeting the family chief as a long-lost visitor although he can't have left home for more than two hours. Moussa's wife dispenses hospitality like a princess from her mud porch. Fifteen children look on while she brews up green tea on a tiny charcoal burner. She is much bigger than him, and towers splendidly in her flowing gown. Her moussereau, the length of cloth which most women wind into extravagant shapes and sport as a headdress, is canary yellow. The tea is tried and tasted by the lady of the house several times before it is considered fit for her husband and myself. When ready, it is served in large glass thimbles. Then we share a tray of pawpaw with a scatter of flies as each child is introduced. All but the youngest are very shy. The three eldest, who are in school, look rigid with fear, which I interpret as a dread of being called upon to say anything in French (the language of their studies but still not their own). Since saving face is crucial, I ignore them studiously in favour of their unpressured younger siblings.

We return to the city basking in Moussa's pride in his sons and daughters. Moussa himself is illiterate, even his name has to be written by someone else. By his industry he has moved his family from the bush behind Koulikoro to the capital, and is not only feeding his entire clan but is sending his children to school.

We made our way back through clouds of dust. Hoardings along the highway announced that going to school is the way ahead. They are interspersed in the miles of sandy scrubland by warnings about Aids, or Sida: it is known by its French name in West Africa. The commonest one is a huge, crudely painted board and shows what looks like a big pink sunflower with a grimace for a face, waving its petals at a huddle of startled men and women. Written above it, in large letters in French, it says: Sida kills, together let's stop Sida. (*Sida tue, ensemble stoppons Sida.*) It's a nice thought, but as Aids scourges Africa, it is going to take far more than that, not least in a country where most people can't read and probably aren't very scared of pink petals.

I can't help wondering how many of the fifteen children in Moussa's compound and how many others under his care will fall prey to the new plague. Tentatively I sound Moussa out for his views on Sida. He works fifteen hours a day for the owner of his taxi, surrounded by the signs of numerous tropical diseases. This new one hasn't registered for him as a threat any greater than the others. When I speak of it he smiles at me as though I am the one who doesn't understand. There is an element of knife-edge in his life which is absent in mine and we both know it.

When it comes to one of his little nephews being blinded by cataracts, we are on safer ground. There is a clinic but it costs more than Moussa will ever earn. His brother has three wives and no work, Moussa explains, I think with a hint of criticism both of his brother for siring quite so many children and of myself for drawing attention to the four-year-old's plight. The child might be blind but he isn't starving, thanks to the pounds of dust Moussa chews daily at the wheel.

From my first days in Mali, I became the honorary godmother to Moussa's brood. For someone with a penchant for protégés, getting thirty-two in one go is a blessing. Moussa says it is destiny that brought us together and I tend to agree. We are each other's benefactors in a deal which leaves me the debtor as he unfolds the treasures of Mali for me.

When the days slack, we cruise the hundred kilometres to Koulikoro again, passing hamlets with names like Manabougou hosting stacks of oranges and firewood, Fougabougou and Noumoubougou with yet more mangoes. Manabougou was marked by an immense dead tree with a hollow heart high in its trunk making a window onto the striated ridge of rock that lines the horizon. The sky is a pale grey haze of heat and dust. By midday it is 43°C. Villagers linger under the blazing sun as though oblivious to it. Drumming up dust with their heels, I see several boys jogging, one even runs. Inside a rusty wire-fenced enclosure, two boys in identical black and white strips hop doubled up like giant black crickets. They are synchronised. 'What,' I ask Moussa, 'are they doing?' He shrugs. 'Training for something. Eating dust.'

On the other side of the road *la brousse*, the bush, claws into the dry land. Balls of fluff drift from false cotton trees. Half an hour out of Bamako, the dustcloud lightens. The thin strips and squares of vegetable plots with all their vibrant greens have given way to a sudden patch of pre-desert. It is a dead land with skeletal trees, skinny eucalyptus and termite tracks. Hamlets are marked from afar more by their piles of firewood and stacks of reeds than by the sandcastle dwellings, which are either going up or falling down. At each centre, a tiny market punches colours into the parched savannah, smudging out either end with its collection of plastic bags.

Now it is dry and fissured stone: a flat, cracked landscape. Now it is a prairie of sparse stubble, of pale gold straw occasionally freckled by dappled and horned ceibu. A herdsman in a pointed thatch-shaped hat strolls with his arms dangling over a long pole across his shoulders: a pose that appears to combine both pleasure and pain.

By Souban, the rocks keep cracking, flat and friable, edging into ashlands. The Niger is not far beyond. It is seen only in surprising silver flashes which could be mirages were it not for a grey-faced woman holding up a large, black, writhing fish by its tail. Then the flashes of water become more frequent and the straggling thorn trees give way to groves of mango. For a while, the desert speaks only from a distance.

There is a steady flow of traffic on the road, mostly lorries and small green buses packed to bursting point with laden passengers. The buses have holes cut out of their sides: they are discs or hearts of makeshift windows. The roofs are piled high with bundles and crates. Some of the buses have names painted on them, of which the most succinct is '*trop chaud*'. I am so hot in the relative luxury of Moussa's car I cannot imagine how anyone survives inside the baking tin buses. My oracle informs me they have no choice. The people who use the road are not tourists. As one of the scratched windscreens announced, 'Needs Must'.

In the mango groves, the trees are heavy with ripe and ripening fruit. And there are walls of mangoes, mounds and pyramids of them, baskets and calabashes of them, and trays and bags of them, all for sale. It would seem impossible to have enough of a market for all the fruit to sell, but Moussa assures me it will all go.

Picking over market stalls full of the stuff of spells and witch doctors, with their various snakes and bats, monkeys' skulls and lizards' guts, foxs' feet, bones and tufts and other fetishes, the rites and rituals of tribal life advertise themselves blatantly. Moussa dismisses such stuff as hocus-pocus but its popularity is obvious. Gradually signs of rigid tradition, of tribal rites and of spiritual meaning pervade almost every moment and every movement, from the obeisance by the plain sandy mosques to the obsessive mounding of mangoes.

Back in Bamako, where mangoes were being sold by the five, I transgressed by picking my own from a small backstreet stall. I chose a particular fine fruit from a lower layer of the vendor's fruit pyramid. The vendor's dismay and distress at the gap thus made could not have been greater if she had been an artist and I had vandalised her sculpture. As I left apologetically she went about repairing the damage, trying various-sized fruits to repair the desecration while sucking her teeth and clucking. From which I surmised that despite the great April glut of mangoes and the general poverty, the eating and selling of the fruit was peripheral to the affair. The essence was in the overall shape, that was what really mattered: not a hollow shape, but one filled with meaning, with spirit. Once again, what appears to be overlapping confusion is minutely ordered, even though order as we know it elsewhere turns on its head here.

One of the strangest and most poignant sights of Bamako are the dozens of girls, with aprons of sacking over their gowns, employed by the government to sweep the edges of the road. Crouching low in the dustbowl with brooms made from bundles of twigs, the pretty girls swirl red dust as they address the thankless task of sweeping their particular patch, raising clouds and covering everything with another pink patina. Of all the jobs, theirs seems to be the most pointless. In a curious way, although every one of the sweepers must know she will never clear so much as a square metre of dust, they make their mark momentarily, like pavement artists, and perhaps it is that mastery which gives them job satisfaction.

A leopard spoke to me in Bamako. It was an ancient, dog-eared carving in a pale wood chewed by insects and time. It came from Mali's Dogon country and stood out conspicuously among the highly polished dark-wood carvings of etiolated women with bare breasts, elephants and hippos, beloved of tribal craftsmen, it would seem, all over Africa. I have never felt tempted by the giant combs, the metre-long forks or the jungle beasts and warriors so dear to both the sons of Africa and its visitors. Back in my childhood, when my father eventually returned from Ghana, he arrived bearing gifts of that ilk which I hid most ungratefully at the back of our nursery cupboard.

In Bamako, trotting behind Moussa, I examined hundreds of yards of cotton, bolts of fine, hand-loomed hessian, and leather in all its shapes and sizes, be it cow, lizard, snake or crocodile; but the wood-carving stalls I spurned. Then the leopard spoke to me, drawing me into a dusty jumble of antiquities in which he alone stood out, or rather crouched.

This was no ordinary feline, no ordinary carving. Larger than a big domestic cat but by no means life-size, my leopard had the air of being very special. I know nothing about African, or indeed, Dogon antiquities, but my leopard told me he was one. His price reflected this rarity to such a degree that I left him open-mouthed in the midst of his jumbled inferiors. Three times on my first visit I ran into his temporary master, who three times offered him to me at drastically lowering prices.

By the time I was ready to leave, my desire and my budget met. Although it was now affordable, I had decided to leave all my spare pennies to Moussa and his wife, and had already handed over the contents of my wallet, minus the 10,000 Cefa airport tax I needed to leave the country. It was the eve of the end of Ramadan, and Bamako was in a frenzy of commerce as the clans gathered to feast on ram. The antique dealer was no exception in his desperation for one last deal. As though to rub in the folly of my not buying the leopard, he chased after our taxi, running alongside while conducting a Dutch auction on the Dogon treasure. I was momentarily tempted to ask Moussa for enough of my money back to pay the derisory ransom required to release the proffered leopard to my custody. The traffic was thick as Ramadan ended and the dealer was able to shadow our taxi for a long while. Time after time I refused the proffered carving. I wanted it as I have rarely wanted anything in my life. On the other hand, Moussa needed his bonus. Had there been a medical emergency, I know he would have handed it back to me, but he would never understand my affinity for the beaten-up piece of wood he hadn't liked the look of from the start. Unlike me, Moussa was unable to overlook the fact that my leopard was already owned, body and possibly soul, by savage woodworm. The body was weak, but the soul had lingered, and it was a good strong message the battered beast sent out.

Back in Italy, I often thought of the leopard I had left behind. Having refused it when it was so cheap and being thrust through my taxi window, I felt I had let him down, betrayed him. Then, in my brief forays through Paris, with its plethora of West African art, I began to look more closely at some of the finer, older carvings in the windows of the finer, older galleries, and realised that my leopard was probably, by any of their standards, pretty special, both in the clean lines of its carving and for its age.

In the interim, with Bamako's dearth of tourists and connoisseurs, and its trickle of businessmen, nobody bought my leopard. He was there waiting for me on my return, his features further blurred by an extra quarter of an inch of dust.

Unlike the Russian amulet that never leaves my neck, the leopard is too big to carry on my person, although I hugged him for most of the twelve-hour trip from Bamako to Quarata, wrapped in old, soiled brown paper which made him the object of distaste to many a fellow passenger. I felt like telling them that the crinkly mummy under his unsavoury swaddling bands was actually a splendid talisman (I didn't though, lest it led me to problems at customs).

Having taken the leopard home, as with the Russian icon and the little Leningrad box, for the Dogon talisman *mi casa es su casa*, now and for ever.

34

Ever since my first trip to Bamako, I have been full of Mali, singing its praises to anyone willing to hear. It is perceived as a good place in the family. It not only made me happy and excited again, but from my return my luck began to change. In the months since I was last there, the dust has settled around us, the debts have been turned around, and a great many other things besides my luck have also changed.

Robbie had his first big exhibition and his first marks of real acclaim. The opening at Maddox Street in London was a gathering of the clans. Family and friends from all over the world were there, almost to a man.

Apart from three short stories I wrote in Bamako, sitting up late and scribbling longhand between the powercuts and the racket of tropical night sounds, I had decided to wait until the exhibition started before recommencing work of my own. One week after the opening, I pulled out the hundred pages I had written on Nevis and buried myself in them again.

Iseult had moved to Paris, and since I wanted to get away

from the responsibilities of the villa for a while, Florence and I took up quarters on the second floor of their Parisian folly. My window looked out over fluted grey slates; the main windows looked out over a corner of the cemetery.

Paris was a city that had threaded in and out of my life without my ever having much attachment to it at the time. Mostly in retrospect, I admired its splendour. At fifteen I had spent a summer in its fourth arrondissement with my father. At sixteen, it had been one end of Jaime's and my commuter run from Milan. At twenty-four, with the five-year-old Iseult, I had lived on and off in a hotel on the Rue de Vaugirard at the Luxembourg end.

In the years between then and Umbria, I went once a year to meet Otto for a few days of his annual pilgrimage. There was a gap of one year when he was unable to lunch, being in prison again in Venezuela. From the time I moved to Italy, my preferred mode of travelling back to London was by train. This requires crossing Paris to change stations. Trains arriving from Italy do so at the Gare de Lyon. Those leaving for London do so from the Gare du Nord. En route, I always paused for a filter coffee and a *croque-monsieur*: a forty-minute interlude to keep my Parisian allegiance topped up.

I had nursed Quarata through eleven winters. I felt my new-found energy should be mine to reconstruct my writing. I had spent enough time stoking fires. Much as I loved the villa, I decided to change base for a while. We would travel back and forth to Umbria, but until the summer came to lessen the chores, I opted out of juggling with its cavernous spaces. It felt like time to turn the coin and see its other face. As it turned out, it wasn't Paris I got to know, it was

Montmartre, and more precisely the triangle defined by the boulevard de Clichy at its base, Abbesses above and rue Lépic with its gourmet street-market linking the two like a dog's hind leg. At first I explored the cemetery with its avenues of famous and unknown graves. I walked through the area known as Blanche, so named for the plaster of Paris quarried there which used to leave a white patina in its wake. Its streets are built over tunnels and pits and still occasionally cave in. We bought our baguettes every day from the same baker, and drank our coffees at the same bar, 'the local' all of a hundred and fifty yards from the pink turreted fantasy in which we were ensconced.

Yet, as the weeks went by, I left that house less and less. There were fortnightly forays to Ghibert's in St Germain to stock up on books, but these fizzled out when I discovered the tiny paper shop at Abbesses would order anything in. Montmartre was a safe haven. I didn't even get lost because the beacon of the Sacre Coeur was as good a guide as a lighthouse is at sea. Florence and I ended up distilling our urban needs to matinée cinemas and the railway stations for the times we headed back to Italy.

The move to Paris had seemed important at the time. It took on a significance in theory that it just didn't have in practice. I didn't need a city, great or small, or any specific place. I was looking for something in Paris, not realising I had already found it. It was like the Zen paintings of the man looking for an ox. I had used all the aids, followed all the stages, I had found and ridden the beast and was left with the blank paper.

Epilogue

My mother worked with maladjusted children in the East End of London in a school in a big Victorian house built by an admiral. Every morning in Bethnal Green the bruised and battered pupils were encouraged to 'let off steam'. The children ran around the playground as though being chased by hornets. She urged them to scream and shout and kick the walls. They rolled around on the tarmac as though in the throes of epilepsy. This letting-off of steam, my mother explained, was the key to survival.

At Montpelier on Nevis, another admiral's house, I realised I was, yet again, following her advice, letting off steam in my own way to avoid an explosion. Twice while we were there the volcano on neighbouring Montserrat let off its steam, spraying our island with a fine white dust. Montserrat itself was knee-deep in volcanic ash, and a grim example of what could happen when the steam-valve blocked.

Back in Umbria it was a source of amusement to some and concern to others that I was a compulsive bottler. I bottled jams, chutneys, fruit, peppers, onions, herbs, aubergines – whatever I could get to stay in a sterilised jar. Morra, the village we lived in, was a hotbed of bottlers. They saw my industry as a mark of sanity. They all did it: laying down stocks of food for the future, shoring up their cantinas against eventual famine. The laying down of hundreds of kilos of tomatoes was an annual ritual. Tomato purée is the Italian penicillin: a wonder drug to cure all ills. I had never lived anywhere in which my own hundreds of jars could sit more naturally on their shelves. Maria, our housekeeper for seven years, used to bring her friends up to see my efforts, proud to exhibit something so natural in what, to them, was my often baffling behaviour. Between August and October, it was a family joke that no one linger in the kitchen lest I preserve them under oil or vinegar.

The rigours of Umbria did not drive me to bottling my hopes – I'd been an ardent maker of jams for as many years as I could remember. It may have looked as though I had archived my energy into jars, but the preserving of perishable things was just a hobby. And the fact that I myself was so emotionally repressed just a coincidence.

In London, during my refugee year after Venezuela, my mother used to encourage me to have faith. 'You'll rise up like a phoenix from the ashes,' she assured me, referring to my reduced circumstances and my lack of fame. I was no phoenix then, but I had risen. The only ashes in my life were the ones that occasionally dropped off the end of my cigarettes. Later, at Quarata, there were all the ashes from all the fires with which, in vain, we tried to heat the palace. Every surface had a layer of dust.

It is important to me to honour my mother's wishes, her zest for life, her generosity of spirit. I have tried to be a dutiful daughter, to fulfil her dreams. I grew up with the sensation of having to live two lives: hers and mine. I had to feel and do more intensely to make up for her broken life. The intensity has not always held, but the intention has – doubly since her early death in 1981. And the image of that phoenix held too.

On Nevis, in the days when the ash drifted across the straits from Montserrat, I felt that perhaps a great change was in the air for me. Maybe it was because I was getting fat but whatever traces of the mythical bird were in me failed to take off. For all that I felt a change coming, and an urge to soar, I was going to need a lot more of a runway to get airborne.

Florence didn't like my fuller figure. She wanted me to have the litheness of a supermodel, the slenderness of her Barbie dolls. Seeing me in my bathing dress on Pinney's beach, she said, 'Mamma, you're fat!' After a week of seeing the local mammas, many of whom looked as though they had swallowed large lumpy pillows whole, she revised her opinion. That new perception intrigued her. Having grown up in a small rigidly traditionalist village, the yardstick of relativity had not sunk in.

Fat is a relative thing. Mine was to fall off at an alarming rate the following year. The secret of the stick figure my daughter had aspired to on my behalf was a diet of undiluted stress. I didn't choose it, but it worked wonders!

Nevis was a lull that restored my strength. The following year was an escalating nightmare which force-fed my life through a funnel into the heap of ashes my mother had foreseen. Now, chastened, I am rising out of those ashes, not as a phoenix, but as myself. This is not an end, but a beginning.

Just as I seemed unable to fall in love or commit myself fully to any man before my mother died (unable to betray our closeness), I seemed to need to go to Africa before I could fully commit myself to life. She had a dread of Africa. It was a threat that hung over my childhood, a place that threatened to take me from her and extinguish our light. When my father went out to live in Ghana, he lobbied, half-heartedly, for me to visit him in Accra. Joanna didn't trust him, he would take me and keep me, and so refused to let me go. Then he was in Zambia and in Tanzania, urging me to join him. The not-inconsiderable negative feelings my mother felt for him were transferred to the continent he lived in. The idea of abduction hovered around our flat. Even a holiday, she assured me, would end in my never coming back. I had to steer clear of Africa, not even think about it; all his enticements, she told me, were a trick. Our sitting room began to fill with library books about eaten missionaries, bilharzia, malaria and tribal wars.

By my early teens, I had put whatever lingering curiosity I had once felt about Africa out of my mind. Such thoughts were disloyal to Joanna. Mentally I transferred the need to trace the African blood in my veins from the source to the halfway station. South America, Guyana, the West Indies were as far back as I went. When, many years later, I learnt of Belle, the princess from Benin who was six foot three and bought as a slave by my great-great-grandfather in Belém, who then married her, I blocked my interest in Benin, transfusing it into a greater interest in Brazil.

I had traipsed around the world finding affinities with places, falling in love with them, feeling I belonged here or there and telling myself it was so. Only in Africa, though, did people come up to me and claim me as their own. Only there was the question not 'Where are you from?' but 'Why have you strayed?' Over and over again, strangers from Timbuktu, from a place I hadn't known existed, a place that was, till then, a family joke, reclaimed me as one of them. The roles reversed. I was used to infiltrating closed communities, trying to persuade the locals that I was one of them, or could be. In Mali, it was the locals who interrogated me as to which family I came from out in the sub-Sahara, and it was I who refused to acknowledge kinship. Timbuktu was the place where all that was irretrievably lost in our family drifted to. It was the homeland of displaced things. I found myself in the right place at the right time in Mali, and found a missing part of me.

Thus West Africa became the first and last of all the good times and good places that have sustained me like amulets through troubled times.

I feel the worst times of my life are past. They have mostly been transformed now into fuel for the fire. The good times are the sparks, the fleeting fireflies that illumine changes.

I don't know exactly where I am going now, but I know I am on my way. And I know that I shall keep returning, *we* shall keep returning, to Africa.

In the last few years, I have lost a few friends and made a few enemies. Skipping tripwires I did my best not to trigger any mines, with a few notable failures. When one is good at things, and strong, failure is harder to accept. Recognising that I am not Wonderwoman has taken some time. Changing from being the one who supports others to the one who has let others down was the hardest part of all. Crawling out from under that particular label, accepting my responsibility from a dung heap of bad luck, has taken a while to do.

When it comes to luck, I have been phenomenally lucky from the word go. My life would have been fatuous if some, at least, of that luck hadn't swung the other way too. In the year 2000, the bad luck clustered. I don't see this as a jinx: I got caught in a vortex which happened to take over my life. It wasn't about me; it just happened. I got caught and kept in to write lines of fear and darkness.

I have emerged from that long tunnel with profound gratitude to the handful of people who stood by me, and with apologies to those whom I let down along the way.

When I left Venezuela, I thought I had been tested and had proved myself. I thought I could live my life resting on those Andean laurels. Yet a real trial has to be equal to the strength of the challenged. I am not Wonderwoman, but I have grown a little stronger than most. A test is not always a visible task, a tangible challenge to which one brings success or failure. Mine was a lesson in survival. The backdrop of lawyers and debt was a mere warm-up, and then a peripheral scourge. The proof of my passing my particular test is my survival. I am still here. Now I can claim that fairytale ending which is, in itself, a beginning.

A little late, perhaps, I am ready to start again. The rest of the family have survived the storm. Iseult has found her vocation in sculpting. After twenty-two years of exile she has also returned to Venezuela to visit the country I snatched her from. The fallout from her long divorce has settled. Felix, her ten-year-old son, has survived, a credit to his clan. Allie, now eighteen and called Alex, is making his way to university. Florence, though only ten, has determined to be a painter. Robbie, in the sixteenth year of our marriage, has finally found the recognition he has both merited and needed for so long.

And I have picked up the novel I started on Nevis and which got pushed into a drawer, mid-way, by the vagaries of life. I went to Montmartre expressly to finish it. I read and reread the existing manuscript but kept finding old memories intruding overly on to its new pages. I had bulky luggage that needed repacking. Sorting the maps and memories has been the last stage of clearing my decks. I needed to realign my stories, to acknowledge the ones that have floated to the surface.

Now they are folded back in their case, I find, as Anne Frank did before me, that, 'In spite of everything, I still believe that people are really good at heart'. Sometimes that goodness is buried so deep it takes a shovel to unearth it. I am ready now, and I am a keen gardener. In their own ways, in their own plots, in their own stories, most of the world is busy digging. I used to think I was different. Now I feel I am not so different, really, from anyone else: the time and the places have been different, that is all.

THE HACIENDA
MY VENEZUELAN YEARS

Lisa St Aubin de Terán

At the age of seventeen Lisa St Aubin de Terán followed her new husband, South American aristocrat and bank robber Don Jaime Terán, to his *hacienda*, deep in the Venezuelan Andes. Once there, Jaime virtually abandoned his new bride to fend for herself. With only two pedigree beagles, a pet vulture and one peasant girl for company, Lisa St Aubin de Terán became *la Doña* – and lived for seven years amongst *la gente*, an illiterate, feudal people who she says 'have been the greatest influence on my life and work'.

'Lisa St Aubin de Terán writes with extraordinary vividness and clarity . . . She faces reality with a courage and skill that left me not knowing which to admire more: her gift as a writer or that she had the guts to carve out a place for herself in such an unforgiving world' *Independent*

'Powerful engrossing' *Observer*

SOUTHPAW

Lisa St Aubin de Terán

Venezuela and Italy, villages and prisons, forests and whore houses are the backdrops to these short stories which are a reflection of the people and the places that have informed this wonderful writer's work.

'The collection contains some of St Aubin de Terán's most satisfying work to date . . . An absorbing storyteller, she finds other people's life stories even more enchanted than her own' *Independent*

'Her vivid, telling sketches of characters in a remote Umbrian village – linger in the memory' *Sunday Times*

'A jubilant sense of place pervades the stories, together with the smell of woodsmoke, acacia blossom and the day's baking' *Sunday Tribune*

ELEMENTS OF ITALY

Lisa St Aubin de Terán

'I have chosen the elements of Italy to sift and sort the mountains of matter. My categories are the four classical elements of **earth**, **water**, **fire** and **air**: four channels to convey the essence of Italy; what it is about, what it looks like, smells like, sounds and tastes like.'

'The charm of Italy is akin to that of being in love' *Stendhal*

'Italians, unlike the thrifty French, are very extravagant with raw materials. They are used not so much with reckless abandon as with a precise awareness of what good quality does for the cooking' *Elizabeth David*

'Italy is mostly an emotion' *Henry James*

'They make love a great deal – and assassinate a little'
George, Lord Byron

JOANNA

Lisa St Aubin de Terán

In the late 1800s 'Poor Florence' grows up under the shadow of the beautiful sister with emerald eyes, eyes that are inherited by Florence's clairvoyant daughter Kitty. After the First World War, Kitty conceives a daughter, Joan, in bitterness at the loss of her lover in battle. Thereafter they begin a life of exile in London. Eventually Joan – now Joanna – begins to understand the terrible inheritance that has shadowed her family for three generations.

On *The Slow Train to Milan*: 'No need to ask whether her second account is as good as her first: it is much, much better' – Anita Brookner, *The Standard*

THE VIRAGO BOOK OF WANDERLUST & DREAMS

Edited by Lisa St Aubin de Terán

In this haunting and unusual collection of writing about longings for flight, the yearnings are as varied as their dreamers. Some want to cross a desert or an ocean, some travel back into memory, some never leave home, some wait patiently for their life. Including writers as diverse as Zora Neale Hurston, Elizabeth von Arnim, Karen Blixen, Angela Carter, Elaine Dundy, Janet Frame, Jessie Kesson, Shena Mackay, Dorothy Parker, Bernice Rubens, Elizabeth Smart, Romaine Brooks and Harriet Wilson, this imaginative and far-reaching anthology is dedicated to women who have had the courage to say 'yes' to life, whether that means daring to go, or daring to stay.